Birnbaum's

Walt Disney World®
without kids

by Pamela S. Weiers

Tom Passavant
EDITORIAL DIRECTOR

Jill Safro
EDITOR

Deanna Caron
MANAGING EDITOR

Todd Sebastian Williams
ART DIRECTOR

Isabel Shamlian
COPY EDITOR

Suzy Goytizolo
EDITORIAL ASSISTANT

Alice Garrard
CONTRIBUTING EDITOR

Alexandra Mayes Birnbaum
CONSULTING EDITOR

THE OFFICIAL GUIDE

HYPERION AND HEARST BUSINESS PUBLISHING, INC.

Table of Contents

8 PLANNING AHEAD

First things first: Lay the groundwork for an unforgettable vacation by timing your Walt Disney World visit to take advantage of the best weather, crowd patterns, and special goings-on. We set forth information about package and ticket options, offer time- and money-saving strategies, and present the keys to the World's extensive transportation system. Our sample mix-and-match schedules will help you plan your days and nights. And a round of specialized advice offers the promise of no regrets.

38 CHECKING IN

Whether it's elegant, rustic, whimsical, or romantic digs you're seeking, you'll find them among Walt Disney World's 18 resorts and brand-new cruise ship, themed as

only Disney knows how. Choose from hotels whose architecture and ambience evoke such locales as New Orleans, Martha's Vineyard, Polynesia, or an early 1900s mountain lodge. Within our listing we explain the advantages of staying on-property and the big draws of each resort. You'll also find recommendations for lodging outside the World's boundaries.

78 THEME PARKS: THE BIG FOUR

Enchanting, engaging, entertaining . . . overwhelming. The Magic Kingdom, Epcot, Disney-MGM Studios, and the new Animal Kingdom (opening this May), can rekindle even the most sluggish sense of wonder. But where to begin? Right here: We've devised strategies to help you make the most of each day. We've also provided an orientation to each park—including an honest-to-goodness Animal Kingdom exclusive; detailed walking tours that highlight the most alluring stops for adults; and lists of touring priorities that rank every attraction. From "Don't Miss" to "Don't Knock Yourself Out," we've scoped out the grownup fun quotient.

142 DIVERSIONS: SPORTS, SHOPPING & OTHER PURSUITS

Because the World's attractions extend way beyond the theme parks, so does our guidance. Here, discover the options, including five first-rate 18-hole golf courses, tennis, boating, fishing, and biking. Die-hard shoppers will have a field day checking out our favorite shops. Our in-depth report on the Disney Institute reveals the creative essence of this adult-minded retreat. For those who prefer soaking and sliding, we dive into all three water parks. We also visit the natural realms of Fort Wilderness and Discovery Island.

182 DINING & ENTERTAINMENT

Here's your insider's guide to adult best bets for full-service restaurants and casual eating spots in the theme parks, resorts, and elsewhere in Walt Disney World—including all the new hot spots at Downtown Disney West Side. We've found (dining) rooms with prime views, cheap eats, sweet treats, afternoon teas, wines by the glass, and hearty microbrews. After dark, you'll know where to go to watch the big game, hear cool jazz, join in a rollicking sing-along, and dance the night away (disco, country, or cheek-to-cheek), how to navigate the new clubs, find a dinner show or a comedy club, or catch a theme park spectacular.

ISBN: 0-7868-8279-4

Printed in the United States of America

A truckload of gratitude to my fabulous supporting cast of family and friends (especially Michael, Mum & Dad, and Marianne) for their patience, understanding, and tireless support. Ears all around! —Pam

Other 1998 Birnbaum's Official Disney Guides

Disneyland
Walt Disney World
Walt Disney World For Kids, By Kids

A Word from the Editors

When you stop to think about it, a Walt Disney World guide for adults makes a lot of sense. Look at it this way: How many kids do you know who have been there alone? As it happens, Disney has been catering to grownup sensibilities for a long time; the most obvious example is one entire theme park, namely Epcot. For true movie mavens, the Disney-MGM Studios is close to heaven. And the new Animal Kingdom, a lush celebration of all creatures great and small, is sure to lure the nature lover out of even the most

The editors at work. (It's a brutal way to make a living.)

civilized, buttoned-down sophisticate. That in mind, we've extended our mission to include a detailed, exclusive, insider report on Animal Kingdom—since a new park, even one as user-friendly as Disney is wont to present, may render more than a few seasoned theme park veterans initially befuddled. Add to the above a new nightlife district and an all-out sports complex, and you have proof positive that the World is expanding in precisely our direction. Chic resort hotels and restaurants, world-class golf courses, and enriching programs at the Disney Institute only add to the allure.

But there's also another, more subtle level on which Walt Disney World has always appealed to grownups. We're referring to the little jokes, both visual and verbal, that keep popping up where you least expect them. More than ever before, Disney's creative efforts are crossing over to the grownup side of the street. Lots of adults, both younger ones ("pre-kid") and older people whose children have flown the coop ("post-kid"), are descending on the parks with needs and notions that are vastly different from those of the parental persuasion.

While this is just the third edition of our guide for adults, we like to think we've come a long way since the original version. Letters from grateful readers have affirmed our instincts and inspired us to pursue our cause with even greater purpose. Clearly, an adult-oriented book is a perfect complement to our ongoing series of Birnbaum Guides to Walt Disney World and Disneyland. We already

We Couldn't Have Done It Without...

Roger Binney

Kim Carlson

Christian Campagnuolo

Jacqui Cintron

Todd Crawford

Walt Disney

Robin Domigan

Gene Duncan

Amy Foley

Richard Gregorie

Karen Haynes

Dan Jue

Rochelle LaMontagne

Tim Lewis

AnnMarie Mathews

Neal McCord

Keith McKlinsey

Joe Rohde

Pamela Ritchie

Beth Stevens

Rick Sylvain

Joel Torme

Bob Weiers

Mike West

publish what we immodestly believe is the definitive annual guide to Walt Disney World. Anyone who wants the complete word on everything there is to see and do there is well advised to accept no substitutes.

The book you hold in your hands is different in several important respects. First, as you may have already noticed from the title page, it is written and edited by one very talented person, Pamela S. Weiers, aided and abetted by the rest of the Birnbaum Disney Guides staff. Pam's distinctive voice, equal parts authority, experience, and humor, makes her the perfect person to lead a tour of this vast enterprise. Second, this book is by no means comprehensive. Rather, it skips the kid stuff and delivers the goods on adult amusements in and around Walt Disney World.

Put another way, this guide is selective in the very best sense. We have spent the past year debating which of the attractions, hotels, and restaurants—both new and old—continue to merit special attention by adults. And Pam, usually accompanied by one or more fellow staffers, has made countless trips to Orlando to put everything to the test.

For the most part, these visits are not the sort we would recommend for the casual traveler. Consider the time Pam and managing editor Deanna Caron made a sweep through 15(!) hotels in one day, looking for the best adult nooks and crannies. The mere memory of it still sends chills up their spines, as does the recollection of a plunge into River Country's unheated (read: almost numbing) Ol' Swimming Hole one cool January afternoon.

The result is that anything that doesn't live up to expectations is bumped from our "standout" list to the "good bets" rankings or banished entirely. Attractions that are awash in a sea of kids are simply given short (or at least shorter) shrift. And when we find something that just tickles us with pleasure, we aren't subtle about mentioning it.

Even with research aplenty, we have to fess up to the fact that not one word of this book would ever have seen print were it not for the dedication and talent of many, many other people. To begin, we owe enormous thanks to the people who manage and run Walt Disney World. It is their willingness to open their files and explain operations to us in the most detailed and timely way possible (not to mention letting us—and only us—publish pictures of their parks and characters) that makes this the Official Guide, even though it is, in fact, written by non-Disney employees.

In the listing at left we've tried to acknowledge all of the Disney staffers, both in the parks and behind the scenes, who contributed their time, knowledge, and experience to this edition. In addition, we want to extend a deep bow to Julie Woodward, Laura Simpson, Diane Hancock, Regina Maher, and Valjean Smoley for the care and effort they've put into this

Author Pamela S. Weiers

project. We would also like to thank our favorite off-site Disney expert, Wendy Lefkon, who edited our guides for many years and is still instrumental in their publication as executive editor at Hyperion.

For their key roles behind the scenes, we salute Shari Hartford and Susan Hohl. We are also indebted to Laura Vitale for her wondrously uncompromising sense of style. Of course, no list of acknowledgments would be complete without our founding editor, Steve Birnbaum, who was surely smiling on this project, as well as Alexandra Mayes Birnbaum, who continues to be a guiding light—to say nothing of a careful reader of every word.

Finally, it is important to remember that Walt Disney World is constantly changing and growing, and in each annual revision we expect to refine and expand our material to serve your needs even better. For the present edition, though, this is the final word.

Have a great visit!
The Editors

Don't Forget to Write

No contribution is of greater value to us in preparing the next edition of this book than your comments on what we've written and on your own experiences and discoveries at Walt Disney World. Please share your insights with us by writing to:

The Editors, Official Disney Guides
Birnbaum's Walt Disney World Without Kids 1998
1790 Broadway, Sixth Floor
New York, NY 10019

Anyone can have a magical time at Walt Disney World with advance planning.

Planning Ahead

There are plenty of hotels, restaurants, and theme park attractions for everyone at Walt Disney World. So why sit down with a book in hand to plan ahead? Because a little attention to detail beforehand—we like to think of it as shopping for fun insurance—pays big dividends once you arrive in the Orlando area. Just ask the couple who had the foresight to book a table at the ultradeluxe Victoria & Albert's dining room before they left home. Or the friends who arrived with admission passes in hand and thereby avoided the ticket line at the entrance to Epcot. Or the golfers who knew about Disney's golf packages and got a coveted midmorning tee time on the Osprey Ridge course during their Easter visit. Our point: You can't be assured of the vacation experience you want without knowing which of the gazillion ways to enjoy Walt Disney World most appeal to you, and how to go about making sure these potential highlights don't become missed opportunities.

This first chapter not only provides the framework for a successful visit; it establishes a vital awareness that helps the information in subsequent chapters fall right in line. On the following pages, you'll find insight on when to visit; advice on tickets, packages, reservations, and how to save money; information on how to get around the World; flexible touring schedules; tips for older travelers, couples, singles, and guests with disabilities; and a whole lot more. This chapter is a straightforward planner that you'll return to again and again—no doubt with greater purpose than the first time through, when you're still eager to learn about Walt Disney World's hotels, theme parks, dining, and nightlife. So go ahead and give it a quick skim if this is your first read, but don't forget to come back.

WHEN TO GO

Much tougher than the (rhetorical) question of *if* you want to visit Walt Disney World is the prickly matter of *when*. In addition to your own schedule, there is the weather to consider; you'd also like to avoid the crowds, although you'd love to get a gander at the Christmas parade or that flower festival you read about in the newspaper. You want to experience Walt Disney World at its best. But when?

Weather and crowd patterns are charted in this section, along with other factors, such as extended park hours, so you can see how possible vacation dates stack up. Timing your visit to meet all expectations may be impossible, but experience suggests certain optimum times. Mid-January through early February, September through early November, and the week after Thanksgiving through the week before Christmas stand out as particularly good times to find oneself in the World.

Taking things one step further, we like to underline the period from the Sunday *after* Thanksgiving to the week *before* Christmas as the ultimate timing for a WDW visit. This is a chance to savor Walt Disney World during one of its least crowded and most festive times of year. The place is wrapped in wonderful holiday decorations, and there are scads of special goings-on, from parades and parties to themed dinners and stage shows.

WDW WEATHER

	Average High (°F)	Average Low (°F)	Average Rainfall (inches)
January	71	49	2.3
February	73	50	3.0
March	78	55	3.2
April	83	59	1.8
May	88	66	3.6
June	91	72	7.3
July	92	73	7.2
August	92	73	6.8
September	90	72	6.0
October	85	65	2.4
November	79	58	2.3
December	73	51	2.2

If your travel dates fall outside the above-mentioned ideal, don't despair. Walt Disney World makes an extracurricular spectacle of itself year-round. This listing highlights holidays and happenings that—for their fanfare, their crowd-drawing potential, and in some instances, their accompanying package deals—are worth factoring into your vacation plans.

Note: We've provided 1998 dates when available, but specifics are subject to change (and often do). For up-to-the-minute details about listed events, be sure to call the number provided or 824-4321 about one month prior to your visit. For additional information about package offerings, turn to "The Logistics" later in this chapter.

Holidays & Special Events

WALT DISNEY WORLD MARATHON (January 11): International competitors and first-time marathoners alike lace up for a 26.2-mile race through Walt Disney World. The course is flat as a flapjack, wending its way through three of the theme parks and Blizzard Beach water park, and past several resort areas. Live bands, Disney characters, and hot-air balloons inspire some 7,000 runners to stay the course. For details, call 939-7810. Vacation packages are available.

LPGA HEALTHSOUTH INAUGURAL (January 17–19): No matter that this tournament debuted in 1995. The name has stuck because it's the first full-field event of the year—an opportunity for women pros to start the season off with a bang. The Lake Buena Vista course serves as the sole venue, and a two-day pro-am precedes the three-day competition. Call WDW-GOLF (939-4653) for details.

INDY 200 (January 22–24): Indy race cars burn rubber on the Walt Disney World Speedway, a one-mile track just south of the Magic Kingdom parking lot.

MARDI GRAS (February): Crescent City jazz bands, Creole and Cajun food, and street performances bring New Orleans' biggest party to Pleasure Island. Also, join the international celebration at Epcot's World Showcase.

SOAP OPERA FESTIVAL (March): Soaps fans might think they've died and gone to Port Charles at this weekend event in the Disney-MGM Studios. Meet stars and writers from ABC daytime dramas, see sets—and yes, audition.

All in the Timing

Factor the following WDW trends and truths into the equation before settling on vacation dates. For up-to-the-minute details on park hours and any attractions closed for refurbishment, call 824-4321.

■ **Shortest Lines, Smallest Crowds:** the second week of January through the first week of February; the week after Labor Day until Thanksgiving; the week after Thanksgiving through the week before Christmas.

■ **Longest Lines, Biggest Crowds:** Presidents' week; the third week of March through the third week of April, especially Easter week; the second week of June through Labor Day, particularly Fourth of July; Christmas through New Year's Day.

■ **Potential Pitfalls:** The water parks and some WDW attractions are sometimes closed for renovations (most often during winter months). Spring break (usually between February and mid-April) lures many students, as do Grad Nites (weekend events in late April and early May).

■ **Extended Hours:** Presidents' weekend; the two weeks surrounding Easter; summer; Thanksgiving week; Christmas through New Year's Day.

What to Pack

- Comfortable shoes
- Sunscreen
- Bathing suit
- T-shirts and shorts for day
- Casual separates for evening (jeans are okay)
- Lightweight sweaters or jackets for summer evenings and when air-conditioning can be chilly; warmer clothing is essential for evening (and often daytime) from November through March
- A jacket for men and a dress or comparable outfit for women if plans include dinner at Victoria & Albert's or another elegant dining spot
- Any sporting togs and equipment for tennis, golf, fishing, jogging, or gym workouts (racquets, clubs, balls, golf shoes, and poles are available for rent)
- Lightweight rain gear and a folding umbrella

EPCOT SCI-TECH ADVENTURE (March): A month-long series of events highlights new inventions and scientific discoveries. Demonstrations galore mean there's no telling what amazing new thingamadoodles you'll have a chance to observe in action.

PLEASURE ISLAND'S ST. PATRICK'S DAY CELEBRATION (March 17): Pleasure Island gets its Irish up with music from the Emerald Isle, drinks along the lines of the Nutty Irishman, and a four-leaf clover of a food fest.

EASTER (April 12): Main Street becomes a bunny trail in a televised parade that makes for a hopping Magic Kingdom. The theme parks have extended hours—and monumental crowds—throughout the Easter season.

EPCOT INTERNATIONAL FLOWER & GARDEN FESTIVAL (April 17–May 31): This flowery event—a fragrant affair featuring some 30 million blossoms—not only makes a glorious perfumery of Epcot; it allows gardeners to learn a trick or two from the folks who care for 10,000 rosebushes and then some. In addition to the character topiaries and elaborate display gardens in full bloom, gardening workshops, behind-the-scenes tours, and dining and entertainment events are featured. Vacation packages are available.

BLACK MUSIC MONTH (June): Pleasure Island and *Vibe* magazine showcase all genres of black music from gospel to rap, R & B, reggae, jazz, and dance.

FOURTH OF JULY CELEBRATION: Double-fisted fireworks at the Magic Kingdom, Epcot's Illumi-Nations, and the Disney-MGM Studios' stunning symphony of music and fireworks (Sorcery in the Sky) are glorious. But you pay a price: It's the busiest day of the summer.

DISNEYANA (September): For serious Disney enthusiasts, this five-day convention is the be-all and end-all. The event generally alternates between Disneyland and Walt Disney World; this year it's in California.

EPCOT INTERNATIONAL FOOD & WINE FESTIVAL (late October–November): The temptation to eat and drink your way around World Showcase is intensified by gourmet and healthy cooking demonstrations, samples of exotic specialty dishes, international wines by the glass, and worldly desserts.

PLEASURE ISLAND JAZZ FEST (October): Jazz greats from various eras bring live music to the fore in this weekend festival.

WALT DISNEY WORLD/OLDSMOBILE GOLF CLASSIC (October 22–25): In this exciting tournament, now in its 28th year, top PGA Tour players compete alongside amateurs on three classic WDW venues: the Palm, Magnolia, and Lake Buena Vista courses. The drama builds until the final day, when the Magnolia's fickle 18th hole has been known to twist fates. For more information, see the "Golf" section in the *Diversions* chapter, or call WDW-GOLF (939-4653).

FESTIVAL OF THE MASTERS AT DOWNTOWN DISNEY MARKETPLACE (November): One of the South's top-rated art shows, it draws upwards of 200 award-winning exhibitors from around the country. The three-day festival tends to be least crowded on Friday and Sunday mornings. Vacation packages are available.

DISNEY'S MAGICAL HOLIDAYS (November 27–December 31): The whole wide World is positively aglow with holiday spirit, and it doesn't stop at decorations: You can even ice-skate at the Marketplace. Nightly tree-lighting ceremonies are held in three of the parks. The Magic Kingdom celebrates with Mickey's Very Merry Christmas Parade. Epcot invites guests to enjoy a candlelight procession and a choral celebration of holidays around the world. The Disney-MGM Studios mesmerizes with an enveloping display featuring some four million twinkling lights. Vacation packages are available; see "Joy to the World" below.

NEW YEAR'S EVE CELEBRATION (December 31): The theme parks are open after midnight, attracting huge throngs and presenting such high-spirited fun as "Auld Lang Syne" à la Space Mountain. Double-size fireworks are launched over the parks, which are still decked out in full Christmas regalia. Many of the resorts have special celebrations. And for serious partyers, Pleasure Island unleashes the New Year's Eve spectacular it's been rehearsing for the past 364 nights in a special-admission blowout complete with big-name acts.

Joy to the World

To take advantage of the extra festivity on tap during the Christmas season, consider booking a Jolly Holidays vacation package. Available from November 27 through December 24, packages include admission to the Jolly Holidays Dinner Show. For details, call 800-828-0228. The Magic Kingdom hosts Mickey's Very Merry Christmas Party, another special-ticket event, on several nights during the first two weeks of December.

Cruise Patrol

For the vacation *and* the vacation after the vacation, consider a Disney Cruise Line package. After a three- or four-day romp in the theme parks, you'll cruise the Bahamas on a ship fit for Mickey. Staterooms go from basic to luxe, corresponding with accommodations at Disney resorts, and easy transfers are the rule. See *Checking In* for more information.

THE LOGISTICS
Should You Buy a Package?

Travelers who like the idea of paying for their vacation in one lump sum that includes accommodations, transportation, and park admission have a wealth of choices when visiting Walt Disney World. As a rule, these package plans offer some savings over the total cost of the included vacation elements purchased separately; but their real hallmark is convenience—a completely organized vacation with a few perks thrown in for good measure.

Vacation plans put forth by Disney tempt with such extras as unlimited bicycle rentals or golf; meals at WDW restaurants; and unlimited admission to Pleasure Island and the water parks, as well as to the theme parks. Specifics vary, but basic package offerings range from the economical Classic Plan to the top-of-the-line Grand Plan. Additional packages are built around the needs of golfers or honeymooners, and still others are tied to a season or special event. Featured accommodations include hotels on and off WDW property; some deals incorporate discounted airfare. The Disney Cruise Line launches its first ships this year, providing a seamless Walt Disney World–cruise vacation (to learn more, see above margin and *Checking In*). For details on the many packages offered by the Walt Disney Travel Company, call 800-828-0228.

Other operators with plans featuring WDW and off-property hotels include Delta Dream Vacations (800-872-7786), American Express Vacation Travel (800-937-2639), and AAA (for members only; inquire at the nearest AAA office).

Because the value of any package depends wholly on your needs, we have provided a checklist to help you quickly narrow the choices. If you think you might be interested in buying a package, call for brochures, then use these guidelines to help determine which plan, if any, suits you.

The right package: (1) Saves you money on precisely the type of lodging, transportation, and recreation you want. (2) Includes meaningful extras (meals at restaurants of your choice, for example), as opposed to fluff like welcoming cocktails and so-called privileges that are actually services available

to all WDW guests. (3) Fits like a glove. You wouldn't buy a pair of gloves that were two sizes too big no matter what the sale price; nor should you buy a package that encompasses much more than you can reasonably expect to enjoy. Example: If this is your first visit and you have three days to spend, you'll have your hands full just exploring the theme parks, so a package whose main appeal is unlimited admission to other attractions is probably not worth your while. Alternatively, if you're looking to golf yourself silly, you'll get a lot of wear out of a package that allows for unlimited tee times.

Money Matters

A few points of interest related to green matter and its plastic counterparts: Traveler's checks, American Express, Visa, MasterCard, and The Disney Credit Card are acceptable for most charges at Walt Disney World. Full-service and fast-food restaurants in the parks all accept credit cards; refreshment stands operate on a cash-only basis. WDW resort guests who leave a credit card imprint upon check-in may use their hotel ID card to charge meals at full-service and fast-food restaurants, purchases at shops and lounges, and recreational fees.

As for banking services, there are a slew of ATMs accessible to WDW guests. Locations include Main Street, Adventureland, and Tomorrowland in the Magic Kingdom; the entrances to Epcot, the Disney-MGM Studios, and Animal Kingdom; Germany and the walkway between Future World and World Showcase in Epcot; the Transportation and Ticket Center; Pleasure Island; Downtown Disney Marketplace, and Downtown Disney West Side. ATMs can also be found in the lobby of all WDW resorts. For full-service banking, there is a SunTrust branch opposite the Downtown Disney Marketplace (open 9 A.M. to 4 P.M. weekdays, until 6 P.M. Thursday, with drive-in teller service from 8 A.M. to 6 P.M.; 828-6106).

Cost-Cutting Tips

■ Consider accommodations with kitchen facilities to save on food costs. Or rent a small refrigerator (available at WDW resorts for a $5 nightly fee).

■ Compare lunch and dinner menus at a favored restaurant. The same dishes are often available for less at midday.

■ When choosing a place to stay, don't break the budget for a resort packed with amenities you won't have time to enjoy.

■ Join the Magic Kingdom Club to net discounts on certain WDW resort rates (pending availability), golf fees, meals at select theme park restaurants, purchases at Marketplace shops, and more. Many companies offer free membership as an employee perk. Two-year family memberships are $65 ($50 for individuals or couples 55 and older); call 800-893-4763.

■ Call for a free Orlando Magicard (800-551-0181). It offers discounts on Orlando-area accommodations, restaurants, and attractions.

Keep in Mind

■ All admission passes are nontransferable.

■ Passes bought before Animal Kingdom's debut must be upgraded to include the new park.

■ When we say that any unused days on a multi-day pass may be used on a future visit, we mean that these days don't expire until you do.

■ As long as you have at least one day remaining on your Four-Day Value Pass or Four-Day Park Hopper Pass, you can upgrade to a Five-Day World Hopper Pass by paying the difference.

■ If you want to do things like spend the afternoon in the Magic Kingdom and then head to Epcot for dinner and IllumiNations viewing, you need a Four-Day Park Hopper Pass, a Five-Day World Hopper Pass, or a Length of Stay Pass.

Admission Options

The first thing visitors need to understand is the name game: Disney defines a ticket as admission good for one day only; multi-day admission media are called passes. Once you know this, you're ready to consider your options. Note: For the purposes of this section the term *parks* is understood to mean the Magic Kingdom, Epcot, and Disney-MGM Studios. Adult admission prices quoted include sales tax and were correct at press time, but are likely to change with the opening of Animal Kingdom this May. Ticket options for Animal Kingdom were *not* determined at press time; the following does not apply. Call 824-4321 to confirm current prices.

ONE-DAY TICKET ($42.14): Good for one-day admission to one park only.

FOUR-DAY VALUE PASS ($142.04): Valid for one day in each of three parks, plus one additional day at the park of your choice; includes unlimited use of WDW transportation. This pass need not be used on consecutive days; any unused days may be used on a future visit.

FOUR-DAY PARK HOPPER PASS ($159.00): Valid in three parks for four (not necessarily consecutive) days; includes unlimited use of WDW transportation. Any unused days may be used on a future visit.

FIVE-DAY WORLD HOPPER PASS ($217.30): Valid in three parks for five (not necessarily consecutive) days; includes unlimited use of WDW transportation; allows admission to Typhoon Lagoon, Blizzard Beach, River Country, Discovery Island, and Pleasure Island for up to seven days from the first use of the pass. Any unused park admissions may be used on a future visit.

LENGTH OF STAY PASS: Available to WDW resort guests only. Valid for the duration of a guest's stay for admission to three parks, as well as Typhoon Lagoon, Blizzard Beach, River Country, Discovery Island, and Pleasure Island; includes unlimited use of WDW transportation. Prices are $99.64 for two days, $143.10 for three days, $175.96 for four days, $204.58 for five days, $231.08 for six days, $255.46 for seven days, $277.72 for eight days, $297.86 for nine days, and $315.88 for ten days.

THEME PARK ANNUAL PASS ($285.14; $256.52 for renewal): Valid for unlimited admission to three parks for one year; includes unrestricted use of WDW transportation and free parking.

PREMIUM ANNUAL PASS ($380.54; $342.38 for renewal): Valid for unlimited admission to three theme parks, the water parks, Discovery Island, and Pleasure Island for one year; includes unrestricted use of WDW transportation.

Medical Matters

Although quality medical care is readily available at Walt Disney World, travelers with chronic health problems are advised to carry copies of all prescriptions and ask their physicians to provide names of local doctors. Diabetics should note that WDW resorts will provide refrigeration for insulin. More generally:

■ Report emergencies to 911 operators or nearby Sandlake Hospital (351-8550).

■ Each theme park has a First Aid Center staffed by a registered nurse. In the Magic Kingdom, it's next to Crystal Palace; at Epcot, it's in the Odyssey Center, between Mexico and Test Track; at the Studios, it's next to Guest Relations; in Animal Kingdom, it's near the Creature Comforts shop in Safari Village.

■ For nonemergency medical care, Centra Care Walk-In Medical Care (239-6463) at 12500 South Apopka-Vineland Road is open 8 A.M. to midnight weekdays and 8 A.M. to 8 P.M. weekends. HouseMed (239-1195) operates a walk-in treatment center: MediClinic, just east of I-4 on U.S. 192, is open 8 A.M. to 9 P.M. daily. Courtesy transportation is provided to both clinics.

■ HouseMed can also refer you to the closest pharmacy, deliver medications, or send a physician to your hotel room (239-1195 or 396-1195).

The Pass Word

Admission passes may be purchased at the Orlando International Airport, at the theme park entrances, at any WDW resort, at any Hotel Plaza Blvd. resort, and at the Transportation and Ticket Center (a bus and monorail hub near the Magic Kingdom). WDW resort guests may charge passes to their rooms. Cash, traveler's checks, personal checks (with presentation of driver's license and major credit card), Visa, MasterCard, American Express, and The Disney Credit Card are also accepted.

Passes can be bought in advance at The Disney Store; by calling 824-4321 (multi-day passes only; allow two to three weeks for processing); or via mail order (allow three to four weeks). To receive passes by mail, send a check or money order (including $2 for handling) payable to Walt Disney World Company to: Walt Disney World; Box 10030; Lake Buena Vista, FL 32830-0030; Attention: Ticket Mail Order. Passes are also available through Disney's Web site; see page 30 for details.

Tips for Drivers

■ During major events, WDW traffic is frequently rerouted. Follow detour signs, as directed.

■ State law requires use of headlights in the rain.

■ Running near empty? The stations opposite Pleasure Island, near the BoardWalk, and in the Magic Kingdom Auto Plaza are open 24 hours. The AAA Car Care Center, also in the Plaza, provides service (824-0976).

■ Be alert to slippery roads when it rains, as a fine layer of oil (a.k.a. Florida ice) accumulates between drizzles.

■ Call security (824-4777) for towing on WDW property. Riker's Wrecker Service (352-0842) provides 24-hour towing off-property.

■ For traffic reports and news, tune to 90.7 FM (National Public Radio), 580 AM, or 740 AM.

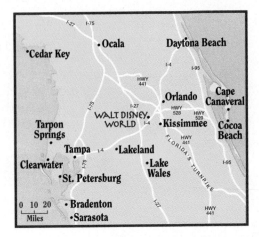

GETTING AROUND

Before you can find your way around Walt Disney World, you must first have a firm sense of where you are (and where you are not). While Walt Disney World is closely associated with the city of Orlando, it is actually located about 22 miles southwest of Orlando proper in a much smaller community called Lake Buena Vista.

The most important highway in the Orlando area is unquestionably I-4, which runs southwest to northeast, cutting through the southern half of Walt Disney World before bisecting Orlando and winding up just shy of Daytona Beach at I-95 (a major coastal artery). All the area's other major highways intersect I-4. Among the more frequently traveled is Route 435 (a.k.a. Kirkman Road), a north–south route that links I-4 to the major hotel-and-business thoroughfare called International Drive, known locally as I-Drive.

Will you need a car during your stay? Only if you plan to spend time touring and exploring outside the World. Most area hotels offer buses to and from Walt Disney World. And Disney's own resorts and parks are serviced by a legion of buses, monorail trains, and boats, which provide efficient means of getting from point to point within WDW borders. This transportation is available to visitors staying at WDW resorts and to those with a multi-day park pass (guests with a one-day ticket to any of the theme parks or River Country have limited access). If you think reliance on mass transit will cramp your style, by all means, rent a car. Disney's transportation is convenient (departing from most areas every 15 to 20 minutes, a bit less frequently during the off-season), but it can accommodate only limited spontaneity. If you decide to get around by car, note that parking at any of the theme parks costs $5 per day (it's free for WDW resort guests).

The following listing—a compilation of WDW transportation to key destinations—is a quick reference for when you simply need to know how to get somewhere in the World. Schedules coordinate with park hours (service begins about one hour prior to park opening, even on special early-entry days, and continues until one hour after park closing), so there's little chance of being stranded. Call 824-4321 to confirm available routes. We have also included options for guests at the Hotel Plaza Blvd. resorts, which have separate bus service.

MAGIC KINGDOM: From the Grand Floridian, Contemporary, and Polynesian: monorail (the Contemporary also has a walkway). From Epcot: monorail to the TTC, then transfer to the TTC–Magic Kingdom monorail or ferry. From the Disney-MGM Studios, Animal Kingdom, Downtown Disney, and the Hotel Plaza Blvd. resorts: buses to the TTC, then transfer to ferry or monorail. From Fort Wilderness and the Wilderness Lodge: boats. From all other WDW resorts: buses.

EPCOT: From the Swan, Dolphin, Yacht Club, Beach Club, and BoardWalk: walkway or boats to the International Gateway entrance, near World Showcase's France pavilion. From the Grand Floridian, Contemporary, and Polynesian:

Directions from Orlando Airport

The distance is about 22 miles. For the most direct route, take the airport's North Exit, head west on Route 528 (a.k.a. the Beeline Expressway) to I-4 west, and turn off at the appropriate WDW exit; tolls are $1.25. If this route is congested, take the South Exit, and follow the Central Florida Greeneway (Route 417) to State Road 536, which leads right to WDW; tolls total $2.

Get off at **Exit 27** for the Hotel Plaza Blvd. resorts.

Take **Exit 26B** for Epcot, Animal Kingdom, Typhoon Lagoon, Old Key West, Caribbean Beach, Swan, Dolphin, BoardWalk, Yacht Club, Beach Club, Dixie Landings, Port Orleans, Disney Institute, or Downtown Disney (Marketplace, West Side, and Pleasure Island).

Use **Exit 25** for Magic Kingdom, Disney-MGM Studios, River Country, Blizzard Beach, Fort Wilderness, Discovery Island, Disney's Wide World of Sports, Grand Floridian, Contemporary, Polynesian, Wilderness Lodge, All-Star Sports, All-Star Music, or Coronado Springs.

For those without wheels, Mears Motor Shuttles is an economical alternative to the $35 or so taxi tab, at about $14 one way or $25 round-trip. The shuttles serve all area hotels, and make the trip every 10 to 25 minutes around the clock. Call 423-5566 for reservations.

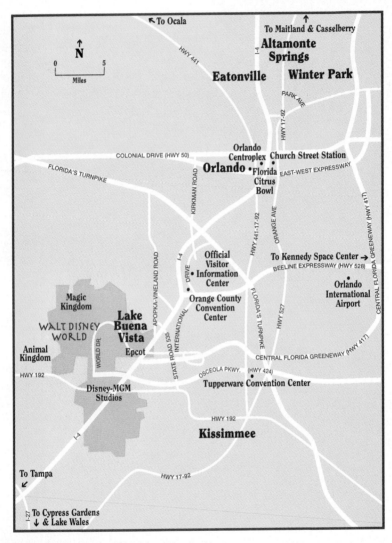

local hotel monorail to the TTC, then switch for the TTC-Epcot monorail. From the Magic Kingdom: express monorail to the TTC, then switch for the TTC-Epcot monorail. From Fort Wilderness and Downtown Disney: buses to the TTC, then transfer to the TTC-Epcot monorail. From Disney-MGM Studios, Animal Kingdom, other WDW resorts, and Hotel Plaza Blvd. resorts: buses.

DISNEY-MGM STUDIOS: From the Swan, Dolphin, Yacht Club, Beach Club, and BoardWalk: water launches. From Fort Wilderness and Downtown Disney: buses to the TTC, then transfer to the Disney-MGM Studios bus. From the Magic Kingdom, Epcot, Animal Kingdom, all other WDW resorts, and Hotel Plaza Blvd. resorts: buses.

ANIMAL KINGDOM: From the Magic Kingdom, Epcot, Disney-MGM Studios, Downtown Disney, WDW resorts, and the Hotel Plaza Blvd. resorts: buses (perhaps with a brief stop at Blizzard Beach).

DOWNTOWN DISNEY: From the Disney Institute: walkway or bus. From Port Orleans, Dixie Landings, and Old Key West: boats or buses. From the Magic Kingdom, Epcot, the Grand Floridian, Contemporary, and Polynesian: monorail to the TTC, then transfer to the Downtown Disney bus (direct buses take guests from these locations after 4 P.M.). From the Disney-MGM Studios, Animal Kingdom, Wilderness Lodge, and Fort Wilderness: buses to the TTC, then switch for the Downtown Disney bus. From all other WDW resorts: buses.

FORT WILDERNESS/RIVER COUNTRY: From the Wilderness Lodge: bus or bike path. From the Magic Kingdom and the Contemporary: boats. From Epcot, the Grand Floridian, Contemporary, and Polynesian: monorail to the TTC, then transfer to the bus to Fort Wilderness. From the Disney-MGM Studios, Animal Kingdom, Downtown Disney, and Hotel Plaza Blvd. resorts: buses to the TTC, then change for Fort Wilderness bus. For all other WDW resorts: bus to Downtown Disney, switch for bus to the TTC, then take Fort Wilderness bus. Note: Visitors who are planning to arrive by car must park in the Fort Wilderness parking lot, then take an internal bus to River Country, Pioneer Hall, and all other Fort Wilderness destinations.

TYPHOON LAGOON: From Fort Wilderness and the Wilderness Lodge: buses to the TTC, then transfer to the Typhoon Lagoon bus. From the Grand Floridian, Contemporary, and Polynesian: monorail to the TTC, then change for the Typhoon Lagoon bus. From the TTC, all other WDW resorts, and Hotel Plaza Blvd. resorts: buses.

BLIZZARD BEACH: From WDW resorts and Hotel Plaza Blvd. resorts: buses.

DISCOVERY ISLAND: From the Magic Kingdom, Contemporary, Fort Wilderness, and River Country: boats. Discovery Island admission ticket or WDW resort ID necessary to ride.

Meet the TTC

Think of the Transportation and Ticket Center (TTC) as the friendly neighborhood hub. Easily the most "connected" place in the World, the TTC is equipped to shuttle guests to most WDW locations. It is most important as a traffic-free link between Epcot and the Magic Kingdom, since WDW's two monorail loops merge here. The TTC also provides connections for day visitors and guests whose resorts do not offer direct transport to certain parts of the World. Parking is available and costs $5 per day (free to WDW resort guests). Park admission passes may be purchased here.

MIX & MATCH
SAMPLE SCHEDULES

The task of deciding how your days at Walt Disney World will be spent only seems daunting. Yes, there is a lot of ground to cover. Beyond the obvious (the Magic Kingdom, Epcot, Disney-MGM Studios, and the new Animal Kingdom) there's a splashy trio of water parks, a quintet of fine 18-hole golf courses, an armada of pleasure boats, a nightlife metropolis, and tons of shopping opportunities. It all sounds quite unwieldy, but you'd be surprised how much fits neatly into a week's vacation.

Rather than provide cues that require cue cards, we've taken the liberty of simplifying matters. To that end, we have carved Walt Disney World's most compelling recreational options for adults into concise activity and touring modules whose contents can generally be accomplished in a day or half day (as allotted). To complement these daytime schedules, we've included evening and rainy day supplements. Fully intended to be mixed and matched (and

Did you know...

Walt Disney World encompasses 45 square miles, an area about twice the size of Manhattan.

expanded or compressed) at your whim, the schedules offer our best guidance and tips to each individual park or diversion; we leave it to you to decide if, when, and how fast. The plans work in tandem with the detailed descriptions provided in the *Theme Parks*, *Diversions*, and *Dining & Entertainment* chapters. We refer you to these chapters for more information, and encourage cross-referencing during the planning stages. For a sense of location, turn to the Walt Disney World map on the inside back cover or the detailed park maps provided in the *Theme Parks* chapter.

Before we set you loose on the schedules, a few general touring guidelines are in order. First, we have allotted five self-contained days to the theme parks—including one day each at Animal Kingdom, the Magic Kingdom, and the Disney-MGM Studios; and two days at Epcot—because this is the minimum amount of time necessary to cover the adult essentials at an unharried pace. As for order, we suggest spending the first day at Animal Kingdom (keep in mind that it may be very crowded), and devoting successive days to touring Epcot, the Disney-MGM Studios, the Magic Kingdom, and Epcot (for an encore). If five days swallow your entire visit, we recommend a day exploring each park, with a flexible day to revisit your favorite attractions or take advantage of another pursuit that's caught your eye. These schedules are ideally used at times when extended evening hours are in effect at the parks, but smaller crowds during the off-season can help you cover the same territory. WDW resort guests participating in the early-entry program at the theme parks should take advantage of attractions open during this time and slip into the schedule after the park's official opening.

A Day at Animal Kingdom

■ Arrive at least a half hour before the park's posted opening time, and prepare to bond with the crowds waiting to enter. (Animal Kingdom opens in May).

■ Pick up a guidemap at Guest Relations. If you haven't made previous arrangements, try to secure priority seating for an early dinner at Rainforest Café.

■ Resist the urge to conduct an informal wildlife census in The Oasis, and walk straight for the bridge to Safari Village. The animals will be here all day. Minimal lines for your two biggest priorities, Countdown to Extinction and Kilimanjaro Safaris, won't.

■ Neglect to have breakfast? Pause at Tuskers or a food cart to silence the growls.

■ Give The Tree of Life a quick once-over, but don't stop to inspect it now. (We promise to come back later.) Instead, head directly for the first brachiosaurus skeleton on your right. In DinoLand U.S.A., make the thrilling acquaintance of Countdown to Extinction. The morning jolt should keep you running for the rest of the day. Also, take a peek at The Boneyard before it's overrun with little diggers.

■ Next, go to Africa (take the bridge back to Safari Village and bear right around The Tree of Life). Make tracks for Kilimanjaro Safaris, and dally on the Gorilla Falls Exploration Trail before breaking for an early lunch (a quick bite at a fast-food spot in Harambe).

■ After lunch, poke around the shop in Harambe. When afternoon crowds descend, hop on the Wildlife Express to Conservation Station—and get your fill of all the interactive exhibits at journey's end.

■ For a (mostly) relaxing ride, circle the park on the Discovery River Boats (board near Africa).

■ *Now* see the movie in The Tree of Life. Be sure to check out the animal carvings on the tree and all around the shops of Safari Village.

■ Return to DinoLand U.S.A. for a leisurely walk back in time on the Cretaceous Trail. While you're here, slot in a time to see the show at the Theater in the Wild (check your guidemap for the schedule).

■ If there's time before dinner, snoop on the little critters in The Oasis.

■ No fireworks here (imagine the stampede!). As an alternative, experience dinner as entertainment at thunderstorm-prone Rainforest Café. If you have other plans, consider stopping in for an after-dinner Margarilla or Spotted Chocolate Monkey.

Photographic Details

Whether you need film, a battery, or a camcorder loaner, the theme parks are prepared to provide. Camcorders ($30 per day with a $450 deposit) may be rented at the Camera Center in the Magic Kingdom, the Camera Center and World Traveler in Epcot, The Darkroom in the Disney-MGM Studios, and Garden Gate Gifts at Animal Kingdom. Refundable deposits may be charged to American Express, MasterCard, or Visa. Two-hour film processing is available (where you see a Photo Express sign) at the theme parks, WDW resorts, and Downtown Disney.

Be Prepared

■ If you want to see a dinner show—particularly the Hoop-Dee-Doo Musical Revue, the World's toughest ticket—reserve a table in the same breath that you book your hotel. Reservations are taken up to two years in advance; call WDW-DINE (939-3463).

■ Arrange for priority seating at WDW restaurants (up to 60 days in advance) by calling WDW-DINE.

■ If you or one of your traveling companions has a disability, request the *Walt Disney World Guidebook for Guests with Disabilities* (see "Customized Tips" in this chapter for details) before leaving home.

■ Call 824-4321 to confirm park hours in effect during your visit, and plan an itinerary using the schedules provided in this chapter.

•CONTINUED ON NEXT PAGE

A Day at Epcot

■ Note that guests are often permitted to enter the park a half hour before Future World's scheduled opening.

■ If you were unable to secure priority seating arrangements for lunch or dinner before your arrival, head for Guest Relations straightaway to book a table at one of the international restaurants of World Showcase. Pick up a guidemap while there.

■ If you haven't had breakfast or could use a cup of java, stop in at Fountain View Espresso and Bakery.

■ Visit Test Track, Wonders of Life (your priorities here: Cranium Command and Body Wars), and The Land.

■ This should take you up to 11 A.M., when World Showcase opens. Consider grabbing an early bite at The Land's Sunshine Season Food Fair before crossing over from Future World into World Showcase.

■ View *O Canada!* at the Canada pavilion and *Impressions de France* at the France pavilion. Backtrack to take in the shops, gardens, and pub at the United Kingdom pavilion before fully exploring France.

■ Aiming to reach The American Adventure and catch the next show there before dinner (check your guidemap for showtimes), pause en route to take in the compelling street entertainment, shops, gardens, and art galleries in Morocco and Japan.

■ After dinner, return to Future World and visit Spaceship Earth (if you have time, pop into Innoventions for a peek).

■ Keep an eye on the time so you can secure a good spot around World Showcase Lagoon (we recommend the area between Italy and The American Adventure) to watch the evening's performance of IllumiNations.

A Day at the Disney-MGM Studios

■ Arrive before the posted opening time, as doors often open a half hour early.

■ Pick up a guidemap at Guest Relations; note that many attractions have set showtimes, and some don't open until later in the morning.

■ Haven't had breakfast yet? Consider stopping by the Starring Rolls Bakery for a quick croissant.

■ If you were unable to book a table for dinner before leaving home, stop at the kiosk at Hollywood Junction (the corner of Hollywood and Sunset boulevards) and make priority seating arrangements for the 50's Prime Time Café or the Hollywood Brown Derby. Note: This plan assumes a quick lunch taken whenever your personal lunch bell rings (good bets are Hollywood & Vine and Backlot Express).

■ If you're up for a couple of 13-story drops, head directly for The Twilight Zone Tower of Terror on Sunset Boulevard (but do so *before* you eat). For something much tamer, you might try to get a jump on the notoriously long line at Voyage of The Little Mermaid.

■ Afterward, head across the park to take in Star Tours, Jim Henson's Muppet*Vision 3-D, and The Hunchback of Notre Dame show. Stroll down New York Street. Next, see The Magic of Disney Animation, The Great Movie Ride, and SuperStar Television. Note that the Hercules parade passes through these parts around 2 P.M. (twice during busy seasons), and plan accordingly.

■ Having taken care of your highest touring priorities, check your guidemap and slot in times before or after dinner to see what you can of Indiana Jones Epic Stunt Spectacular, the Studio Backlot Tour, Backstage Pass to 101 Dalmatians, and The ABC Sound Studio.

■ Make note of when the last performance of Beauty and the Beast Live on Stage takes place, and make a point of seeing it then.

•CONTINUED FROM PREVIOUS PAGE

■ If you're a golfer, reserve tee times as far in advance as possible—60 days ahead if you're staying at a WDW resort or a Hotel Plaza Blvd. resort, 30 days ahead if you're not—to secure your preferred time(s) and venue(s). For visits during WDW's peak links season (see "Sports" in the *Diversions* chapter for details), consider a golf package, which allows you to reserve tee times up to 90 days in advance. Lessons may be reserved up to a year ahead. Call WDW-GOLF (939-4653).

■ Note that tennis lessons may be booked up to a year in advance (call 824-3578), and guided Fort Wilderness fishing trips may be reserved up to two weeks ahead (call 824-2621).

■ A few days before you leave home, make a quick round of calls to confirm all travel arrangements, including flight, rental car, airport transfers, and lodging.

In the Evening Hours

Here's more than a week's worth of activities for your consideration. For a complete guide to after-dark amusements, see our "Nightlife Guide" in the *Dining & Entertainment* chapter.

■ Attend a dinner show (all require advance reservations, and our favorite, the Hoop-Dee-Doo Musical Revue, requires more forethought than any other).

■ For a cheap thrill (just $6 per person) and an early night, take a hayride at Fort Wilderness.

■ Grab a partner and play the coolest tennis at Walt Disney World. There are a couple dozen WDW courts lighted for night play. The courts at the Dolphin and Swan are open 24 hours.

•CONTINUED ON NEXT PAGE

■ Between attractions, check out the interesting shops and the Sunset Ranch Market. For a relaxing breather, slip into the Catwalk Bar or the Tune-In Lounge.

A Day at the Magic Kingdom

■ Plan to be in the parking lot at least 45 minutes before the park is scheduled to open, so as to be at the Central Plaza end of Main Street before opening time.

■ Pick up a guidemap at City Hall. While here, if you haven't booked a table in advance, make any desired priority seating arrangements for lunch or dinner. (We recommend Liberty Tree Tavern or Tony's Town Square, preferably for an early lunch.)

■ If you haven't had breakfast, grab a bite at the Main Street Bake Shop.

■ When the park opens, see what you can of the top priorities, at your own pace. It's good to begin with Space Mountain and Alien Encounter, then move on to take in Splash Mountain, Big Thunder Mountain Railroad, Pirates of the Caribbean, The Haunted Mansion, The Hall of Presidents, and The Timekeeper.

■ Pausing for lunch when your priority seating time arrives or hunger calls, begin a second sweep of the park, targeting such attractions as the Walt Disney World Railroad, Carousel of Progress, Cinderella Castle, Liberty Belle Riverboat, Country Bear Jamboree, and Diamond Horseshoe Saloon Revue. Stop to check out any shops and entertainment en route that catch your eye.

■ About 20 minutes before the afternoon parade (daily at 3 P.M.): Either camp out on Main Street or head for Fantasyland to see as many key attractions—Peter Pan's Flight, Legend of the Lion King, and It's A Small World—as possible before the crowds swell back to normal.

■ Spend the rest of the day tying up loose ends on your touring checklist and perusing the shops on Main Street (while you're there, check out the Main Street Cinema).

■ Consider arranging to have dinner at a restaurant accessible via monorail (perhaps California Grill at the Contemporary resort or Narcoossee's at the Grand Floridian resort). Return to the park in time to snare a spot on Main Street to watch the SpectroMagic parade if it's scheduled during your visit (generally busy seasons and some weekends). If there are two runnings of the parade, aim to see the later one.

Another Day at Epcot

■ Follow the initial guidelines provided in the first Epcot touring schedule.

■ Visit Journey Into Imagination (your priorities here: Honey, I Shrunk the Audience and Image Works), The Living Seas, and the Universe of Energy.

■ Once World Showcase has opened (at 11 A.M.), cross over into this area of the park, beginning this time with Mexico. Be sure to wander into the pyramid (and don't miss the artifacts exhibit and the handicraft market). For lunch, we recommend watermelon juice from Mexico's Cantina de San Angel and a sandwich from Norway's Kringla Bakeri og Kafé, followed by a soft pretzel at Germany's Sommerfest.

■ Moving along into Norway, ride Maelstrom, pop into the Stave Church Gallery, and then head for China to take in the film and gardens. Stroll through Germany and Italy, as well as any World Showcase pavilions you didn't get enough of on your first day (France and its pastries are not far).

■ Return to Future World, and make your way through Innoventions, being sure to notice the fiber-optic sidewalks and to try at least one of the virtual reality exhibits. There's a lot to see in these two buildings, so allow time to explore.

■ If you have dinner reservations at a World Showcase restaurant, consider prefacing the meal with a drink at the United Kingdom's Rose & Crown Pub, Japan's Matsu No Ma, or the Cantina de San Angel in Mexico.

•CONTINUED FROM PREVIOUS PAGE

■ Try the Disney Institute's killer dinner-and-show combo, about $27 per person, and completely different every night (reserve ahead).

■ For dining as event, book a table at Victoria & Albert's, Artist Point, Bistro de Paris, California Grill, Yachtsman Steakhouse, or Flying Fish Café.

■ If ready-made nightlife appeals, go club-hopping at Pleasure Island. One stop, many different venues, plus a New Year's Eve street party every night. Or swing by Downtown Disney West Side, Pleasure Island's new neighbor, to check out the options.

■ Take a wine tour. Martha's Vineyard at the Beach Club resort takes crushed grapes seriously, and pours wines both by the glass and by the "flight" (two-ounce samples that follow a theme).

■ Prefer the grain to the grape? Beer lovers' hangouts include BoardWalk's working brewpub, Big River Grille & Brewing Works; Crew's Cup lounge at the Yacht Club resort; and The Laughing Kookaburra Good Time Bar at Buena Vista Palace.

■ For a nostalgic evening, stroll the boards at BoardWalk, where everything from saltwater taffy to a classic dance hall and dueling pianos awaits.

Rainy Day Inserts

The sun will come out tomorrow (or maybe in a few hours). In the meantime, here are some great ways to pass the time.

■ See a movie with all the comforts in the 24-screen AMC Theatres at Downtown Disney West Side.

■ Shop your way through Downtown Disney Marketplace, and out beyond Walt Disney World, where outlets and antiques centers will keep you dry.

■ Call Disney's Wide World of Sports to find out if you can catch an indoor event (363-6600 for schedules).

■ Sink into a sofa in the lobby of the Grand Floridian, and simply listen to the graceful music. Or curl up in front of the fireplace at Wilderness Lodge.

•CONTINUED ON NEXT PAGE

A Day at the Disney Institute

■ Not ready to commit to a Disney Institute vacation? Pique your curiosity about this experiential resort by getting acquainted with it as a day guest.

■ You'll have free rein to choose from any available programs, trying your hand at animation, gourmet cooking, rock climbing, or radio broadcasting, to name just a few of the participatory experiences offered. For broadest program choice, reserve as far in advance as possible (two weeks ahead).

■ Arrive early, and count on wanting to stay into the evening to take in whatever performances are happening that night (they're included in the day rate). For inspirational and efficient dining, include a cooking session. Allow time to check out the incredibly endowed Sports & Fitness Center.

Water Parks (Half Day)

■ Choose from River Country, an old-fashioned swimming hole nestled into a cove of Bay Lake; Typhoon Lagoon, seven times the size of River Country, with one of the world's largest wave pools; and Blizzard Beach, WDW's newest and biggest water park, themed as a ski resort.

■ Whichever you visit, be at the gate when the park opens, as these places frequently fill up before noon during the warmer months. When the water parks reach a certain capacity, only guests arriving via WDW buses are admitted until crowds subside, usually about 3 P.M. When they hit peak capacity, no one is admitted until the throngs ease up.

■ Blizzard Beach's relative novelty (it opened in 1995), makes it extremely popular; guests should expect lots of company and ask an attendant to point out any quiet zones.

■ Note that you may bring a picnic lunch and nonalcoholic beverages into any of the water parks, and while fast food is available, it's fun to BYO.

■ Typhoon Lagoon and Blizzard Beach each feature a lazy waterway perfect for a cool respite from the water slide traffic. Grab one of the inner tubes and settle in for a relaxing ride.

■ River Country offers a brief, but pretty and extremely peaceful, nature trail that winds through egret territory on the lake's edge; peer through a trailside telescope for a view across the lake.

Golf (Half Day)

■ Essential for anyone who has even a minor passion for the game, Disney's five outstanding 18-hole courses challenge golfers of all abilities. Demand requires that you reserve space as far in advance as possible—up to 60 days ahead for WDW resort and Hotel Plaza Blvd. resort guests, and up to 30 days for others—to secure your preferred venue and time.

■ Morning tee times, the toughest to come by, provide the most comfortable temperatures; but consider, too, the significant savings afforded by twilight rates, in effect year-round, usually after 3 P.M.

■ Beginners might want to start with the Lake Buena Vista course, which, while no pushover, offers a forgiving layout. Experienced golfers should not miss Osprey Ridge or Eagle Pines. The nine-hole Oak Trail practice course is yet another great skill sharpener.

■ For fun puttering around, Disney's 18-hole Fantasia Gardens miniature golf course provides a *Fantasia*-themed escape, complete with entertaining bits of sorcery. For mini golf that deftly approaches real golf, Fantasia Fairways packs all manner of exaggerated contours, devilish water hazards and sand traps, unique doglegs, and challenging par 3s and par 4s into its 18 holes.

Downtown Disney Marketplace (Half Day)

■ A great afternoon or evening outing on the last day of your visit, this bustling shopping enclave boasts the biggest stash of Disney merchandise anywhere. And it's open until 11 P.M.

■ Be sure to poke into the World of Disney, where Disney characters take their place on an astounding array of goods—from jewelry, clothing, and office accessories to decorative items for the home. Also check out the Christmas Chalet, 2R's Reading and Riting, The Art of Disney, Gourmet Pantry, and Team Mickey's Athletic Club.

■ Additional temptations include the food (especially at adjacent Pleasure Island's Portobello Yacht Club), the delectable raw bar at Fulton's Crab House, and the strawberry margaritas at Cap'n Jack's Oyster Bar.

■ For people-watching, sipping lemonade, eating a take-out sandwich or salad alfresco, or simply taking a load off your feet, consider the do-it-yourself sidewalk café formed by the array of waterfront tables here.

•CONTINUED FROM PREVIOUS PAGE

■ Get a massage. The World's two spas and several of its health clubs have licensed massage therapists on hand, and they too need something to do on a rainy day. Of course, the clubs' personal trainers may also be able to spare an hour or so.

■ Take afternoon tea at the Grand Floridian's Garden View lounge.

Internet users can simply enter *http://www
.disneyworld.com* to
receive an interactive
preview or update on
WDW's offerings on the
World Wide Web.
Packed with sophisticated graphics,
the Web site is ever
changing. Among its
more valuable features:
interactive maps, ticket
sales, a reservations
desk, "live" images from
the theme parks, details
on special events, and
a wealth of information
on everything Disney.

■ Shopped out? Rent a boat from the marina for an excursion on Buena Vista Lagoon. The Gourmet Pantry's got fixings for a pontoon-bound picnic.

Boating (Half Day)

■ When you add up all the Water Sprites, sailboats, pedal boats, canoes, pontoons, and such, Walt Disney World's marinas have the country's largest fleet of pleasure boats. All provide a great intermission from the theme parks' hubbub.

■ The sailing's best on Bay Lake and Seven Seas Lagoon; for Water Sprites, we like the running room of Buena Vista Lagoon at Downtown Disney Marketplace. Canoeing the canals of Fort Wilderness is quite peaceful in the morning.

■ If you're up for trying something new—and brave enough to hover 200 feet over Bay Lake—check out the parasailing operation at the Contemporary resort's marina.

Fishing (Half Day)

■ The two-hour guided fishing trips that ply the World's waters several times daily rank among the most relaxing interludes available to WDW visitors.

■ As for timing, consider the appeal of being out on Seven Seas Lagoon, bonding with friends and the (rather large) largemouth bass that reside there, while the rest of the World is gulping down breakfast and running for the parks.

■ While WDW's various guided catch-and-release trips offer similar experiences, we recommend outings on Bay Lake and Seven Seas Lagoon for the biggest catches; the Marketplace's or Dixie Landings' early-morning gigs are great for singles and twosomes, who can save by paying by the seat (rather than by the boat).

Discovery Island (Half Day)

■ The perfect antidote to theme park overdose, this lushly landscaped island wildlife sanctuary is a terrific retreat. And it's totally covered with shade.

■ Check the schedule upon arrival, and see the next Feathered Friends show.

■ Before or after showtime, follow the path on a clockwise tour of the island. Don't rush, as the enjoyment's in the leisurely observation of 100-some species.

■ Bring your own picnic lunch (or stop by the Thirsty Perch); bypass the main picnic area for tables tucked into a pleasantly removed alcove by the toucan exhibit.

CUSTOMIZED TIPS
Guests with Disabilities

Walt Disney World has long earned kudos from guests with disabilities because of the attention paid to their needs. Still, familiarization with the World as it relates to one's personal requirements is essential, and to this end, the comprehensive *Walt Disney World Guidebook for Guests with Disabilities* is required reading. The guide is available at all wheelchair rental locations (as well as City Hall in the Magic Kingdom and Guest Relations at Epcot, Disney-MGM Studios, and Animal Kingdom). However, we strongly recommend getting hold of this publication well before you leave home to become familiar with procedures and accessibility. To do this, send a written request to Walt Disney World Guest Communications; Box 10000; Lake Buena Vista, FL 32830. Note that the extensive information provided is also available instantly on Disney's Web site; see the margin on the opposite page for details.

Those interested in guided tours should note: The Society for the Advancement of Travel for the Handicapped (347 Fifth Ave., Suite 610; New York, NY 10016; 212-447-7284) can provide a list of travel agents who are knowledgeable about tours for travelers with disabilities and experienced in arranging both individual and group tours. To receive the listing, send a check or money order for $5. If you prefer to connect directly with a tour operator, consider Flying Wheels Travel (800-535-6790), which can also arrange trips for individuals.

While we defer to the *Walt Disney World Guidebook for Guests with Disabilities* for its comprehensiveness, we offer the following advice as an indication of existing facilities and services:

■ Special parking is available at the theme parks (inquire at Auto Plazas upon entering). Valet parking at Downtown Disney (available from 5:30 P.M. to closing) is complimentary for guests with disabilities.

■ All monorail stations are accessible to guests in wheelchairs *except* the one at the Contemporary resort, which can be reached only by escalator. WDW buses are frequently, but not always, equipped with wheelchair lifts.

■ Most theme park attractions are accessible to guests who can be lifted to and from their wheelchairs with the assistance of a member of their party, and many can accommodate guests who must remain in their wheelchairs at all times. Consult the *Walt Disney World Guidebook for Guests with Disabilities*, a park guidemap, or check in with a host or hostess for additional guidance.

■ Note that all hotels listed in this book's *Checking In* chapter offer rooms specially equipped for guests with disabilities. All WDW resorts are easily explored by wheelchair. While room and bathroom configurations vary among hotels, lending themselves better to guests with certain needs, all but the Polynesian resort offer roll-in showers. For assistance in selecting a WDW hotel whose public areas and barrier-free rooms best serve your specific requirements, ask to speak to someone in the Special Requests Department when you call Central Reservations (934-7639). The representatives are extremely informed.

Important Phone Numbers

Central Reservations:
W-DISNEY (934-7639)

Donald Duck: **Unlisted**

Lost and Found:
824-4245

Priority Seating:
WDW-DINE (939-3463)

Walt Disney Travel
Company: **800-828-0228**

WDW Information:
824-4321

Weather: **824-4104**

• • •

AMC Theatres: **827-1300**

Behind-the-Scenes
Tours: **939-8687**

Centra Care Walk-In
Medical Care: **239-6463**

Disney's Racquet Club:
824-3578

Downtown Disney
Marketplace: **828-3800**

Golf Reservations/
Lessons: **WDW-GOLF (939-4653)**

Pleasure Island:
934-7781

Sandlake Hospital:
351-8550

■ Wheelchairs are available for rent at each of the theme parks, as are Electric Convenience Vehicles (ECVs). At the Magic Kingdom, the rental area is just inside the main entrance on the right; at Epcot, rentals are available inside the entrance plaza on the left, at the gift shop to the right of the ticket booths, and at the International Gateway; at the Disney-MGM Studios, rentals are handled at Oscar's Super Service, just inside the entrance; Animal Kingdom rentals are at Garden Gate Gifts near the entrance to the park. Wheelchair rentals cost $5 per day, and require a $1 refundable deposit. Guests planning to visit more than one park on the same day may obtain a replacement wheelchair at the next park with no additional charge or deposit (just be sure to save your receipt and return the wheelchair by the end of the day). Due to the limited number of ECVs, they usually sell out within the first couple of hours the parks are open. The cost to rent an ECV is $30 (plus a $10 refundable deposit) per park per day.

■ Areas along the parade routes in the Magic Kingdom and Disney-MGM Studios are earmarked for guests using wheelchairs. Similarly, several prime spots around the lagoon at Epcot are set aside for guests in wheelchairs wishing to view Illumi-Nations. Arrive early, as these areas are filled on a first-come, first-served basis. See park guidemaps for exact locations.

■ For guests who are sight impaired, the theme parks offer cassettes designed to accentuate enjoyment of each park through detailed description. A $25 refundable deposit is required for use of a tape recorder.

■ Guests who use telecommunications devices for the deaf (TDDs) can call 827-5141 for WDW Information. Complimentary TDDs are available for guest use at City Hall in the Magic Kingdom; at Guest Relations in Epcot, the Disney-MGM Studios, and Animal Kingdom; and at Guest Services in Downtown Disney Marketplace.

■ Assistive listening devices, which amplify attraction sound tracks for the benefit of guests who are hearing impaired, are available (with a $25 refundable deposit) at City Hall in the Magic Kingdom and at Guest Relations in Epcot, Disney-MGM Studios, and Animal Kingdom. Scripts are also available at each attraction for hearing-impaired guests. For live performances, guests can request sign language interpretation; to make arrangements, call 824-4321 (voice) or 827-5141 (TDD) at least two weeks in advance. Also, a new Reflective Captioning Device that projects dialogue onto a panel placed in front of guests is becoming available for use in theater shows. Inquire at Guest Relations.

Older Travelers

Walt Disney World is a friendly and welcoming place, but its sheer enormity and energy level, and its mere heat, particularly during the summer, have the potential to overwhelm. While knowing what to expect is half the battle, knowing how to plan accordingly is even more important. The keys to an enjoyable, relaxed visit for older visitors apply to everyone (although the stubborn younger crowd will likely resist). Our suggestions:

■ Familiarize yourself with the areas you plan to visit by reading Walt Disney World literature before you arrive.

■ Plan your visit for one of the least crowded times of year (see "When to Go" earlier in this chapter). Also note that Florida residents net discounts on selected nonpeak dates. Call 824-4321 for details.

■ Don't be shy about asking Disney employees for directions or advice. They are always happy to help out.

■ Consider enlisting the services of a private guide to usher you through the theme parks. Eventures Unlimited Inc. (826-0055 or 800-356-7891) charges $20 per hour (with a four-hour minimum, plus admission for the guide).

■ In the parks, eat early or late to avoid mealtime crowds, and snack on the juices and fresh fruit sold at stands. Touring takes energy.

■ Protect yourself from the sun by wearing sunscreen and a hat. Be sure to cover your legs (as sunlight reflecting off the pavement leaves them vulnerable to sunburn) and the back of your neck.

■ Drink lots of liquids, and take frequent rest stops in the shade (for the best locales in each park, see the "Quiet Nooks" lists in the margins of the *Theme Parks* chapter).

■ Don't underestimate the distances to be covered at Epcot; the park is bigger than the Magic Kingdom and the Disney-MGM Studios combined, and visitors often log a few miles in a full day of touring. However you're getting around, take it slowly. Broken into small increments with plenty of air-conditioned or

For Woofers & Meowers

No pets other than service animals are permitted in the theme parks. Travelers may lodge Fluffy or Fido in one of WDW's five air-conditioned Pet Care Kennels, opt for a designated pet site at the Fort Wilderness resort and campground, or call the Orlando/Orange County Convention and Visitors Bureau (363-5871) to locate one of the number of area hotels that allow pets. WDW's kennels are available for day or overnight stays, and may be found near the TTC; at the entrances to Epcot, the Disney-MGM Studios, and Animal Kingdom; and at Fort Wilderness, where the facility is next to an open field. WDW resort guests pay $9 for overnight pet stays, including food; others pay $11. Day rates are $6 and include one feeding. Pets must have proof of vaccination. For kennel hours and other information, call 824-6568.

WDW Resort Phone Numbers

All-Star Music: **939-6000**

All-Star Sports: **939-5000**

Beach Club: **934-8000**

BoardWalk: **939-5100**

Caribbean Beach: **934-3400**

Contemporary: **824-1000**

Coronado Springs: **939-1000**

Dixie Landings: **934-6000**

Dolphin: **934-4000**

Fort Wilderness: **824-2900**

Grand Floridian: **824-3000**

Old Key West: **827-7700**

Polynesian: **824-2000**

Port Orleans: **934-5000**

Swan: **934-3000**

The Villas at the Disney Institute: **827-1100**

Wilderness Lodge: **824-3200**

Yacht Club: **934-7000**

tree-shaded breaks, it's not so tiring. The launches that cross World Showcase Lagoon provide a nice break for weary feet, but only when there are no long queues. Lots of older travelers who enjoy walking around the other parks choose to treat themselves to a wheelchair here. As in the other parks, wheelchairs and Electric Convenience Vehicles are easily rented at the park entrance. (When Animal Kingdom opens this May, you'll want to heed the same advice.)

■ For a nostalgic evening out, spend a few hours strolling along the BoardWalk. Be sure to stop into Atlantic Dance, where retro-swing music (forties-style tunes with a nineties spin) played by live bands will have you twirling on the dance floor.

Single Travelers

While Walt Disney World may not exactly be the last word for singles in search of romance (single rates are available only at the Disney Institute), the fact is, singles and independent travelers can have an absolute blast here.

The novelty of being solo in a sea of groups invites friendly conversation from WDW employees and fellow visitors alike. The freedom to set one's own course—pausing to chat with the young World Showcase employees born and educated in the country their pavilion represents, for example—truly enhances the WDW experience. And there is no shortage of places and situations for meeting people. Some ideas:

■ Pleasure Island's clubs typically attract lots of locals on weekends. The polished atmosphere of Stone Crab lounge at Fulton's Crab House is a happening social setting as well. The clubs that recently opened at Downtown Disney West Side also attract a hip crowd.

■ Teppanyaki Dining Rooms and the Biergarten restaurant at Epcot, where smaller parties are seated together, offer especially convivial settings.

■ Some of the World's more compelling restaurants have an area with counter seating, which helps take the sting out of dining solo. These noteworthy spots include the California Grill, Flying Fish Café, Narcoossee's, Fulton's Crab House, and Portobello Yacht Club.

■ The water parks and hotel swimming pools are great spots for friendly encounters, provided you don't mind meeting people in your bathing suit.

■ The Disney Institute's interactive programs and inherently friendly atmosphere—there are even community tables in the dining room—make it a great destination for singles.

- At WDW's 18-hole golf courses, company is a given; players are assigned to a group when tee times are allotted.
- The casual atmosphere along the BoardWalk makes it a fun place to people-watch, and the slew of eateries, shops, and clubs provide interesting diversions.
- If you're a tennis player sans partner, consider the "Tennis Anyone?" program at Disney's Racquet Club.
- Tour programs are engaging alternatives to exploring Epcot's World Showcase solo (see page 116 for details).

Couples

There is a place for lovebirds at Walt Disney World. Actually, there are many spots in the World perfectly suited to those with romantic intentions. The Magic Kingdom's nostalgic carousel-and-castle combo invokes enchantment in the truest fairy-tale tradition. Epcot's World Showcase has the aura of a whirlwind tour (and inspiration for a future trip?), with 11 countries as exotic and far-reaching as Japan and Morocco (and it has even bottled France). The Disney-MGM Studios recaptures an era of starry-eyed elegance. And what could be more titillating than sharing a surprise-filled safari through Africa at the new Animal Kingdom? By day, there is romance in the theme parks for those already inclined to hold hands; by night, the parks sparkle with an intensity that inspires sudden mushiness in those who never considered themselves the type, and that's *before* the fireworks displays.

As the themed resorts of Walt Disney World go about transporting guests to various times and places, they make quite a few passes through settings straight out of the vacation fantasy textbook. From the endearing Victorian charms of the Grand Floridian to the exotic island getaway that is the Polynesian, it's safe to say that Disney has romantic notions that go way beyond heart-shaped tubs. You won't find a more picture-perfect setting than the wondrously rustic Wilderness Lodge, marked by geysers, waterfalls, steamy hot springs, and the grandest stone fireplace you've ever seen. At the nostalgic BoardWalk resort,

Keeping the Faith

Among the religious services most convenient for Walt Disney World guests are those held at the Polynesian resort. Every Sunday at the Polynesian's Luau Cove, a Protestant service is offered at 9 A.M., and Catholic masses are held at 8 A.M. and 10:15 A.M. For information on local Protestant and Catholic parishes, call the Christian Service Center at 425-2523.

Jewish visitors may attend Conservative services at Temple Ohalei Rivka (11200 Apopka-Vineland Rd.; 239-5444) or Reform and Shabbat services at the Congregation of Liberal Judaism (928 Malone Dr.; 645-0444), near Winter Park. Muslim services are held at Jama Masijid (11543 Ruby Lake Rd.; 238-2700).

The Most Romantic Places in the World

RESORTS
Wilderness Lodge
Grand Floridian
Polynesian
Port Orleans
BoardWalk
Yacht Club

RESTAURANTS
Victoria & Albert's
Bistro de Paris
Artist Point
Yachtsman Steakhouse
California Grill
Liberty Tree Tavern
Maya Grill
Portobello Yacht Club
Cinderella's Royal Table
San Angel Inn

LOUNGES
Martha's Vineyard
Pleasure Island Jazz
   Company
Atlantic Dance
Garden View
Matsu No Ma
Tambu

nestled courtship chairs and romantic rides along the waterfront in unique rolling chairs provide memorable locales for the whispering of sweet nothings.

And there's more. Consider a restaurant that starts with candlelight, then takes things a step further by setting the dining room inside a Mayan pyramid fitted out with such decorative flourishes as a moonlit river and a smoking volcano. (See the left margin and the *Dining & Entertainment* chapter for more of our romantic picks.)

Those couples with bigger things in mind, like tying the knot, might consider "I do"–ing it here. While no one yet has likened Mickey Mouse to Eros, newlyweds have beaten such a path to Mickey's doorstep over the years that Walt Disney World rates as the most popular honeymoon destination in the country. In fact, more than 1,000 couples flock to Walt Disney World each year to exchange vows. Why this place, you ask? For some couples it's a matter of mutual Disney adoration, a sense of getting things off to a magical start; for others it's a convenient answer to the dilemma posed by the bride being from one area of the country and the groom, from quite another (they figure if everybody's going to be traveling for the wedding, they might as well get a vacation out of it). Still others see it as an opportunity to, for example, have a semblance of a Polynesian-style honeymoon without the hassle of actually *going* there.

WEDDINGS: In these parts, the sky is truly the limit. Intimate weddings for up to six guests start at $2,500; for larger affairs, figure $12,500 minimum. WDW coordinators work with couples from six months to a year in advance to create a wedding tailored to their specifications—from elegant affairs without a hint of Disneyana to the sort in which the bride arrives in Cinderella's coach and Goofy "crashes" the reception. These wedding gurus are equipped to handle most any imaginable detail and, indeed, a litany of unimaginables.

The possibilities are infinite and growing. Evening nuptials in the theme parks (which hover in the $45,000 range) take place after park closing and allow couples to take their vows in front of Cinderella Castle in the Magic Kingdom or in a traditional English courtyard in Epcot's World Showcase, among other places. For an extra $15,000, a free-spending couple can get a sprinkling of pixie dust and a personal exhibition of Fantasy in the Sky fireworks.

Then there's the Wedding Pavilion—a dainty structure reminiscent of a Victorian summerhouse that sits on a lushly landscaped man-made island between the Grand Floridian and Polynesian resorts. Surrounded by roses, palm trees,

and beaches, the glass-enclosed pavilion seats 250 and offers a prime view of Cinderella Castle, perfectly framed in a window behind the altar. Picture Point—a trellised archway set among the pavilion's gardens, with the castle prominently in the backdrop—is also an option for ceremonies with up to six guests. For couples still in the planning stages, the tasteful on-site wedding salon is like a three-dimensional bridal magazine.

Indoor and outdoor settings for weddings are also available at many WDW resorts; the garden-bound gazebo at the Yacht Club, Sunset Point at the Polynesian, and Sea Breeze Point at the BoardWalk are popular spots to tie the knot.

Wedding packages vary broadly, depending upon the type of ceremony and reception desired, and include discounted rates at certain WDW resorts for family and friends attending the wedding. For additional information about weddings at Walt Disney World, call 828-3400.

HONEYMOONS: Most WDW resorts have designated suites. You needn't buy a honeymoon package to get special treatment; just let the reservations agent know that you're newlyweds. For information on packages, call 800-827-7200.

A Match Made in Heaven?

Couples tying the knot at Walt Disney World have incorporated Disneyana in some rather interesting ways. Take the bride who wore Mickey ears with her veil. Or the couple who chose to walk back up the aisle to "Zip-A-Dee-Doo-Dah." Certainly, the bride and groom who exchanged Donald and Daisy caps instead of wedding rings set a precedent.

37

At Walt Disney World, there's a hotel to suit every taste, budget, and mood.

Checking In

Like a photograph whose mood changes depending upon the frame in which it is displayed, a Walt Disney World vacation is colored by the context in which it is experienced. Guests have quite a variety of frames—rather, resorts—from which to choose, and each yields a unique perspective on the World. Some hotels imbue the mousedom with surprising elegance; others render it especially whimsical, homey, or romantic. Looking for grand seaside digs or a home base straight out of New Orleans? They're here. Something Polynesian? No problem. From campsites and economy-priced rooms to villas and suites, there are accommodations in Cinderella's neighborhood to suit most every taste and billfold.

If you're the sort who favors a gilded frame for your vacation, you'll find the chandelier quotient you're looking for—and a rich Victorian aura—at Disney's turreted Grand Floridian resort. Here, the WDW experience is defined by private verandas, a whirlpool surrounded by roses, and room service that delivers the likes of chocolate-covered strawberries "dressed" in tuxedos.

If rustic romance is more your style, your ultimate WDW roost is the Wilderness Lodge, which patterns its grandeur after National Park Service lodges of the early 1900s. The resort's soaring totem poles and tepee chandeliers, bubbling hot spring, and roaring waterfall have forever altered our conception of a log cabin.

If you simply must make every dollar count, the All-Star Sports and All-Star Music resorts come through with perfectly comfortable accommodations starting at $74 a night. The brightest dwellings you'll ever want to call home, augmented by three-story sports and music icons, ensure you'll not forget for a moment that you're staying on WDW turf.

Amenities Checklist

While there are significant differences in the amenities provided at Disney's value and deluxe properties, certain conveniences are provided at all WDW hotels. Namely: voice mail, clock radios, in-room safes, guest laundry facilities, dry-cleaning service, and either room service or more limited food delivery options. Also, every WDW resort now has an ATM in the lobby.

If you're not quite sure what you want, that's fine, too. This chapter provides descriptions of every WDW resort, from the overall atmosphere to the rooms, facilities, and amenities. In addition to the basic rate information, you'll find summaries of each hotel's big draws, plus tips that will help you make a choice that's in line with your budget, interests, and touring priorities. We've covered all of the Disney-owned resorts and their favored siblings, the Swan and Dolphin, plus the new Disney Cruise Line. Careful readers will easily discern those we recommend most highly for adults (hint: look for clues in the "Big Draws" category). Be aware, too, that within each entry the information provided is selective, encompassing details most relevant to the adult visitor. When it comes to the Hotel Plaza Blvd. resorts—seven properties that are within Disney's borders but independently managed—we've included our top three choices for adults. Finally, for those willing to give up the convenience of staying on-property, we've also listed some hotels worth considering outside the World's boundaries. So think about what's important to you in a resort and in this trip to Walt Disney World. Then read on for all the information you need to choose the perfect frame.

WALT DISNEY WORLD RESORTS

Unless otherwise noted, all phone numbers are in area code 407.

As an example of the meticulous theming that is a hallmark of the Disney hotels, consider Port Orleans, a moderately priced resort designed to evoke New Orleans' French Quarter. As you check in, you might catch the aroma of fresh beignets wafting over from the resort's food court, decorated as a Mardi Gras warehouse. The lobby has French horns for light fixtures and restrooms with such great jazz coming over the speakers they could almost impose a cover charge.

In addition to compelling theming, Disney's resorts are marked by staffs trained to bend over backward to ensure guests' happiness, and well-kept, comfortably furnished accommodations comparable in size to those found outside WDW borders. There are also practical advantages to staying on-property. Chief among these benefits are convenience and easy access to Disney services. Other privileges enjoyed by WDW resort guests include free use of WDW transportation; early admission to the Magic Kingdom, Epcot, and Disney-MGM Studios on designated days; discounted golf fees; and the option to reserve tee times on Disney golf courses up to 60 days prior to their check-in date. At all WDW resorts except the Swan and Dolphin, amenities also include free package delivery and the ability to charge meals and merchandise back to one's room.

This resort listing is organized according to price tiers—Deluxe, Moderate, and Value—with the exception of the Home Away From Home category, used to distinguish all-suite and villa-type accommodations. These categories are consistent with Disney's rating system for its resorts (explained on page 43). But consider location as well as price, particularly if you know you'll be spending a lot of time touring a particular theme park. The "Vital Statistics" section of each entry will help you place the resorts on the World map. You'll notice in this listing that certain twosomes are earmarked as "sister resorts"; these are adjacent properties that feature complementary designs and shared facilities. With the exception of Port Orleans and Dixie Landings, whose greater separation and distinct identities we feel merit individual attention, sister resorts' descriptions are combined.

We've packed in as much detail as possible about the offerings at each resort, but to learn more about restaurants and lounges, see our recommendations in the *Dining & Entertainment* chapter. For further details about WDW transportation, including a description of options at the Transportation and Ticket Center (TTC), consult *Planning Ahead.* For additional information on recreational opportunities available at the resorts, turn to the "Sports" section of the *Diversions* chapter.

The Last Word On...

RESERVATIONS

While there are more than 25,000 rooms available on-property, they're in high demand; to get your first choice, book well in advance, especially if you plan to visit during summer or holiday periods. Call W-DISNEY (934-7639) to make reservations for all but the independently owned Swan and Dolphin resorts (numbers provided in listing).

CHECKING IN

The check-in time for WDW resorts is 3 P.M., except at The Villas at the Disney Institute and Old Key West, where it is 4 P.M., and Fort Wilderness, where campsite check-in is 1 P.M. Check-out time is 11 A.M.

•CONTINUED ON NEXT PAGE

Deluxe
BoardWalk

This fetching resort and entertainment complex recaptures an ephemeral (if not fictional) period in eastern seaboard history. It has all the charm of a close-knit shore village awash in sun-bleached pastels. The name comes from the 48-foot-wide boardwalk out back, where you'll find a lively piano club, a swinging dance hall, and a major-league sports bar, not to mention a bakery and a brewpub. When hunger calls, you can sit down to a seafood dinner or buy a slice of pizza from a restaurant window. For dessert, try a caramel apple from the sweetshop or cotton candy from a vendor. Located lakefront directly opposite the Yacht Club and Beach Club, BoardWalk completes this seaside community in exceedingly romantic fashion. The Board-Walk Inn (a 378-room deluxe hotel) and Disney's BoardWalk Villas Resort (517 villas styled in the tradition of family vacation cottages) share a lobby. Filled with antique miniatures of early boardwalk amusement rides, the lobby fronts an inviting porch with rocking chairs. A sweeping staircase leads to the resort's main recreation area as well as to the restaurants, shops, and clubs of the BoardWalk entertainment district.

BIG DRAWS: Intimate charm, an entertainment zone right out back, and a walkway to Epcot.

WORTH NOTING: Guestrooms at the BoardWalk Inn are comparable in size to those at Disney's other deluxe properties, and offer two queen-size beds plus a child's daybed. Decorative touches include curtains imprinted with images and inscriptions from old postcards, and French doors that open to private patios or balconies. Two-story suites feature a master bedroom loft (with king-size bed and adjoining bath with whirlpool tub), a living room with a wet bar, and a private garden enclosed in a white picket fence. Single-story concierge rooms are similarly appointed (no gardens, alas).

Disney's BoardWalk Villas Resort is the newest Disney Vacation Club property (see page 55 for club details); because its accommodations are equipped with either a wet bar or a full kitchen, it falls into Disney's Home Away From Home category. Villas, decorated in the eclectic fashion of seaside cottages, feature balconies (or patios), travel trunk coffee tables, and carousel-print curtains. Studios offer a bedroom with a queen-size bed and a double sleeper sofa; plus a

Mickey Rates the Resorts

Disney's ranking system for its resorts provides a convenient framework for considering WDW lodging options. Categories reflect not only price, but the style of the accommodation and the level of service. The hotels fall into Deluxe, Moderate, and Value classifications. Home Away From Home encompasses villa-type lodgings (and the Wilderness Homes at Fort Wilderness), while Disney's Campground category is occupied solely by the Fort Wilderness campground.

For the sake of clarity and comparison, we have used these same categories in this chapter, with a few exceptions for Fort Wilderness and other properties with two types of accommodations.

In general, here's what to expect in our categories:

■ Deluxe properties (rates for double rooms range from $175 to $395 per night) are defined by large, graciously appointed rooms, several restaurants, and such amenities as 24-hour room service.

■ Home Away From Home (starting rates from $35 to $295) applies to villas, vacation homes, all-suite hotels, trailer homes, and campsites.

■ Moderate properties (rates from $119 to $155) represent comfortably sized rooms, full-service restaurants as well as food courts, and bellman luggage service.

■ Value properties (rates from $49 to $109) offer fewer frills and smaller yet adequate quarters. Meals are provided at food courts or lobby lounges only. Recreation options are usually limited to swimming pools and arcades.

•CONTINUED FROM PREVIOUS PAGE

RATES

Figures provided in resort entries were correct at press time, but prices are subject to change.

■ **Value** rates apply January 1, 1998, through February 12, 1998, and August 23, 1998, through December 22, 1998, for all WDW properties except the Swan and Dolphin; they further extend July 5, 1998, through August 22, 1998, for all Home Away From Home and Deluxe WDW resorts except the Swan and Dolphin. Value seasons at the Swan and Dolphin are mainly January and May through mid-December.

■ **Regular** rates are in effect April 26, 1998, through July 4, 1998, for all WDW resorts except the Swan and Dolphin; they further extend July 5, 1998, through August 22, 1998, for all Moderate and Value WDW resorts. Regular seasons at the Swan and Dolphin are mainly February through April, and late December.

■ **Peak** rates apply February 13, 1998, through April 25, 1998, and December 23, 1998, through December 31, 1998, for all WDW resorts except the Swan and Dolphin.

BoardWalk Tips

■ Waterfront rooms at the Inn afford a glimpse of Epcot's IllumiNations fireworks. The Disney-MGM Studios' Sorcery in the Sky fireworks can be seen from some of the villas.

■ Take advantage of the resort's more romantic assets—rolling cart rides on the board-walk, nestled courtship chairs, and the capacity for sunset cocktails on the waterfront.

■ Ask about organizing an IllumiNations fire-works cruise (arranged at the children's club).

■ Inn guests should be sure to stop and read the curtains. The fabric was created using imprints of vintage Atlantic City postcards.

■ Stop by the Wyland Galleries to see some awe-inspiring paintings, sculptures, and jewelry depicting marine life.

wet bar with microwave, coffeemaker, and small refrigerator. Larger villas (with one, two, or three bed-rooms) have a dining room, fully equipped kitchen, laundry facilities, whirlpool tub, and VCR. They also have a king-size bed in the master bedroom, a spa-cious living room with a queen sleeper sofa, and two queen-size beds or a queen-size bed and double sleeper sofa in any additional bedrooms.

Both properties have 24-hour room service. Room amenities include hair dryers and an iron (with board). A convention center provides access to busi-ness services. BoardWalk guests have exclusive use of the amusement park–themed pool, two quiet pools, and three whirlpools. Other recreational offerings include two clay tennis courts, a health club (massages by appointment), and croquet. Bikes, in-line skates, pedal-driven carts, fishing poles, and inner tubes may be rented. A poolside library rents books.

Where to eat: Big River Grille & Brewing Works (microbrews, pub food); BoardWalk Bakery (baked goods); ESPN Club (all-American sports bar, ball-park menu); Flying Fish Café (creative American, steak and seafood); Seashore Sweets' (saltwater taffy and ice cream); and Spoodles (Mediterranean fare).

Where to drink: Atlantic Dance (elegant dance club); Belle Vue Room (cocktails and cognac flights, board games, old-time radio); Jellyrolls (dueling pianos); and Leaping Horse Libations (poolside refreshments).

VITAL STATISTICS: BoardWalk guests have enviable access to Epcot, the Disney-MGM Studios, and the Fantasia Gardens Miniature Golf complex. Board-Walk; 2101 N. Epcot Resorts Blvd.; Box 10000; Lake Buena Vista, FL 32830-1000; 939-5100; fax 939-5150.

Transportation: Boat or walkway to Epcot's International Gateway entrance. Boats to the Disney-MGM Studios. Buses to the Magic Kingdom, Animal Kingdom, Typhoon Lagoon, Blizzard Beach, Downtown Disney, and other WDW resorts.

Rates: At the Inn, standard rooms start at $249 in value season, $264 regu-lar, and $279 peak; concierge rooms begin at $385 value, $405 regular, and $420 peak; and suites begin at $575. A $25 per diem charge applies for each extra adult (beyond two) sharing a room. At the Villas, studios start at $249 value, $264 regular, and $279 peak; one-bedroom villlas begin at $305 value, $325 regular, and $340 peak; two-bedroom villas start at $410 value, $499 reg-ular, and $520 peak; and three-bedroom villas start at $1,100.

Contemporary

First impressions might suggest that the enormous A-frame tower of this legendary resort is simply a 15-story concrete tent that's been pitched here, a stone's throw from Space Mountain, for the benefit of the monorail trains regularly schussing through it. And the Contemporary is certainly defined by a futuristic sophistication. But there's more to the Contemporary—namely, artistic reverie that plays out in bold decor, from the lobby to the sleek guestroom furnishings; three eateries, including a critically acclaimed restaurant with a market-inspired menu; and terrific views of the Magic Kingdom or Bay Lake, particularly from rooms in the resort's tower (the higher, the better).

BIG DRAWS: Location. Monorail service. Extensive water sports options. Ideally suited for serious tennis players.

WORTH NOTING: Guestrooms here are, on average, larger than at any other WDW resort hotel; most feature two queen-size beds plus a daybed (king-size beds may be requested). Amenities at the 1,041-room resort include 24-hour room service. Concierge services are available to suite guests. On the basis of its top-notch tennis facility alone, the Contemporary would be a recreational hub; but it also boasts a recently renovated pool area (with free-form pool, quiet pool, and two whirlpools), parasailing, a boat rental marina, and a health club (massages by appointment). Waterskiing and fishing excursions may be arranged. A convention center offers business services. Note that the Contemporary's theming doesn't exude an especially cozy ambience and rarely comes off as romantic.

Where to eat: California Grill (West Coast cuisine and a 15th-floor Magic Kingdom vista); Concourse Steakhouse (casual for its genre); Chef Mickey's (breakfast and dinner character buffets); and Food and Fun Center (24-hour snacks).

Contemporary Tips

■ The California Grill is among the World's best restaurants. The lounge here offers informal wine tastings each Friday at 5 P.M.

■ Rooms in the resort's garden buildings generally do not yield notable views, which is why their rates are lower than in the tower.

■ Tennis players will do well to stay in the north wing because of its proximity to the resort's six lighted courts.

■ The marina here is full of choices for sailors, from Water Sprites and sailboats to Seariders, which are faster than the Sprites and (conveniently) unavailable to the under-18 crowd. It's also parasailing central.

■ Tower guests have especially convenient access to business services at the convention center. Guests staying in the south wing are especially close to the pool and marina areas.

Grand Floridian Tips

■ For optimum quiet and a striking panorama, request a lagoon-view room.

■ Rooms on upper floors afford the greatest privacy.

■ You can sit on the beach or grass and watch the fireworks over Cinderella Castle with little or no company.

■ Consider a honeymoon room for your second (or third) honeymoon.

■ The pair of tennis courts here have clay surfaces and a resident pro.

■ Book dinner at Victoria & Albert's way in advance—that is, before you leave home.

■ The resort is surprisingly popular with families, considering the posh surroundings.

Where to drink: California Grill Lounge (emphasis on wine and panoramic views); Contemporary Grounds (lobby coffee bar); Outer Rim (comfy alcove overlooking Bay Lake); and Sand Bar (poolside refreshments).

VITAL STATISTICS: The Contemporary, which has the Magic Kingdom virtually in its front yard and Bay Lake right out back, is the only hotel with a walkway, and one of just three on the monorail line, to that park. Monorail links extend the resort's neighborhood to the Polynesian and the Grand Floridian, and provide for convenient commutes to Epcot. Contemporary; 4600 N. World Dr.; Box 10000; Lake Buena Vista, FL 32830-1000; 824-1000; fax 824-3539.

Transportation: A monorail resort (platform is reached from the fourth floor, and is not wheelchair accessible). Walkway or monorail to the Magic Kingdom. Monorail to the TTC; from there, monorail or bus to Epcot and buses to Typhoon Lagoon and Downtown Disney. Direct buses to Disney-MGM Studios, Animal Kingdom, and Blizzard Beach. Boats to Fort Wilderness and River Country.

Rates: Standard rooms start at $209 in value season, $229 regular, and $244 peak; tower rooms are $290 value, $310 regular, and $325 peak; suites start at $665. A $25 per diem charge applies for each extra adult (beyond two) sharing a room.

Grand Floridian

This romantic slice of Victorian confectionery, a quick hop (and a world apart) from the Magic Kingdom, eloquently recalls the opulent hotels that beckoned high society to Florida at the turn of the century. The Grand Floridian's central main building and five guest buildings—snow-white structures laced with verandas and turrets, and topped with gabled roofs of red shingle—sprawl over 40 manicured acres of Seven Seas Lagoon shorefront. On these grounds, not an eyeful lacks for towering palms, stunning lake views, or exquisite rose gardens. The resort's magnificent lobby—Victoriana in excelsis—features immense chandeliers, stained-glass skylights, and live piano and band music that might inspire spontaneous dancing. Guestrooms exude bygone elegance, with old-fashioned armoires, marble-topped sinks, and room service delivered atop lace-covered tablecloths.

BIG DRAWS: The height of luxury with a view of Cinderella Castle. Great for a honeymoon or an escape to a kinder, gentler era. And the monorail stops here, too.

WORTH NOTING: Standard accommodations at this 900-room resort are larger than those at most deluxe hotels in the World and include two queen-size beds, plus a daybed; many rooms have terraces. Amenities include hair dryers, special toiletries, bathrobes, minibars, nightly turndown,

24-hour room service, and newspaper delivery. Concierge rooms and suites are located on the upper floors of the resort's main building. The resort offers some of the best restaurants on-property, including Victoria & Albert's. Traditional afternoon tea is served in the Garden View lounge. The Electrical Water Pageant and the Magic Kingdom fireworks can be seen from most lagoon-view rooms. A convention center offers access to business services. Boats may be rented, waterskiing and fishing excursions may be arranged, and volleyball equipment is available. The Grand Floridian Spa & Health Club is among WDW's most complete fitness facilities and one of only two spas on-property. The vast swimming pool and the rosebush-ringed whirlpool are open 24 hours, with quiet hours in effect at night. A white-sand beach offers respite from the pool din.

Where to eat: Citricos (market fresh Mediterranean dinners; tapas menu); Gasparilla Grill & Games (24-hour snacks); Grand Floridian Café (all-day Floridian fare); Narcoossee's (steak and seafood waterside); 1900 Park Fare (buffet breakfast and dinner); and Victoria & Albert's (six-course dinners).

Where to drink: Garden View (cocktails and afternoon tea); Mizner's (classic cocktails); Narcoossee's (yards of beer in a lagoonside setting); and Summerhouse (beachside refreshments).

VITAL STATISTICS: The Grand Floridian's prime Seven Seas Lagoon locale allows for fast access to the Magic Kingdom. Proximity to the Palm and Magnolia links pleases golfers. The monorail stretches the hotel's neighborhood beyond the adjacent Polynesian resort to include the Contemporary resort and provide for easy commutes to Epcot. Grand Floridian; 4401 Floridian Way; Box 10000; Lake Buena Vista, FL 32830-1000; 824-3000; fax 824-3186.

Transportation: A monorail resort (platform is on the hotel's second floor). Monorail or boat to the Magic Kingdom. Monorail to the TTC to connect with the monorail to Epcot and buses to Typhoon Lagoon and Downtown Disney.

Bygone Era

At the Grand Floridian, it's not uncommon to see housekeepers twirling peach-colored parasols as they promenade along the footpaths in Victorian dress.

Polynesian Tips

■ Tahiti and Fiji tend to be calmer than other guest buildings because they are generally reserved for adult guests, but there's a catch: their location near Luau Cove, where the lively Polynesian Luau dinner show is held nightly.

■ Moorea is a good choice for its relative seclusion and Magic Kingdom views (request a lagoonside room).

■ Rooms on upper floors afford the most privacy.

■ Tucked down below Sunset Point in front of Moorea is a beach that many guests don't realize is there.

■ Couples celebrating their honeymoon or anniversary should alert their reservation agent to the occasion (they'll receive a complimentary bottle of champagne).

Direct buses to the Disney-MGM Studios, Animal Kingdom, and Blizzard Beach. Water launch to the Polynesian resort.

Rates: Standard rooms start at $294 in value season, $314 regular, and $329 peak; concierge rooms begin at $495 value, $425 regular, and $440 peak; and suites start at $638. A $25 per diem charge applies for each adult beyond two sharing a room.

Polynesian

This resort echoes the romance and beauty of the South Pacific with enchanting realism. Polynesian music is piped throughout the lushly landscaped grounds, which feature white-sand beaches, tiki torches that burn nightly, and sufficient flowers to perfume the air. Sprawled amid tropical gardens are 11 two- and three-story village longhouses, all named for Pacific islands, where 853 guestrooms are located. But the Polynesian's centerpiece and primary mood setter is unquestionably the Great Ceremonial House, which (in addition to the usual front desk, shops, and restaurants) contains a huge, three-story-high garden that all but consumes the atrium lobby.

BIG DRAWS: A breathtaking, you-are-there South Sea ambience makes the Polynesian exceptionally romantic and helps to explain the resort's busy wedding calendar. Plus convenient monorail service.

WORTH NOTING: Standard guestrooms, comparable in size to those at the Contemporary, are roomy, and feature two queen-size beds plus a daybed. Those in Oahu, Moorea, and Pago Pago are slightly larger. Decor includes ti leaf–shaped mirrors, bamboo accents, and batik cloth draped over and behind the beds. All third-floor rooms (and second-floor rooms in the Bali Hai, Oahu, Moorea, and Pago Pago buildings) have balconies. Room service is offered until midnight. A concierge lounge with a choice view of the Magic Kingdom is a comfy retreat for guests in Tonga and all-suite Bali Hai, the resort's most luxurious accommodations. In addition to the themed pool there is a second, more removed pool. Near Oahu, a grassy knoll known for good reason as Sunset Point offers a hammock. The resort boasts three white-sand beaches and great vantage points on Magic Kingdom fireworks and the Electrical Water Pageant. Boats may be rented, waterskiing and fishing excursions may be arranged, and a 1¼-mile trail invites jogging around the tropical grounds.

Where to eat: Captain Cook's Snack Company (24-hour grazing); Coral Isle Café (all-day casual fare); and 'Ohana (family-style Pacific Rim dinners featuring grilled meats).

Where to drink: Barefoot Bar (poolside refreshments) and Tambu (tropical drinks and setting).

VITAL STATISTICS: The Polynesian is located on the shore of Seven Seas Lagoon directly opposite the Magic Kingdom, and offers both an enviable view and fast access to the park. Monorail links extend the resort's neighborhood beyond the adjacent Grand Floridian to include the Contemporary and provide for convenient commutes to Epcot. Golfers appreciate having the Palm and Magnolia courses nearby. Polynesian; 1600 South Seas Dr.; Box 10000; Lake Buena Vista, FL 32830-1000; 824-2000; fax 824-3174.

Transportation: A monorail resort (platform on second floor of the Great Ceremonial House). Water launches to the Magic Kingdom and the Grand Floridian. Monorail to the Magic Kingdom and the TTC. From the TTC, monorail or bus to Epcot, and buses to Typhoon Lagoon and Downtown Disney. Direct buses to Disney-MGM Studios, Animal Kingdom, and Blizzard Beach. (Note: The TTC is within walking distance.)

Rates: Standard rooms start at $269 in value season, $289 regular, and $305 peak; concierge rooms begin at $335 value, $355 regular, and $370 peak; suites start at $580. A $25 per diem charge applies to each extra adult (beyond two) sharing a room.

Swan & Dolphin

The motto for these whimsical yet sophisticated resorts might be "expect the unexpected." Certainly, noted architect Michael Graves designed these postmodern bookends with entertainment in mind. At the Dolphin, a 27-story triangular tower is flanked by buildings that are topped by two 56-foot-tall dolphin statues and covered in a mural of banana leaves. One restaurant has the gastronomic sensibility of a serious steak house—and chandeliers hung with monkeys. In short, guestrooms with such decorative touches as cabana-like doors do not preclude access to a first-rate fitness center or a showroom with Cartier gems. It's more of the same playful luxury next door at the Swan, which carves its own distinctive silhouette with 46-foot namesake statues perched atop its (12-story) central building and facades accented with turquoise waves.

F.Y.I.

All WDW resorts offer rooms equipped for guests with disabilities, as well as nonsmoking rooms. For more detailed information, inquire with Central Reservations (934-7639). For more specifics related to travelers with disabilities, see the "Customized Tips" section of the *Planning Ahead* chapter.

Swan & Dolphin Tips

- Request a corner room with a king-size bed at the Dolphin, and if it's available, you'll get two balconies for the price of one.

- Both the Swan and Dolphin feature large convention centers. If you're visiting for pleasure, check the name-badge quotient before you book.

- Swan and Dolphin guests who pay a $5 surcharge upon check-in receive a morning paper and use of the Dolphin's health club for the length of their stay.

- Four tennis courts (located at the Dolphin) are kept lighted all night.

- Catch the sunset or IllumiNations fireworks from the large picture window on the Swan's ninth floor.

The Swan has 758 rooms, about half as many as the Dolphin, and its rooms tend toward bird lamps and pineapple-stenciled headboards.

BIG DRAWS: Luxury in a lighthearted wrapper. Exceptional facilities. And you can walk to Epcot and BoardWalk.

WORTH NOTING: The Swan (managed by Westin) and the Dolphin (operated by ITT Sheraton) are the only two WDW hotels whose value season extends through the summer months. Guests staying at either of the two hotels have access to the restaurants and recreational activities at the other, and may charge any meals and activities enjoyed at the sister hotel to their room tab. Such charging privileges do not extend to beyond the two hotels. Guestrooms at the Swan and Dolphin are comparable to those at Disney's other deluxe resorts. Whereas standard rooms at the Dolphin feature two double beds, queen-size beds are the rule at the Swan (king-size beds are available at both). Room amenities at both hotels include minibars and 24-hour room service, plus nightly turndown at the Swan, and coffeemakers, hair dryers, and ironing boards and irons at the Dolphin. Club-level rooms at the Dolphin are located in the resort's tower; at the Swan they are on the top two floors of the hotel's main building. The Swan's fitness center is complimentary; the Dolphin's Body By Jake health club is among the most complete facilities on-property. In addition to a white-sand beach with a volleyball net and boat rentals, the resorts share a lap pool, a sprawling grotto pool with waterfalls, a small rectangular pool, and several whirlpools. IllumiNations fireworks are visible from both hotels.

Where to eat: At the Swan: Garden Grove Café (greenhouse setting with Gulliver-themed dinner) and Palio (Italian bistro). At the Dolphin: Coral Café (casual all-day dining); Dolphin Fountain (ice cream parlor); Harry's Safari Bar & Grille (grilled steaks and seafood); Juan & Only's (authentic Mexican fare); and Tubbi's (cafeteria with 24-hour convenience store).

Where to drink: At the Swan: Kimono's (cocktail lounge with sushi bar); Lobby Court (coffees, occasional cigar menu); and Splash Grill (poolside refreshments). At the Dolphin: Cabana Bar & Grill (poolside refreshments); Copa Banana (tropical spot with karaoke, big-screen TVs); Harry's Safari Bar (for cocktails, beer by the yard); and Only's Bar & Jail (sangria, specialty margaritas).

VITAL STATISTICS: The Swan and Dolphin offer exceptionally easy access to Epcot, the Disney-MGM Studios, BoardWalk, and the Fantasia Gardens Miniature Golf complex. Located side by side on the shore of Crescent Lake, a virtual stone's throw from World Showcase, the hotels are flanked by BoardWalk on one side and the Yacht Club and Beach Club on the other. Walt Disney World Swan; 1200 Epcot Resorts Blvd.; Box 10000; Lake Buena Vista, FL 32830-1000; 934-3000; fax 934-4499. Walt Disney World Dolphin; 1500 Epcot Resorts Blvd.; Box 10000; Lake Buena Vista, FL 32830-1000; 934-4000; fax 934-4099.

Transportation: Boat or walkway to Epcot's International Gateway entrance. Boats to the Disney-MGM Studios. Buses to the Magic Kingdom, Animal Kingdom, Typhoon Lagoon, Blizzard Beach, and Downtown Disney.

Rates: At the Swan and Dolphin, standard rooms begin at $265 in value season and $295 regular, club-level rooms are $385 value and $410 regular, and suites begin at $610. A $25 per diem charge applies for each extra adult (beyond two) sharing a room. Reservations for either hotel can be made by calling 800-227-1500 or visiting the resort's Web site (*http://www.swandolphin.com*).

Wilderness Lodge

Rustic romance infuses every inspired detail of this resort, patterned after the grand National Park Service lodges of the early 1900s. Hidden away on an isolated shore of Bay Lake, the Wilderness Lodge is surrounded by towering pine

forests that provide a drumroll of sorts along the winding road leading to the dramatic timbered hotel. The soaring atrium lobby kindles the spirit of the great American West with hand-painted tepee chandeliers, an imposing pair of totem poles, a bubbling hot spring, and an 82-foot-tall fireplace whose layered stones replicate the Grand Canyon's strata. As if Bay Lake weren't a sufficiently beautiful backdrop, the resort's natural landscape is supplemented by a roaring waterfall, a swimming area surrounded by boulders and wildflowers, and a steaming geothermic meadow complete with geyser. Guestrooms are located in two wings that extend back from the lobby to the lakefront, forming a U-shaped frame around the inner courtyard. In other words, the Wilderness Lodge is no mere log cabin in the woods.

BIG DRAWS: Luxury. Undeniable romance. The bottom line: a truly extraordinary setting at a considerable value.

Wilderness Lodge Tips

■ Daily tours offer a closer look at the resort's architecture or its restaurants.

■ Courtyard and lake-view rooms are especially romantic, with audio accompaniment that includes waterfall gushing, brook babbling, and geyser eruptions. Woods views provide considerable quiet.

■ Junior suites are a good value here, given their spaciousness. Honeymooners should request room 7084, for its fireworks views and big whirlpool tub.

■ Some rooms come with a queen-size bed and a bunk instead of two queen-size beds. Be sure to make your preference known.

■ It's possible to order Artist Point's amazing berry cobbler from room service.

WORTH NOTING: The 728 guestrooms, all of which have balconies or patios, are slightly more compact than those at Disney's other deluxe resorts, and feature two queen-size beds. Colorful quilted bedspreads, buffalo lamps, and armoires etched with mountain scenes maintain the theme. Room service is available for breakfast and dinner, and includes selections from the resort's excellent Pacific Northwest restaurant, Artist Point. The four corridors ringing the lobby offer more than an extraordinary view of the lobby itself; they also provide access to porches overlooking the courtyard and contain cozy nooks with sofas and tucked-away fireplaces. The resort is so laden with Hidden Mickeys (images of Mickey Mouse placed out of context, for example, in a fireplace screen) that scavenger hunts are held to locate them. Fire Rock Geyser faithfully spouts off 120-foot water plumes at the top of every hour from 7 A.M. until 10 P.M. A white-sand beach fronts the lake. Waterskiing and fishing excursions can be arranged. Boats and bicycles may be rented, volleyball equipment is available, and a three-quarter-mile path ideal for biking and jogging leads to Fort Wilderness. The hotel affords a great view of the Magic Kingdom fireworks and Electrical Water Pageant. Wilderness Lodge Mercantile is a standout among resort shops.

Where to eat: Artist Point (sophisticated Pacific Northwest cuisine); Lobby Coffee Bar (continental breakfast); Roaring Fork (round-the-clock snacks); and Whispering Canyon Café (lively family-style dining).

Where to drink: Territory (western-style watering hole) and Trout Pass (poolside refreshments).

VITAL STATISTICS: The Wilderness Lodge is located on a shore of Bay Lake, with the Contemporary and Fort Wilderness as its nearest neighbors. It has the fastest commute to the Magic Kingdom among non-monorail resorts, and unrivaled access to Fort Wilderness. It's also well located for golfers who plan to play on a few of the WDW links. Wilderness Lodge; 901 W. Timberline Dr.; Box 10000; Lake Buena Vista, FL 32830-1000; 824-3200; fax 824-3232.

Transportation: Boat launch to the Magic Kingdom and Contemporary. Direct buses to Epcot, the Disney-MGM Studios, Animal Kingdom, Blizzard Beach, and the TTC. From the TTC, buses to Typhoon Lagoon and Downtown Disney. Walkway to Fort Wilderness and River Country.

Rates: Standard rooms begin at $175 in value season, $195 regular, and $210 peak; suites start at $560. A $25 per diem charge applies for each extra adult (beyond two) sharing a room.

Yacht Club & Beach Club

This inspired duo conjure such a heady vision of turn-of-the-century Nantucket and Martha's Vineyard you'd swear you smelled salt in the air. Certainly, architect Robert A. M. Stern's two-part evocation of the grand old seaside hotels has the gulls fooled. The Yacht Club and Beach Club stretch along a picturesque shoreline complete with white-sand beach, swimming lagoon, lighthouse, and marina. As the five-story gray clapboard structure of the Yacht Club gives way to the sky-blue Beach Club (the two are connected), the interior motif shifts from seriously nautical to seashore whimsical. The Yacht Club has a rich, exclusive feel to it—there's a stunning globe anchoring the lobby, and polished brass abounds. Next door at the Beach Club, beach umbrellas act as pillars and clambakes are a nightly occurrence.

BIG DRAWS: Gracious accommodations. Compelling theming. Exceptional swimming area. Some of the World's finest restaurants and lounges. Enviable access to Epcot and the Disney-MGM Studios.

WORTH NOTING: There are 630 guestrooms at the Yacht Club and 583 rooms at the Beach Club. All are comparable in size to those at Disney's other deluxe resorts; as a rule, they feature two queen-size beds and a daybed (king-size beds are available). At the Yacht Club, rooms maintain the nautical theme with such touches as brass-trimmed bathroom mirrors patterned after portholes; most rooms have good-size balconies. The Yacht Club also offers concierge rooms. At the Beach Club, guestrooms keep the seashore motif with the likes of cabana-style striped curtains. Amenities at both resorts include minibars, newspaper delivery, and 24-hour room service.

A three-acre mini water park called Stormalong Bay earns the Yacht Club and Beach Club bragging rights to the best resort swimming area in the World; the sprawling lakefront pool, open only to hotel guests, includes sections with jets and sandy bottoms, swirling current loops, and slides (traditional whirlpools also stand by). Each resort also has a smaller satellite pool and whirlpool, so removed you must seek them out. The resorts' Ship Shape Health Club is among the most extensive fitness centers at a WDW property. Boat rentals and two tennis courts are offered, fishing excursions can be arranged, and volleyball and croquet equipment is available.

Gullible Gulls

At the Yacht Club and Beach Club, the gulls perch on posts along the resorts' pier, perhaps thinking themselves pretty slick indeed for having crossed the Atlantic so quickly (France and the rest of Epcot's World Showcase are just around the bend).

Yacht Club & Beach Club Tips

■ Rooms on the upper floors afford the greatest privacy.

■ The stunning views belong strictly to those with lake-view rooms.

■ At both resorts, it's a lengthy walk to the lobby from the outermost reaches of guest wings.

■ At the Beach Club, second- and fourth-floor rooms have balconies; rooms on the fourth floor are slightly larger.

■ Balconies at the Yacht Club are bigger than those at the Beach Club, which are standing room only.

■ The Beaches & Cream Soda Shop may serve the best burgers in the World.

■ There's a great hideaway table for two tucked into the Ale and Compass lounge at the Yacht Club.

Where to eat: At the Beach Club: Cape May Café (character breakfasts and clambake buffets). At the Yacht Club: Yacht Club Galley (all-day casual dining) and Yachtsman Steakhouse (a New York–style chophouse). Shared by both hotels is the Beaches & Cream Soda Shop (a classic soda fountain).

Where to drink: At the Beach Club: Martha's Vineyard (cloud nine for wine lovers) and Rip Tide (lobby niche). At the Yacht Club: Ale and Compass (cozy lobby nook) and Crew's Cup (well-heeled beer emporium). For poolside refreshments, there's Hurricane Hanna's Grill.

VITAL STATISTICS: The Yacht Club and Beach Club enjoy extraordinary proximity and enviable access to Epcot, the Disney-MGM Studios, BoardWalk, and the Fantasia Gardens Miniature Golf complex. Located side by side on a shore of Crescent Lake that offers a footpath to Epcot's International Gateway entrance, these sister resorts are joined lakeside by the BoardWalk, Swan, and Dolphin. Yacht Club; 1700 Epcot Resorts Blvd.; Box 10000; Lake Buena Vista, FL 32830-1000; 934-7000; fax 934-3450. Beach Club; 1800 Epcot Resorts Blvd.; Box 10000; Lake Buena Vista, FL 32830-1000; 934-8000; fax 934-3850.

Transportation: Boats or walkway to Epcot's International Gateway entrance near the France pavilion. Boat launches to the Disney-MGM Studios. Buses to the Magic Kingdom, Animal Kingdom, Typhoon Lagoon, Blizzard Beach, and Downtown Disney.

Rates: Standard rooms at both resorts begin at $260 in value season, $280 regular, and $295 peak; concierge rooms, available only at the Yacht Club, start at $385 value, $405 regular, and $420 peak; Yacht Club and Beach Club suites start at $550. A $25 per diem charge applies to each extra adult (beyond two) sharing a room.

Home Away From Home
Disney's Old Key West Resort

Pastel-hued clapboard guesthouses with tin roofs and white picket fences set the cheerful tone of this Key Westerly retreat. Here, unassuming luxury dovetails with an intimate, laid-back atmosphere to create the look and feel of a friendly resort community. A sprawling village, it is bounded by the wooded fairways of the Lake Buena Vista links, and anchored at its center by a lighthouse that overlooks the main swimming area and moonlights as a sauna. A picturesque waterway called the Trumbo Canal flows from the heart of the resort, eventually uniting with the Buena Vista Lagoon. Spacious accommodations equipped with kitchens may set this resort apart, but what gives the place cachet is its incredible warmth and homeyness. Every doorstep in its two- and three-story guest buildings is fronted with a mat that reads WELCOME HOME.

BIG DRAWS: Spacious accommodations, ideal for longer stays. Homey and soothing environs. Value for groups. Convenience of kitchens. Well located for golfers.

WORTH NOTING: This resort, formerly the Disney Vacation Club Resort, was renamed in part to emphasize its compelling theming over its status as the first Vacation Club property (see below). It features studio accommodations and one-, two-, and three-bedroom villas. The villas have a distinctly Key West feel, and are decorated in light woods with ceiling fans and color schemes of seafoam green and mauve. Each studio features a large bedroom with two queen-size beds; a wet bar with a microwave, coffeemaker, and small refrigerator; and a spacious bathroom. Larger villas offer a dining room, fully equipped kitchen, laundry facilities, whirlpool bathtub, and VCR. They also feature a king-size bed in the master bedroom, two queen-size beds in each additional bedroom, and a spacious living room with queen-size sofa bed. All accommodations have balconies. Boats and bicycles are available for rent. Volleyball, basketball, and shuffleboard courts and equipment are on hand. The three tennis courts tend to be quiet and accessible. The main swimming area, complete with a huge whirlpool and sauna, supplements three quiet pools. There is a small fitness center, and the

Join the Club?

Frequent visitors who have come to consider Walt Disney World a home away from home might consider joining the ranks of the Disney Vacation Club. For a one-time price and annual dues, members receive certain benefits, and net stays at Disney's Old Key West Resort or Disney's BoardWalk Villas Resort. They can also stay at resorts well beyond WDW borders, including Disney's Hilton Head Island Resort and, just two hours from Walt Disney World, Disney's Vero Beach Resort. For details about the Vero Beach property, see page 58.

Old Key West Tips

■ For a waterfront setting that's pleasantly removed from the main recreation area, request a villa in the Turtle Shack vicinity. Numbers 43 and 44 are good calls, given their water views and close proximity to swimming pool, snack bar, tennis court, and bus stop alike.

■ Try the conch fritters sold at the snack bars.

■ It's possible to have a whole Key lime pie from Olivia's Café delivered to your room.

■ All accommodations but the studios feature whirlpool bathtubs.

■ One-bedroom villas yield more than twice the space of a studio for a relatively small jump in cost.

resort's winding streets lend themselves well to jogging or cycling. Conch Flats Community Hall offers table tennis, board games, and video rentals.

Where to eat: Good's Food to Go (poolside snacks) and Olivia's Café (casual all-day dining with Key West flourishes). Grills and picnic tables are available. Pizza delivery from Dixie Landings is offered until midnight. Conch Flats General Store stocks groceries.

Where to drink: Gurgling Suitcase (tiny spirited pub) and Turtle Shack (poolside refreshments).

VITAL STATISTICS: This resort is well located for golfers, with three WDW courses close by. It also enjoys easy access to Downtown Disney, and good proximity to Epcot and the Disney-MGM Studios. Disney's Old Key West Resort; 1510 N. Cove Rd.; Box 10000; Lake Buena Vista, FL 32830-1000; 827-7700; fax 827-7710.

Transportation: Buses to the Magic Kingdom, Epcot, Disney-MGM Studios, Animal Kingdom, Typhoon Lagoon, Blizzard Beach, and Downtown Disney. Boats to Downtown Disney.

Rates: Studios are $224 in value season, $239 regular, and $254 peak; one-bedroom villas are $295 value, $315 regular, and $330 peak; two-bedrooms are $410 value, $430 regular, and $450 peak; and three-bedrooms are $850 value, $870 regular, and $885 peak.

Fort Wilderness Resort & Campground

No fewer than 700 acres of woodland just hopping with rabbits combine with WDW's largest lake to provide the foundation for Fort Wilderness, a retreat that relies wholly on the great outdoors for atmosphere. A place that's as much about recreation as low-key accommodations, it is brimming with inspiration for nature walks, fishing, and canoeing. Shaded campsites are arranged on 28 loops, linked by throughways. While some of the 1,192 sites are designated for tents, most are devoted to RV camping; 408 spots sport air-conditioned Wilderness Homes, comfortable units that are comparable to well-equipped trailer homes.

BIG DRAWS: Natural setting. Value. And recreation galore.

WORTH NOTING: Almost all loops have at least one air-conditioned comfort station equipped with restrooms, showers, laundry facilities, telephones, and an ice machine. Campsites range in length from 25 to 65 feet. All sites offer a barbecue grill, picnic table, and 30/50-amp electric outlet. Most include sanitary-disposal connections, and nearly half have cable television hookups. Wilderness Homes are separated from other campsites in eight loops. Each air-conditioned unit has a fully equipped kitchen, a living room with a TV, and a full bathroom. While most offer both a double bed and bunk bed in the bedroom and a pull-down bed in the living room, some models skip the bunk. Wilderness Cabins are the newest option. The cozy log cabins sleep six, and offer the comforts of a Wilderness Home, plus a dining room and a deck. Pets are welcome at designated campsites ($3 per day). Recreational options (described in the *Diversions* chapter) include swimming, boating, biking, and fishing. The Hoop-Dee-Doo Musical Revue dinner show is presented here nightly (for details, see the *Dining & Entertainment* chapter).

Where to eat: Most guests cook their own meals (supplies are sold at Meadow Trading Post and Settlement Trading Post), but there's also Trail's End Buffet (home-style dining).

Where to drink: Crockett's Tavern (cocktail service).

VITAL STATISTICS: Fort Wilderness occupies Bay Lake's southern shore; while convenient mainly to its own vast recreational options, it also offers ready access to the Magic Kingdom, and closely borders the Osprey Ridge and Eagle Pines golf courses. Fort Wilderness; 4510 N. Fort Wilderness Trail; Box 10000; Lake Buena Vista, FL 32830-1000; 824-2900; fax 824-3508.

Transportation: Electric golf carts and bikes can be rented to supplement the internal bus system that links all campsites and recreation areas (buses circulate at 20-minute intervals). Boats to the Magic Kingdom and Contemporary. Buses from Settlement Depot to Blizzard Beach and Animal Kingdom, and from the visitor parking lot to the TTC. From the TTC, monorails service the Magic Kingdom, Epcot, and the Contemporary, Polynesian, and Grand Floridian; buses cover all other bases.

Rates: Preferred sites with full hookups, including water, electricity, sewage, and cable TV, are $49 in value season, $59 regular, and $64 peak; sites with full hookups minus the cable TV are $39 value, $54 regular, and $59 peak; sites with electricity hookups only are $35 value, $45 regular, or $49 peak. There is a limit of ten persons per campsite, and a $2 per diem charge applies to each extra adult (beyond two) sharing a site. Rates for Wilderness Homes are $179

Fort Wilderness Tips

■ Bikes and electric carts are, sudden rains aside, the preferable means for getting around.

■ Tent campers should request loop 1500 or 2000 to avoid RV gridlock.

■ Views of Magic Kingdom fireworks and the Electrical Water Pageant are readily available.

■ RV campers will find greater privacy and quiet on loops 1600 through 1900 (note that these are also the pet loops).

A Great Beach Add-on

A stay at Disney's Vero Beach Resort—an oceanfront Disney Vacation Club property just two hours away by car—combines nicely with a WDW vacation. The resort roughly reprises the homey comforts of Disney's Old Key West Resort (described on page 55).

Among its assets are endless beach and proximity to manatee retreats and sunken ships fit for dive trips (this is the Treasure Coast, after all). A tropical tangle separates the resort from the beach. For more information, call 934-7639.

value, $199 regular, and $214 peak; rates for Wilderness Cabins are $199 value, $219 regular, and $234 peak; maximum occupancy is six, and a $5 per diem charge applies to each extra adult (beyond two) sharing a unit.

The Villas at the Disney Institute

This community of villas stretching from the fairways of the Lake Buena Vista golf course to the shores of the Buena Vista Lagoon meshes rustic charm with casual comforts for a relaxed atmosphere. Spread over a lightly wooded and canal-crossed expanse, the peaceful resort offers few hints of its Disney parentage. Among the five types of accommodations are high-rise treehouses set back in the woods, skylight-blessed fairway villas, and cedar-sided all-suite bungalows that ring a small lake.

BIG DRAWS: Rustic and relaxing environs. Golf close at hand. Efficiency kitchens. Convenient access to the Disney Institute. Value for groups.

WORTH NOTING: The only accommodations without full kitchens are the Bungalows, each of which features a living area, a bedroom with two queen-size beds and a balcony (or patio), and a wet bar with a microwave, coffeemaker, and a small refrigerator. Town Houses are either one-bedroom (with a queen-size bed in the bedroom and a sleeper sofa in the living room) or two-bedroom (with a queen-size bed in the loft bedroom, two twins in the second bedroom, and a queen sleeper sofa in the living room). The roomy Fairway Villas have cathedral ceilings, and offer a queen-size bed in one bedroom, two double beds in the other, and either a pull-down bed or a sleeper sofa in the living room. The Treehouse Villas—truly unique and secluded accommodations—offer three bedrooms, two bathrooms, and a utility room in two-story octagonal houses-on-stilts. Grand Vista Homes are luxurious villas whose amenities include stocked refrigerators and nightly turn-down. Lodging for guests with disabilities is available solely in the Fairway Villas. Decor is on the drab side for a Disney accommodation.

The resort has a built-in temptation in the Disney Institute and its extensive fitness center and spa. Bungalows, Town Houses, and certain facilities are largely reserved for guests participating in programs. (For information about Disney Institute vacation packages, see the *Diversions* chapter.) Recreational options available to all guests include the nearby golf course; six swimming pools; a whirlpool; four clay tennis courts (although frequently in use for Disney Institute programs); and canoe, bike, and golf cart rentals.

Where to eat: Seasons Dining Room (four themed dining rooms serving all meals); Reflections Coffee & Pastries (snack bar); and Dabblers (a gift shop stocked with fancy food items, wine, beer, and limited groceries). Groceries from Dabblers and from Gourmet Pantry at the Marketplace may be ordered by phone.

Where to drink: Seasons Terrace Lounge (for beer and cocktails) supplements options at nearby Downtown Disney.

VITAL STATISTICS: The Villas at the Disney Institute, located on the northern shore of Buena Vista Lagoon, has unsurpassed proximity to the Lake Buena Vista links and Downtown Disney. Epcot, Typhoon Lagoon, and the Disney-MGM Studios are also nearby. The Villas at the Disney Institute; 1960 N. Magnolia Way; Box 10000; Lake Buena Vista, FL 32830-1000; 827-1100; fax 934-2741.

Transportation: Buses to the Magic Kingdom, Epcot, Disney-MGM Studios, Animal Kingdom, Typhoon Lagoon, Blizzard Beach, and Downtown Disney. Paved paths to the Downtown Disney Marketplace.

Rates: Bungalows are $199 in value season, $219 regular, and $234 peak; one-bedroom Town Houses are $245 value, $265 regular, and $280 peak; two-bedroom Town Houses are $330 value, $350 regular, and $365 peak; Treehouse Villas are $365 value, $385 regular, and $399 peak; Fairway Villas are $385 value, $415 regular, and $430 peak; and Grand Vista Homes begin at $995.

The Villas at the Disney Institute Tips

■ Unless you're a night owl, the resort's Town Houses are too close to Pleasure Island for comfort.

■ Paved pathways leading to Downtown Disney allow guests to reach this area by golf cart and, in the case of the nearest villas, by foot.

■ If it's space you're after, the two-bedroom Town Houses have about 50% more footage than the Treehouse Villas—and cost less.

■ Dabblers gift shop is as inspired as they come. Wares reflect Disney Institute programs (such as cooking, gardening, or spa products); books and music offerings change in sync with visiting artists and authors.

■ The resort's crisscrossing pathways (ideal for jogging) can be confusing to navigate. Also note that most walkways are dimly lit at night.

Caribbean Beach Tips

■ For optimum privacy, request a room on the second floor.

■ Aruba, linked by bridge to Old Port Royale, is a good choice for both proximity and seclusion.

■ For honeymoon-style isolation, request a room in Trinidad South. Located just off the main loop, its buildings and beach are especially secluded.

■ Martinique tends to be the liveliest village.

■ The 1.4-mile promenade circling Barefoot Bay is ideal for jogging, biking, and skating. Bikes and boats may be rented. A special length-of-stay option is available for boat renters.

Moderate

Caribbean Beach

In this colorful evocation of the Caribbean, the spirit of the islands is rendered via an immense lake ringed by white-sand beaches and villages representing Barbados, Martinique, Trinidad, Jamaica, and Aruba. Each village is marked by clusters of two-story guest buildings that transport you to the Caribbean with cool pastel facades, white railings, and vivid metallic roofs. The separate Custom House reception building resembles one you might encounter at a tropical resort. Lush landscaping adds to the ambience. And Old Port Royale, which houses the resort's eateries and opens out to its main recreation area and themed pool, takes cues from an island market.

BIG DRAWS: Excellent value. Cheery environs with a convincingly Caribbean feel.

WORTH NOTING: The resort has a total of 2,112 rooms. Slightly larger than those at Disney's other moderately priced resorts, they feature two double beds (king-size beds are available) and soft-hued decor. Amenities include a minibar and coffeemaker. Room service, which ventures just a touch beyond pizza, is offered from 4 P.M. until midnight. The resort's 45-acre centerpiece, Barefoot Bay, is larger than World Showcase Lagoon. Villages are sprawled around it in a way that can make travel between some guest areas cumbersome despite footbridges and "local" buses. The resort's sole whirlpool is nestled into its bustling themed pool. Each village offers its own beach, quiet pool, and array of courtyards.

Where to eat: Captain's Tavern (for hearty American fare with limited Caribbean influence) and a food court featuring six counter-service options.

Where to drink: Banana Cabana (poolside refreshments) and the above-mentioned Captain's Tavern (beer, wine, and cocktails).

VITAL STATISTICS: Caribbean Beach is off on its own but well situated for pursuits other than the Magic Kingdom, with Epcot, the Disney-MGM Studios, and Blizzard Beach close at hand on one side and Typhoon Lagoon and Downtown Disney nearby on the other. Caribbean Beach; 900 Cayman Way; Box 10000; Lake Buena Vista, FL 32830-1000; 934-3400; fax 934-3288.

Transportation: Buses stop at each village en route to the Magic Kingdom, Epcot, the Disney-MGM Studios, Animal Kingdom, Typhoon Lagoon, Blizzard Beach, and Downtown Disney.

Rates: Rooms begin at $119 in value season, $129 regular, and $139 peak. A $15 per diem charge applies for each extra adult (beyond two) sharing a room.

Coronado Springs

This sprawling resort, which opened in August 1997, is founded on myth. No matter that this "lost kingdom of riches" arrives much too late to appease its namesake explorer's disappointment over failing to find the fabled Cibola in northern Mexico or the American Southwest. The architecture takes its cue from these areas, with brightly tinted buildings accented by tile roofs, soaring columns, and arched entryways. In a vibrant interpretation of paradise found, three clusters of regionally themed guest buildings ring the 15-acre Lago Dorado lagoon. The terra-cotta Casitas occupy a citylike landscape that segues into a rural area. Here, pueblo-style Ranchos invite guests to dwell among cacti adjacent to a dry streambed. In the resort's third section, the scenery shifts once more, with rocky beaches and festive Cabanas filling the horizon. Guestrooms in the three areas are similarly appointed with brilliant yellow, scarlet, or deep blue accents. Walkways lead from guestroom areas to the resort's main recreation area (dominated by a five-story Mayan pyramid) and the central building that holds its temporal treasures: an intricately tiled rotunda lobby, complete with a Spanish-urn fountain; waterfront eateries and lounge; and a gift shop carrying Mexican handicrafts.

BIG DRAWS: An excellent value in an enchanting setting. Pleasantly removed from the bustle. A standout among the moderates for its health club, suites, and business hotel perks. Enviable proximity to Animal Kingdom.

Coronado Springs Tips

■ Coronado Springs' status as a convention property yields perks for all guests: namely a health club, salon, and rooms equipped with a coffeemaker and extra phone jack.

■ January, May, September, and October are popular convention months. Most groups are housed in the Casitas area.

■ Limited room service is available from 4 P.M. to midnight.

■ The palm-fringed beaches of the Cabanas area make it an especially romantic setting. A bonus: More than half of the rooms offer water views.

■ Ranchos are centrally located; Casitas are closer to the health club and convention center.

■ A trail behind the Ranchos area is lighted at night for moonlight strolls.

Dixie Landings Tips

- For both atmosphere and minimal walking, request a room in the Magnolia Bend's Oak Manor or lodge number 18 or 27 in the resort's Alligator Bayou section.

- The Sassagoula River Cruise is a pleasant outing in addition to being a convenient means of transportation.

WORTH NOTING: Guestrooms at this 1,967-room resort are smaller than those at Disney's deluxe hotels, but comfortable and inviting. Decor reveals Mexican and southwestern influences, and reflects the distinctive style of each guest area. Standard rooms feature two double beds (some king-size beds are available). Amenities include a coffeemaker, iron and ironing board, room service, and an extra phone jack. Most of the resort's 46 suites are located in the Casitas area. In addition to a large themed pool—which has a 22-person whirlpool and a sand volleyball court on the side—there is a quiet pool in each guest area. The entire resort is surrounded by protected wetlands, offering seclusion and greenery. A nature trail wraps behind the Ranchos area. La Vida health club houses the Casa de Belleza salon. Bikes and boats may be rented. The nearly mile-long path around the lake, known as the Esplanade, is ideal for biking and jogging. A large convention center offers access to business services.

Where to eat: Maya Grill (Southwest flavors) complements offerings at the Pepper Market (food court resembling an outdoor market).

Where to drink: Francisco's (waterfront lounge with southwestern snacks) and Siesta's pool bar.

VITAL STATISTICS: Coronado Springs is located on the shore of a small lake near Animal Kingdom and Blizzard Beach. Coronado Springs; 1000 W. Buena Vista Dr.; Box 10000; Lake Buena Vista, FL 32830-1000; 939-1000; fax 939-0425.

Transportation: Buses stop at each guest area en route to the Magic Kingdom, Epcot, the Disney-MGM Studios, Animal Kingdom, Typhoon Lagoon, Blizzard Beach, and Downtown Disney.

Rates: Rooms begin at $119 in value season, $129 regular, and $139 peak; suites start at $238. A $15 per diem charge applies for each extra adult (beyond two) sharing a room.

Dixie Landings

Southern hospitality takes two forms at this 2,048-room resort: pillared mansions with groomed lawns and *Gone With the Wind* elegance and, farther upriver, rustic homes with tin roofs and rough-hewn bayou charm that are tucked among trees and bushes. Guestrooms located in the three-story Magnolia Bend Mansions and the two-story Alligator Bayou Lodges are similarly appointed. The man-made Sassagoula River winds through the heart of the resort, curling around its main recreation area like a moat. Bridges link guest lodgings with this area and the steamship-style building that houses the resort's eateries, gift shop, and check-in facilities.

BIG DRAWS: An excellent value. An exceedingly lovely natural setting.

WORTH NOTING: Rooms are smaller than those at Disney's deluxe hotels, but pleasantly inviting. Each features two double beds (some king-size beds are available). This is a large, sprawling resort with twice as many rooms as its sister resort, Port Orleans; some accommodations are a bit removed from the central building or the nearest bus stop. Room service delivers pizza from 4 P.M. to midnight. Bikes and boats may be rented. The resort's extensive pathways are well suited for joggers, and a carriage path leads to Port Orleans. Five quiet pools (open 24 hours, provided they stay quiet) are sprinkled through the Bayou and Mansion guest areas. A whirlpool is located near the main pool. Catch-and-release fishing excursions are offered, as is a stocked, secluded fishing hole (cane poles available). Guests may use the themed pool at Port Orleans in addition to the one here.

Where to eat: Boatwright's Dining Hall (casual restaurant specializing in Cajun and southern cuisine) and Colonel's Cotton Mill (sprawling food court).

Where to drink: Cotton Co-Op (fireplace and evening entertainment) and Muddy Rivers (poolside refreshments).

VITAL STATISTICS: Dixie Landings is located on a bank of the Sassagoula River and offers fast commutes to Downtown Disney, not to mention its sister resort, Port Orleans (reachable by boat or carriage path). Epcot and the Disney-MGM Studios are close at hand, as are three of WDW's 18-hole golf courses. Dixie Landings; 1251 Dixie Dr.; Box 10000; Lake Buena Vista, FL 32830-1000; 934-6000; fax 934-5777.

Transportation: Buses stop at guest areas en route to the Magic Kingdom, Epcot, Disney-MGM Studios, Animal Kingdom, Typhoon Lagoon, Blizzard Beach, and Downtown Disney. Water launches, known as the Sassagoula River Cruise, travel to Port Orleans and Downtown Disney.

Rates: Rooms begin at $119 in value season, $129 regular, and $139 peak. A $15 per diem charge applies for each extra adult (beyond two) sharing a room.

Port Orleans

New Orleans' historic French Quarter is evoked in this resort's prim row house–style guest buildings, which are wrapped in ornate wrought-iron railings and set amid romantic gardens, quiet courtyards, and tree-lined city blocks. Old-fashioned lampposts add to the ambience, as do signs denoting such streets as Rue D'Baga and Café Au Lait Way. The resort is entered via Port Orleans Square, an airy atrium with adjoining one-story buildings that house the hotel's front desk, gift shop, and arcade on one side, and its restaurant, lounge, and food court on the other. (Follow the French horn chandeliers to the Mardi Gras mural to check in.) Guestrooms are located in seven three-story buildings, which are set on either side of the central thoroughfare that begins just beyond Port Orleans Square and ends at the resort's large themed pool. The whole enclave is set alongside a stand-in Mississippi known as the Sassagoula River.

Port Orleans Tips

- This is too pretty a place to wake up to a view of the parking lot, so consider reserving a room overlooking the gardens or splurge on riverscape digs.

- Of the buildings with riverfront rooms, number 1 is nicely isolated.

- Note that pool views can spoil the ambience.

- Request a top-floor room for optimum quiet.

- Experience Port Orleans' romantic atmosphere via a bike ride along the river.

- Don't miss the fresh beignets (a true taste of the Big Easy), whose aroma regularly wafts through the food court. And try the gumbo.

- Although there is no quiet pool here, guests can swim in the five located at Dixie Landings next door (the two at Magnolia Bend are within walking distance).

BIG DRAWS: A terrific bang for the buck. The truly charming environs rank among Disney's most memorable. Easily the least sprawling and most manageable of the moderately priced resorts.

WORTH NOTING: The pretty, homey rooms are a bit smaller than those at Disney's more expensive hotels, but are perfectly comfortable. Each of the 1,008 rooms features two double beds (some king-size beds are available). The vast food court and the hearty fare at Bonfamille's Café earn repeat guests. Room service is limited to pizza (4 P.M. to midnight). A Dixieland band often entertains in the main courtyard; a street artist is available for portraits. Lobby restrooms, fitted with tall, old-fashioned toilets, have piped-in jazz worthy of a sound track. A carriage path—ideal for jogging, strolling, and biking—wends alongside the river to Port Orleans' sister resort, Dixie Landings, less than a mile upriver. Bikes and boats may be rented. A large whirlpool is centrally located. In addition to the fantasy swimming pool here, Port Orleans guests are permitted use of Dixie Landings' themed pool; they can also take advantage of its secluded fishing hole (catch-and-release only). The Sassagoula River Cruise is a pleasant outing, in addition to being a convenient mode of transportation.

Where to eat: Bonfamille's Café (a dining room with French Quarter–style and Creole cooking) and Sassagoula Floatworks & Food Factory (food court with Mardi Gras ambience and inexpensive fare).

Where to drink: Mardi Grogs (poolside refreshments) and Scat Cat's Club (for specialty drinks and evening entertainment).

VITAL STATISTICS: Port Orleans enjoys special access to Downtown Disney via the Sassagoula River Cruise, which also links it with Dixie Landings, its sister resort upriver. It's close to Epcot, the Disney-MGM Studios, and three 18-hole golf courses as well. Port Orleans; 2201 Orleans Dr.; Box 10000; Lake Buena Vista, FL 32830-1000; 934-5000; fax 934-5353.

Transportation: Buses to the Magic Kingdom, Epcot, the Disney-MGM Studios, Animal Kingdom, Typhoon Lagoon, Blizzard Beach, and Downtown Disney. Water launches to Dixie Landings and Downtown Disney.

Rates: Rooms begin at $119 in value season, $129 regular, and $139 peak. A $15 per diem charge applies for each extra adult (beyond two) sharing a room.

Value

All-Star Sports & All-Star Music Resorts

Bright in a manner normally reserved for toy packaging, these fun-loving resorts exist at the intersection of entertainment architecture and pop art. Picture a landscape in which three-story football helmets, surfboards, cowboy boots, and maracas are the norm, and you have an idea of the oversize sense of whimsy that governs the All-Star Sports and All-Star Music resorts. Identical in all but their telltale preoccupations, the adjacent properties are separate entities. Each has its own utterly felicitous central check-in building, complete with food court, and its own signature swimming pools. Each features ten improbable-looking guest buildings that are divided into five distinct (sports or music) themes

All-Star Stats

The sports and music icons at the All-Star resorts are sooo big that...

■ The jukeboxes at the rock 'n' roll guest building could hold 4,000 compact discs, enough music for 135 days.

■ It would take more than nine million tennis balls to fill one of the tennis cans holding court at All-Star Sports.

■ The boots doing the two-step at All-Star Music measure a whopping size 270.

All-Star Sports & All-Star Music Resorts Tips

■ These resorts attract families with small children in droves. All-Star Music tends to have a higher ratio of adults to children than its sportive compatriot.

■ For maximum quiet, request a third-floor room in a building away from the food court or main pool action (at All-Star Music, it's Broadway or country music; at All-Star Sports, tennis or basketball).

■ Reservations are required for luggage assistance upon checkout; call the night before.

■ Budget-conscious? Note the value season dates on page 43 for the cheapest rates available on-property.

■ Unless you plan to drive everywhere, request a room near the lobby (i.e., bus stop).

and 1,920 thematically correct rooms. Sports fans have a larger-than-Shaquille O'Neal raison d'être in the All-Star Sports resort's homages to basketball, baseball, football, tennis, and surfing. The All-Star Music resort makes equally exaggerated overtures to calypso, jazz, Broadway, rock, and country music.

BIG DRAW: All the advantages of staying on WDW turf at a fraction of the cost of its other resorts.

WORTH NOTING: Requests for specific sport or music genres cannot be guaranteed, but are likely to be met, considering the resorts' enormous capacity (384 rooms per theme, five themes per resort). Rooms are, not surprisingly, the smallest of those at any WDW resort hotel. While spare, they're perfectly adequate, if perhaps a tad lacking in drawer space. In all rooms except those equipped for travelers with disabilities, there's sufficient space under the beds to stash a suitcase. Sports and music themes are maintained with a great deal more subtlety—bedspreads, curtains, light fixtures—in guestrooms than on the startling grounds. Rooms with king-size beds are available on request, as are additional amenities such as down pillows and hair dryers. On-site recreation is limited to arcades and two whimsically designed pools at each resort. Pizza delivery, plus beer and wine, is available until midnight. All-Star guests have special marina privileges at Caribbean Beach, where one fee provides unlimited boat rentals.

Where to eat: At All-Star Sports: End Zone (a vast sports-themed food court). At All-Star Music: Intermission (same food stands, different theme).

Where to drink: At All-Star Sports: Team Spirits pool bar. At All-Star Music: Singing Spirits pool bar.

VITAL STATISTICS: All-Star Sports and All-Star Music have excellent proximity to the Disney-MGM Studios and Blizzard Beach; Epcot and Animal Kingdom are also close at hand. All-Star Sports; 1701 W. Buena Vista Dr.; Box 10000; Lake Buena Vista, FL 32830-1000; 939-5000; fax 939-7333. All-Star Music; 1801 W. Buena Vista Dr.; Box 10000; Lake Buena Vista, FL 32830-1000; 939-6000; fax 939-7222.

Transportation: Buses to the Magic Kingdom, Epcot, Disney-MGM Studios, Animal Kingdom, Typhoon Lagoon, Blizzard Beach, and Downtown Disney.

Rates: Rooms begin at $74 in value season, $84 regular, and $89 peak. A $10 per diem charge applies to each extra adult (beyond two) sharing a room.

Disney Cruise Line

The first thing to understand about the new Disney Cruise Line's one-week vacations, which pair a WDW resort stay with a cruise: *Disney Magic* and its sister ship, *Disney Wonder* (set to debut in December), are *not* floating Fantasylands.

The 1,750-passenger *Disney Magic* is casually elegant, designed to recapture the majesty of early ocean liners. It's equipped to satisfy even the most savvy of cruisers, with a mix of traditional seafaring diversions, classic Disney touches, and an occasional quirky surprise (such as the restaurant whose decor changes from strictly black and white to total Technicolor over the course of a meal). Recreation areas are designed to lure families and adults sans kids to altogether different parts of the ship. There's even a pool and a restaurant earmarked for adults only.

Lest anyone forget who owns this vessel, Disney characters crop up from stem to stern, with some incarnations more subtle than others. A bronze statue of Mickey as helmsman greets arriving guests; character silhouettes line the grand staircase; and a life-size statue of Goofy hangs over the stern (he's painting the ship, not suffering from seasickness). Characters of the flesh-and-fur variety are also on hand to mix, mingle, and otherwise assist the captain.

By day, fun in the sun alternates with lunch, indoor distractions, and catnaps. When the sun goes down, the focus shifts to dining and hitting the deck that's home to Beat Street, a Pleasure Island–like cluster of adults-only party spots.

Disney Cruise Line vacations begin with a stay at a WDW resort. After transferring to Port Canaveral, guests embark on a three- or four-day cruise to the Bahamas (Cruise-only packages are also available). En route to Castaway Cay, Disney's enchanting Bahamian isle, the ship makes an extended pit stop in busy Nassau. How nice it is to know that only Disney Cruise Line can call at Castaway.

Land Ho!

On the final day of each Cruise Line vacation, Disney deposits guests on Castaway Cay (key), its charted, yet private isle. With all the perks of an isolated tropical paradise, an afternoon at Castaway Cay is sure to cure even the most severe cases of Gilligan envy. Disney has allowed the island to retain its natural beauty while accommodating a variety of activities, including volleyball, snorkeling, biking, and hiking. The 1,000-acre Bahamian island features a mile-long stretch of secluded sand reserved for adult sun worshipers, as well as those seeking scuba lessons and open-air massage. There's also a restaurant, bar, and more for Bahama mamas and papas to explore.

Disney Cruise Line Tips

- Expect high demand during Disney Cruise Line's inaugural season, and book vacations well in advance; early-booking discounts may apply.

- If you're certified in scuba, bring proof: There's fantastic diving in the pristine waters off Castaway Cay.

- Resort IDs can be used to charge incidentals such as drinks, minibar snacks, salon services, and traditional cruise gratuities to servers and cabin crew.

- Unlike a trip around World Showcase, in which you merely *feel* like you've left the country, on a Disney Cruise Line vacation you really do. Pack a passport (or birth certificate).

BIG DRAWS: The ultimate surf-and-turf experience, Disney-style. Private island rendezvous. Adults, teens, and tots are unlikely to step on one another's toes.

WORTH NOTING: Each room has a safe, TV, hair dryer, minibar, and telephone with "land line." Facilities include three pools, a sports deck with golf net, an ocean-view fitness center, and a spa. In addition to nightclub-style entertainment, the ship boasts adult-oriented enrichment programs and two theaters: Buena Vista Theater shows first-run movies and classic Disney films; the glitzy Walt Disney Theatre hosts an original Broadway-style production each evening.

Where to eat: A different restaurant each night: Animator's Palate (room undergoes a spectral metamorphosis), Islands Restaurant (Caribbean), Lumière's (French, fairly formal), and Palo (Mediterranean fare, romantic, reserved for adults). Lido Café is a casual daytime spot—kids rule dinner hour. To avoid the crush of pint-sized diners, request the second dinner seating.

Where to drink: In addition to the Promenade Lounge (elegant bar) and the ESPN Skybox (spirited sports bar), there's Beat Street, where you'll find Offbeat (comedy club), Rockin' Bar "D" (dance club that alternates musical themes; country one night, rock 'n' roll the next), and Sessions (intimate piano bar).

VITAL STATISTICS: Shipboard accommodations are, on average, 25% roomier than cabins on other ships. Rooms have a queen-size bed or two twin-size beds. The majority are outside staterooms, with a bath and a half; nearly a third have private verandas.

Transportation: Buses transport guests to Port Canaveral from their resort, where they board *Disney Magic*, unencumbered by luggage; Disney staffers have already sent it to their stateroom. (There's no second check-in. Resort keys open respective staterooms.) When the ship returns to Port Canaveral, guests are bused directly to Orlando International Airport.

Rates: Twelve stateroom categories correspond to comparable rooms in WDW resorts. Moderate resorts yield inside staterooms; deluxe net ocean views. Standard rates for a seven-day vacation begin at $1,229 per person double occupancy during the value season, $1,329 regular, and $1,429 peak. (Seasons differ from those listed for resorts; value season is generally mid-August through mid-December.) The tab includes airfare to Orlando from major U.S. cities, stateroom and WDW resort accommodations, unlimited park admission, shipboard meals and recreation, and ground transportation. To book a Disney Cruise Line vacation, contact a travel agent or call 566-7000.

Resorts on Hotel Plaza Boulevard

The three properties described below occupy a unique position among non-Disney accommodations because they, along with four other hotels, are located inside the boundaries of Walt Disney World, near Downtown Disney; they are within walking distance of the Marketplace.

While convenient location is the chief advantage of staying at a Hotel Plaza Blvd. resort, guests also have other privileges: the ability to book tee times on Disney golf courses 60 days in advance and preferred admission to Planet Hollywood (you get to go to the head of the line before 5 P.M.). The latter benefit is unique to Hotel Plaza Blvd. resort guests—and no small perk, given the mind-boggling waits. All the hotels have car rental desks and Disney-run gift shops; they also sell park tickets and provide free bus service to the Magic Kingdom, Epcot, Disney-MGM Studios, Animal Kingdom, Typhoon Lagoon, Blizzard Beach, and Downtown Disney. Rooms can be booked through the individual hotel or through WDW Central Reservations (934-7639).

Buena Vista Palace Resort & Spa

The largest of the Hotel Plaza Blvd. resorts, Buena Vista Palace is actually a cluster of towers, one of them 27 stories. The grounds are lushly landscaped, with shaded walkways; inside, the decor is elegant. The reception area offers several cozy sitting nooks that invite lingering, and the Island Suite building is set amid secluded courtyards. Many of the 1,014 rooms and suites offer a private patio or balcony, complete with a view of Epcot's Spaceship Earth.

BIG DRAWS: Popular night spots, ranging from romantic to raucous, and first-rate dining rooms.

WORTH NOTING: All guestrooms have ceiling fans, two phones (one bedside, one in the bathroom), voice mail, and 24-hour room service. Four of the

---

Buena Vista Palace Tips

■ The Top of the Palace lounge not only ranks among the most romantic spots in the Orlando area; it also provides a good view of IllumiNations fireworks, serves wine by the glass, and offers patrons a free glass of champagne at sunset.

■ The hotel's European-style spa offers aqua aerobics and salon services, in addition to myriad spa treatments.

■ For the quietest rooms, and those most convenient to the recreation area, choose accommodations in the Island Suite building.

■ The hotel's new telephone system provides computer and fax hookups, speakerphone capability, and voice mail; calls go directly to guests' rooms rather than through the resort operator.

Hilton Tips

concierge rooms feature whirlpool tubs. One- and two-bedroom suites are available. As for recreation, there's a vast health club (personal trainers available); a spa offering massages and aromatherapy; three pools; three lighted tennis courts; a marina with boat rentals; and a sand volleyball court.

Where to eat: Arthur's 27 (rooftop restaurant with an international menu); Outback (specializing in fresh seafood and Black Angus beef); and Watercress Café and Pastry Shop (for 24-hour counter-service baked goods and deli items).

Where to drink: The Laughing Kookaburra (spirited spot known for live entertainment) and Top of the Palace (quiet lounge with a stunning view and entertainment Wednesday through Saturday).

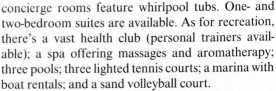

VITAL STATISTICS: The hotel is located right across the road from the Downtown Disney Marketplace. Buena Vista Palace Resort & Spa; 1900 Buena Vista Dr.; Lake Buena Vista, FL 32830; 827-2727 or 800-327-2990; fax 827-6034.

Transportation: Regularly scheduled complimentary bus transport to the WDW theme parks is provided.

Rates: Rooms are from $165 to $270; rates for suites are $270 to $505.

Hilton

Set on 23 landscaped acres, the Hilton has a recently spruced-up facade, with aqua and other beach hues that affirm the hotel's laid-back ambience. The lobby is spacious. The reception desk is backed by two large aquariums. And the 814 rooms are tastefully decorated in mauve, peach, and earth tones.

BIG DRAWS: Directly across the road from the Downtown Disney Marketplace (it has the best proximity of all the Hotel Plaza Blvd. properties). Pool area with adult appeal. Free transportation to all Disney golf courses.

WORTH NOTING: All guestrooms feature minibars, voice mail, and computer hookups; corner rooms have balconies. A health club offers Nautilus and cardiovascular machines. There are two heated swimming pools, and a pair of whirlpools are tucked away under palms and pines. Upscale shops are a plus.

Where to eat: Finn's Grill (Key West setting with oyster bar also serving steak and seafood dinners); Benihana Japanese steak house; County Fair (all-day dining); County Fair Terrace (casual outdoor setting); and the Old-Fashioned Soda Shoppe (snacks from ice cream to pizza).

Where to drink: Rum Largo Pool Bar & Café (for tropical concoctions) and John T's Plantation Bar (an Old South–inspired lobby lounge).

VITAL STATISTICS: Located right across the road from the Downtown Disney Marketplace. Hilton; 1751 Hotel Plaza Blvd.; Lake Buena Vista, FL 32830; 827-4000 or 800-782-4414; fax 827-3890.

Transportation: Regularly scheduled complimentary bus transport is offered to the WDW theme parks.

Rates: Rooms are $195 to $255, and suites are $459 to $759, depending on the season.

Courtyard by Marriott

This 323-room hotel is one of the largest Courtyards in the country. It has a Florida-casual atrium lobby filled with cheerful umbrella-topped tables. Recreational facilities include three heated pools, a whirlpool, and an exercise room with Nautilus equipment.

BIG DRAW: Beautifully decorated rooms that, smallish bathrooms aside, are among the most spacious among the Hotel Plaza Blvd. resorts.

WORTH NOTING: Guestrooms, divided between a 14-story tower and a 6-story annex, are decorated in cool shades of green with tropical-print bedspreads and whitewashed wood furniture. Each room includes a sitting area, computer-data ports, voice mail, clock radio, marble vanity, coffeemaker, iron, and safe. Bathrooms tend to be small, with limited counter space.

Where to eat: 2 Go (breakfast bar); Courtyard Café & Grille (all-day dining, including breakfast buffet); and Village Deli (for snacks, sandwiches, TCBY yogurt, Pizza Hut pizza, beer, and wine).

Where to drink: The Tipsy Parrot lobby lounge serves cocktails; a pool bar is open in warmer months.

VITAL STATISTICS: Two blocks from the Downtown Disney Marketplace. Courtyard by Marriott; Box 22204; 1805 Hotel Plaza Blvd.; Lake Buena Vista, FL 32830; 828-8888 or 800-223-9930; fax 827-4623.

Transportation: Regularly scheduled complimentary bus transport is provided to the WDW theme parks.

Rates: Rooms are $109 to $169 year-round.

Courtyard by Marriott Tips

■ Budget watchers should note that the comfortable rooms here deliver a great bang for the buck.

■ This is a high-rise hotel, unlike many of the national chain's properties, so if you want a picturesque panorama rather than one of nearby Interstate 4, specifically request a courtyard view when making reservations. Courtyard-view rooms cost $10 more; for rooms overlooking the Downtown Disney Marketplace, you pay an extra $20.

BEYOND THE WORLD

When visitors to Walt Disney World consider staying somewhere other than at the on-property resorts, it's normally for one of two reasons. First, many people simply don't realize that Mickey is in the hotel business at all, or that he's so great at it. And second is the notion that Disney accommodations are too expensive. Since the arrival of the All-Star Sports and All-Star Music resorts, the latter objection is less persuasive. But no matter what your style or budget calls for, when it comes to deciphering the options beyond WDW's hotels, the difficulty lies in sorting out the best from all the rest.

Not to worry: We've simplified matters by highlighting our top choices—from luxury to economy. For ease of comparison, this listing places the off-site properties into Disney resort categories consistent with their rate scales and accommodation types. There's Deluxe, Moderate, and Value, plus the Home Away From Home category, used to distinguish all-suite and villa-type lodging options. All of the hotels listed provide transportation to the Disney theme parks; be sure to inquire about current costs and schedules.

Grand Cypress Tips

■ La Coquina serves a champagne brunch on Sunday, when its kitchen is open to guests for tours.

■ Golfers shouldn't miss the resort's New Course, which conjures visions of the Old Course at Scotland's venerable St. Andrews.

■ And don't overlook the nine-hole "pitch and putt" course designed by Jack Nicklaus.

Deluxe

Grand Cypress

The eye-catching 750-room Hyatt Regency Grand Cypress is this destination resort's 18-story centerpiece, while its secluded villas largely remain a well-kept secret. The resort's recreation roster boasts a health club, 45 holes of Jack Nicklaus–designed golf courses (including one 18-hole and three 9-hole layouts), tennis courts, a 21-acre lake with rental boats, a 45-acre nature preserve, fitness and jogging trails, racquetball and volleyball courts, horseback riding, and a waterfall-laden pool area.

BIG DRAWS: Style, service, and great golf. Plus, the lobby's a knockout. It would merit a visit even if Walt Disney World weren't just down the road.

WORTH NOTING: The Mediterranean-style Villas of Grand Cypress dot the fairways. The smaller club suites consist of a spacious bedroom with separate dressing area, large bath, and a patio or balcony. Many of the one- to four-bedroom villas have fireplaces and whirlpools. The villa enclave has its own pool. Hotel guestroom decor is Florida casual. A million-dollar art collection graces the resort's public areas and landscaped grounds. A free-form swimming pool features waterfalls, grottoes, and whirlpools. Golf instruction is available at the on-site Academy of Golf. An equestrian center offers lessons and trail rides. The tennis club has a dozen courts (five are lighted).

Where to eat: At the Villas: Three dining choices include the Black Swan, a sophisticated dining room at the golf clubhouse; the casual Fairways restaurant; and the poolside snack bar. At the hotel: Five dining options include Hemingway's (seafood, steaks, and game) and La Coquina (contemporary cuisine).

Where to drink: Trellises (atrium piano bar); Hurricane Bar (Key West–style); On the Rocks (poolside refreshments); and the White Horse Saloon (country-and-western entertainment).

VITAL STATISTICS: The resort is located adjacent to the Hotel Plaza Blvd. resorts. Villas of Grand Cypress; One N. Jacaranda Blvd.; Orlando, FL 32836; 239-4700 or 800-835-7377; fax 239-7219. Hyatt Regency Grand Cypress; One Grand Cypress Blvd.; Orlando, FL 32836; 239-1234 or 800-233-1234; fax 239-3800.

Transportation: The Hyatt Regency offers shuttle service to the Disney theme parks for $7 round-trip; free transport between the villas and the hotel is provided.

Rates: At the Villas of Grand Cypress, club suites are $210 to $425; one-bedroom villas are $310 to $525; two-bedroom units are $420 to $850; three-bedroom units are $585 to $1,140; and four-bedroom units are $760 to $1,400. At the Hyatt Regency Grand Cypress, guestrooms are from $195 to $380, and suites start at $650.

Peabody Orlando

The only sister property to the famed Peabody in Memphis, this imposing 891-room luxury tower is International Drive's most luxurious hotel. Recreational facilities include a vast heated pool, four lighted tennis courts, and a health club with personal trainers.

BIG DRAWS: Elegance, gracious service, and first-rate dining rooms and facilities.

Peabody Orlando Tips

■ The famous Peabody ducks ceremoniously parade from a private elevator into the three-story atrium lobby, down a red carpet, and into a marble water fountain daily at 11 A.M., then reverse the pomp and circumstance at 5 P.M.

■ Capriccio restaurant offers a champagne brunch on Sunday.

■ Club Capriccio makes the most of the Peabody's exceptional wine cellar with monthly themed wine tastings and seminars, especially popular with local residents.

Best Western Buena Vista Suites Tips

■ The guest service desk here can arrange local transportation or car rental, make dinner reservations, provide currency exchange, and supply information on area attractions.

■ If outdoor amenities are important to you, skip this property. The pool area is small, and there are no grounds other than the parking area. What the hotel does offer is comfortable suites and convenient location.

WORTH NOTING: Nicely appointed guestrooms feature a small television set in the bathroom, nightly turndown service, and daily newspaper delivery. Afternoon tea is served weekdays. The lobby is the site of two daily duck marches.

    Where to eat: Dux (the elegant signature restaurant, where the menu is creative and *no duck* is served); Capriccio (northern Italian cuisine and mesquite-grilled specialties in an exhibition kitchen); and the B-Line Diner (a 1950s-style diner that's open 24 hours).

    Where to drink: Four bars, including The Lobby Bar for nightly live entertainment and daily duck drills.

VITAL STATISTICS: The Peabody is directly across from the Orange County Convention Center and a short drive from Orlando's Official Visitor Information Center. Peabody Orlando; 9801 International Dr.; Orlando, FL 32819; 352-4000 or 800-732-2639; fax 351-0073.

    Transportation: The hotel's whimsical Double-Ducker bus provides regular shuttle service to the four Disney theme parks for $7 round-trip.

    Rates: Rooms are $240 to $300; rates for suites run $450 to $1,350.

Home Away From Home
Buena Vista Suites

This 280-suite hotel is convenient for those who plan to visit other Orlando-area attractions in addition to Walt Disney World. The hotel's highlights include an exercise room, pool, whirlpool, tennis courts, laundry facilities, and gift shop.

BIG DRAW: An all-suite property with full breakfast (even grits) included.

WORTH NOTING: Standard two-room suites have a separate bedroom and a living room with a queen-size sleeper sofa. Each unit has a coffeemaker, refrigerator, two televisions, a VCR (movie rentals are available), two telephones, a safe, and a microwave. The phones are equipped with voice mail and data ports. Deluxe suites feature a king-size bed and a whirlpool tub.

    Where to eat: Patio Grille offers chicken wings and typical grill fare plus made-to-order sandwiches and a variety of snacks.

    Where to drink: Citrus Lounge provides poolside lunch and evening cocktails.

VITAL STATISTICS: The property is situated about 1½ miles from Walt Disney World and is also close to the central tourist strip along International Drive.

Buena Vista Suites; 14450 International Dr.; Orlando, FL 32830; 239-8588 or 800-537-7737; fax 239-1401.

Transportation: Complimentary shuttle service is provided to and from the four Disney theme parks.

Rates: Standard suites range from $129 to $149; deluxe suites are $149 to $169.

Summerfield Suites

This 146-unit property adds another dimension to the all-suite theme: a 24-hour convenience store with microwave entrées and movie rentals. Other amenities include an exercise room, heated pool, whirlpool, and complimentary continental breakfast buffet.

BIG DRAWS: Both one- and two-bedroom suites are unusually spacious. The two-bedroom units are private enough for two couples traveling together.

WORTH NOTING: In addition to a fully outfitted kitchen, each unit features a VCR, an iron and ironing board, a desk in each bedroom, voice mail, and computer hookups. There are no restaurants on the premises, but there is a lobby bar.

VITAL STATISTICS: Summerfield Suites is at the south end of International Drive, opposite the Mercado Mediterranean shopping, dining, and entertainment complex, and convenient to the Disney theme parks and to downtown Orlando. Summerfield Suites International; 8480 International Dr.; Orlando, FL 32819; 352-2400 or 800-830-44964; fax 352-4631.

Transportation: Shuttle service from the hotel to the Disney theme parks is provided for $7 round-trip.

Rates: One-bedroom units (sleeping four) are $169 to $209; two-bedroom units (sleeping six) are $189 to $229; and two-bedroom trio units (sleeping eight) are $209 to $269.

Summerfield Suites Tips

■ Reservations must be made well in advance for stays during peak periods because the inn is frequently booked solid.

■ A sister property in Lake Buena Vista offers complimentary shuttle service to Walt Disney World and is closer to the parks, but we favor the International Drive location because it's more adult-oriented.

■ To have groceries delivered to your room by 6:30 P.M., leave a completed form with the front desk early in the morning.

Clarion Plaza Tips

- Discounted rates as low as $79 are usually available in the spring and fall.

- Don't waste time driving around looking for a parking place when the lot is crowded; check behind the hotel near the meetings area, where spaces are almost always available.

Country Hearth Inn Tips

- The lounge here hosts a happy hour that's popular with locals.

- Don't be surprised if you stumble upon a wedding in the courtyard gazebo.

- A Sunday champagne brunch is served in the Country Parlor.

Moderate
Clarion Plaza

This inviting 810-unit hotel has tastefully decorated public areas and guestrooms, plus an impressive pool area, complete with a waterfall-endowed whirlpool.

BIG DRAWS: A business hotel by design, the property has reasonable rates, lively ambience, and spacious rooms that make it popular with leisure travelers.

WORTH NOTING: The roomy guestrooms and suites are decorated in vibrant colors, and feature safes and separate vanity areas. Facilities include a guest laundry on every other floor.

Where to eat: Jack's Place (complete with caricature sketches à la Manhattan's legendary Sardi's, for seafood and steak dinners, and formidable desserts) and Café Matisse (buffets and à la carte items for breakfast, lunch, and dinner). Lite Bite is a 24-hour bakery and deli.

Where to drink: In the lobby bar and at the Backstage nightclub, where live bands and top local deejays play nightly until 2 A.M.

VITAL STATISTICS: Located on International Drive adjacent to the Orange County Convention Center and near Orlando's Official Visitor Information Center. Clarion Plaza; 9700 International Dr.; Orlando, FL 32819-8144; 352-9700 or 800-627-8258; fax 352-9710.

Transportation: Shuttle service from the hotel to the four Disney theme parks costs $11 round-trip.

Rates: Standard rooms are $135 to $155; suites are $310 to $680.

Value
Country Hearth Inn

This two-story gingerbread-style property with rocking chairs on the porch and homey touches throughout is the closest you'll come to finding quaint accommodations on International Drive. The well-tended, landscaped grounds include a good-size pool and a tropical courtyard.

BIG DRAWS: Charming ambience and reasonable prices.

WORTH NOTING: The hotel's 150 guestrooms feature cherry furniture, colorful drapes and bedspreads, French doors, and verandas. Most have two double beds (some king-size beds are available). Hardwood floors, a patterned tin ceiling, and chandeliers grace the lobby.

Where to eat: Country Parlor (complimentary continental breakfast and à la carte dinner).

Where to drink: The hotel's Front Porch lounge.

VITAL STATISTICS: The inn is across from the Orange County Convention Center (but set back from the street). Country Hearth Inn; 9861 International Dr.; Orlando, FL 32819; 352-0008 or 800-447-1890; fax 352-5449.

Transportation: Hotel shuttles run to and from the four Disney theme parks daily, and cost $9 round-trip.

Rates: Prices range from $49 to $109.

Wynfield Inn Westwood

This three-story, 300-room motel with shuttered windows has the look of a country inn. Landscaped grounds and courtyard with two pools (one heated) make it all the more appealing.

BIG DRAWS: Value. Courteous staff. Somewhat removed from hectic I-Drive.

WORTH NOTING: Guestrooms are pleasantly decorated and feature two double beds, voice mail, safes, and a separate vanity area. Laundry facilities are conveniently located throughout the property.

Where to eat: Snacks are available at the pool bar. The Village Inn restaurant is right next door, and several other options are within walking distance.

Where to drink: The pool bar offers refreshments; complimentary tea and coffee are available.

VITAL STATISTICS: Just off the north end of International Drive, the motel is especially convenient to the airport and downtown Orlando. Wynfield Inn Westwood; 6263 Westwood Blvd.; Orlando, FL 32821; 345-8000 or 800-346-1551; fax 345-1508.

Transportation: There is free scheduled transportation for guests to all the WDW theme parks.

Rates: Standard rooms are $68 to $98.

Wynfield Inn Westwood Tips

■ Request a poolside room to avoid noise from the expressway.

■ There is no charge to place local or 800-number calls from the hotel.

■ There is no restaurant on the premises, but nearby eateries help make up for this by offering Wynfield Inn Westwood guests a 10% discount.

Spectacular fireworks come with the territory at Walt Disney World.

Theme Parks: The Big Four

To experience Walt Disney World's quartet of major theme parks without children is tantamount to celebrating a major holiday without the complication of travel or in-laws. It's positively liberating.

Let the Magic Kingdom runneth over with strollers and too-tired toddlers. Let cumbersome families try to fend off five-headed-monster syndrome. As adults free to roam the Magic Kingdom, Epcot, Disney-MGM Studios, and Animal Kingdom on our own terms, we need not be concerned with such things. We are a distinct minority (read: non-teenaged individuals under no obligation whatsoever to facilitate the entertainment of any young person within 45 square miles) in one of those rare settings in which the minority holds all the advantages.

If we sometimes feel a bit conspicuous touring the parks as unaccompanied adults, it's because we're flaunting the inherent freedom. We're taking advantage of the fact that we're among friends who readily agree that a shaded bench, a nap in a hammock, or a soak in the whirlpool back at the resort really would hit the spot right now. We are free to buzz through the Magic Kingdom at a clip no character-conscious family could maintain, or meander through Epcot's World Showcase pavilions at what might be called escargot pace.

When we see people consumed by a self-imposed game of tag that obliges them to touch each and every attraction, we wish we could somehow interrupt the game and remind them that they are on vacation. The immense array of experiences that constitutes Walt Disney World has a way of inspiring a desire to "collect them all." This is only

The Mouse Is Spoken For

Walt Disney himself supplied the voice for Mickey Mouse from 1929 to 1946.

natural. But by being more selective and pausing to say, "You know, Mickey, as much as I appreciate all the entertainment you've lined up, I just don't have time to do everything," you'll wind up with a much more enjoyable and satisfying experience.

Each park has stuff on its shelves that we want in our shopping cart. It's easy to rationalize visiting all four; they're specialty stores, after all, and the Magic Kingdom may have such essentials as Splash Mountain and Pirates of the Caribbean, but it just doesn't sell Cranium Command or that 3-D movie we like so much, Honey, I Shrunk the Audience. For these, we have to go to Epcot. And although we can find a lot of our favorites here, we can't get The Twilight Zone Tower of Terror; it's available solely at the Disney-MGM Studios. Certainly, such newfound novelties as Kilimanjaro Safaris and Countdown to Extinction are Animal Kingdom exclusives.

That's okay. We like to immerse ourselves in the inspiring atmospheres that make these parks so distinct. When we're at the Magic Kingdom, we take one look at Cinderella Castle and simply cease to function as adults. Suddenly we are in the amusement business, with only ourselves to please. It's funny—a lot of the adults we've met there are similarly engaged. In any case, we've never had even the slightest problem entertaining ourselves in the Magic Kingdom.

In Epcot, it's easy to retain our adult sensibilities, as the point of Epcot in the first place is to be something other than an amusement park (although there's certainly plenty of funny business going on in, say, Cranium Command). The highly conceptual, experiential environs of Future World nudge our curiosity, engage our interest, and heighten our awareness. But when we need a change of pace, we move on to the Magic Snackdom, otherwise known as World Showcase. Granted, there is much more to this part of Epcot than compelling snacks from 11 different countries. One day, we got so caught up watching drummers in Japan we almost let seagulls get away with our soft pretzels from Germany.

Unless otherwise noted, all phone numbers are in area code 407.

When we're at the Disney-MGM Studios, savoring the relaxed atmosphere of this starry-eyed tribute to 1930s Hollywood, we're inclined to become a bit starry-eyed ourselves. The place has such a sophisticated air, a cozy nostalgia, a plucky sense of fun.

Although we have yet to experience Animal Kingdom firsthand, we know from our extensive preview how it will feel to enter this epic new realm: like avid adventurers bound for distant lands and bygone eras. We have no doubt in Disney's ability to momentarily persuade us that we've traveled to Africa on safari. And we are prepared to expect the unexpected.

We believe the parks are best explored in a certain order, especially your first time out. Starting with the least character-intensive theme parks lets you ease into Disneyana gradually, so that by the time Mickey Mouse appears in butter form at your dinner table, you've been conditioned to expect it.

Devote day one to Animal Kingdom (opening this May) so you're not champing at the bit. Preempt the fantasy zones with a day at Epcot and you'll sooner appreciate it on its own merit. Follow your first day at Epcot (it takes at least two to cover both Future World and World Showcase effectively) with a day at the Disney-MGM Studios. This works well for two reasons: Enchantment is a great chaser for enlightenment, and the Disney-MGM Studios ups the character presence a bit without overwhelming. If you're raring to meet Mickey or eager for a closer look at Cinderella Castle, spend your fourth day exploring the Magic Kingdom and your fifth finishing up at Epcot. (In this chapter, the parks are presented in the order they were created at Walt Disney World: the Magic Kingdom, 1971; Epcot, 1982; the Disney-MGM Studios, 1989; and Animal Kingdom, 1998.) After you've toured each park, spend any remaining days exploring other compelling corners of the World and revisiting favorite attractions—preferably between soaks in a soothing whirlpool.

Ears to the Ground

Woman in mid-thirties pleading with her companions in the midst of serious Adventureland foot traffic: "But I LOVE It's A Small World." About ten minutes later, the group was doubling back toward Fantasyland.

Magic Kingdom

The Magic Kingdom is usually open from 9 A.M. to 7 P.M.; park hours are extended during holiday periods and summer months. Call 824-4321 for up-to-the-minute details. One-day park admission is $42.14 for adults (see *Planning Ahead* for ticket options). Prices are subject to change.

As once-upon-a-timish and happily-ever-afteresque a place as exists, the Magic Kingdom is sure proof that you can judge a park by its largest icon (in this case, Cinderella Castle). While it is the most character-intensive, and certainly the strongest kid magnet of all the parks, flying elephants couldn't keep us away.

What puts the Magic Kingdom on the adult map? For starters, it's manageable. Unlike in the far larger Epcot, the essentials here are easily traversed in a leisurely day. High on the list of imperatives is a threesome of rides—Space Mountain, Splash Mountain, and Big Thunder Mountain Railroad—that make the Magic Kingdom the thrill seeker's park of choice. What it lacks in culture, fine cuisine, and opportunities to imbibe, it more than makes up for in magic. Disney has made a real art of coaxing folks into a state of wonderment that seldom occurs in adulthood, and this park represents that art taken to its highest level. Even if the singsongy tune accompanying Fantasyland's It's A Small World drives you crazy, odds are good that your brand of enchantment lies around the corner. It's a rare adult who doesn't fall under the spell of the Magic Kingdom's ballroom of waltzing apparitions, its heavy-breathing ode to an alien encounter, or its convincing den of leering pirates. For bouts of nostalgic whimsy, there are kiddie rides such as Peter Pan's Flight that don't aspire to recapture the magic of childhood so much as momentarily revive it.

Of course, a gazillion children can have a way of getting on one's nerves after a while, so some strategies are in order. First, master the art of noticing children only when they are being cute. We've gotten so good at this that during a recent visit to the park we recall seeing but one child: a girl about four years old whose eyes nearly doubled in size at the sight of Cinderella. To keep the "magic barometer" from falling, either make quick work of the park or weave in and out of major traffic zones (Fantasyland and Frontierland are generally the most crowded areas). Seek refuge in the quiet nooks described in the margins of this chapter and in such havens as The Hall of Presidents and the Main Street Cinema; for a bigger break, indulge in a leisurely lunch at the Grand Floridian or another of the resorts that are easily accessible via a quick trip on the monorail.

GUIDING PRINCIPLES: Know thy touring priorities. Know thy path of least resistance. These commandments are the basis for any enjoyable theme park visit—but they take on even greater importance for adults venturing through the Magic Kingdom.

Of course, you can't exactly determine your priorities or your route without first knowing your turf. Therefore, the section that follows is designed to offer a telling preview for first-time visitors and a timely review for returnees.

Structured as a counterclockwise walking tour through the seven themed "lands" that comprise the park, it provides a geographical orientation to the Magic Kingdom while also taking a critical inventory of the attractions as they relate to adults. Land by land, it highlights the adult essentials, points out redeeming and unfortunate characteristics of the nonessentials, and flags the newest additions. For the sake of easy reference, we've also included a Touring Priorities list ranking the park's best adult bets. To learn the most efficient touring strategies, consult the Hot Tips in the margins of this section and the flexible tour plan provided in the *Planning Ahead* chapter.

For information on how to get to the Magic Kingdom via Walt Disney World transportation or by car, see the "Getting Around" section of the *Planning Ahead* chapter. For the goods on Magic Kingdom shops worth exploring, see the "Shopping" section of the *Diversions* chapter. And finally, to find out about the park's best bets for dining, see the book's evaluative "Restaurant Guide" in the *Dining & Entertainment* chapter.

GETTING ORIENTED: No matter what your mode of transportation, you'll arrive at the same set of gates. Go through the turnstiles, past an area with rental lockers, and you're in Town Square, a cul-de-sac at the foot of Main Street that looks straight out to the park's best landmark, Cinderella Castle. At the opposite end of Main Street is an area known as the Central Plaza, or the Hub. It is here that you'll find the **Tip Board**, an information board listing the current waiting times for the park's most popular attractions.

It's helpful to think of the layout of the Magic Kingdom as a tree. Main Street is the trunk; the other six themed areas—Adventureland, Frontierland, Liberty Square, Fantasyland, Mickey's Toontown Fair, and Tomorrowland—dangle at the ends of the tree's gnarled boughs (actually bridges). The first bridge on your left leads to Adventureland; the second, to Liberty Square and

HOT TIPS

■ On Monday, Thursday, and Saturday, guests staying at WDW resorts may enter the Magic Kingdom 1½ hours prior to the official opening time and get an early crack at Space Mountain and all Fantasyland attractions. Early-entry days and attractions are subject to change.

■ Not coincidentally, Monday, Thursday, and Saturday tend to be the most crowded days at the Magic Kingdom.

■ The afternoon parade is a golden opportunity to take advantage of shorter lines at the most popular attractions.

Frontierland; the pathway straight ahead passes through Cinderella Castle on its way to the heart of Fantasyland; another bridge passes to the right of the castle to enter Fantasyland nearest Mickey's Toontown Fair and Tomorrowland; and the bridge on your immediate right leads directly to Tomorrowland. The lands are also linked via a broad footpath that wends its way behind the castle.

A Walking Tour

Let's begin our tour in **Town Square**, which is important as the location of **City Hall**, where a person can make all manner of inquiries and arrangements (no, you can't get married here). Even if you don't need to make priority seating arrangements, exchange foreign currency, check the lost and found, or play Q&A with the informed folks behind the counter, be sure to stop by for a guidemap. Note that the local ATM is under the train station.

Looking back toward the park's entrance from Town Square, you can see that the archway we walked under to get here is actually the foundation of the **Walt Disney World Railroad** depot. A 1928 steam engine that once carted sugarcane across the Yucatán now hauls freight (largely first-time visitors, train buffs, and homesick commuters) on a 21-minute loop around the Magic Kingdom. We recommend the ride for anyone interested in a great overview and a pleasant respite. It's also a fine way (albeit not always the fastest way) to get to Frontierland and Mickey's Toontown Fair if you don't want to walk.

Onward.

Main Street, U.S.A.

Main Street is notable as the tidy strip of storefronts where adults first gawk at, then feel compelled to photograph, Cinderella Castle. Understand, this will probably happen to you. While there's no shame in it, don't be so distracted you overlook the street's turn-of-the-century charm. Amusements here are decidedly low-key. **Main Street Cinema**'s ten-minute film clip about how Mickey hit the big time is cute; if it's a really hot day, it's even cuter. For grooming as entertainment, there's the old-fashioned Harmony Barber Shop (tucked behind the Emporium), where the Dapper Dans sometimes accompany a haircut. By all means, check out their sweet four-part harmonies.

Main Street stays open a good half hour after the rest of the park has closed, although the shops (see "Shopping" in the *Diversions* chapter for tips) tend to

MAIN STREET, U.S.A.

1. Main Street Cinema
2. Walt Disney World Railroad

FRONTIERLAND

7. Big Thunder Mountain Railroad
8. Country Bear Jamboree
9. Frontierland Shootin' Arcade
10. Splash Mountain
11. Tom Sawyer Island
12. Walt Disney World Railroad Station

LIBERTY SQUARE

13. Diamond Horseshoe Saloon Revue
14. The Hall of Presidents
15. The Haunted Mansion
16. Liberty Belle Riverboat

FANTASYLAND

17. Cinderella's Golden Carrousel
18. Dumbo the Flying Elephant
19. It's A Small World
20. Mad Tea Party
21. Mr. Toad's Wild Ride
22. Peter Pan's Flight
23. Legend of the Lion King
24. Skyway to Tomorrowland
25. Snow White's Adventures
26. Ariel's Grotto

MICKEY'S TOONTOWN FAIR

27. Donald's Boat
28. Mickey's Country House
29. Minnie's Country House
30. Toontown Hall of Fame
31. The Barnstormer at Goofy's Wiseacres Farm
32. Walt Disney World Railroad Station

TOMORROWLAND

33. Astro Orbiter
34. Take Flight
35. Alien Encounter
36. Tomorrowland Speedway
37. Space Mountain
38. The Timekeeper
39. Walt Disney's Carousel of Progress
40. Skyway to Fantasyland
41. Tomorrowland Transit Authority

· · · · · · · · · Parade Route

ADVENTURELAND

3. Jungle Cruise
4. Pirates of the Caribbean
5. Swiss Family Treehouse
6. The Enchanted Tiki Birds

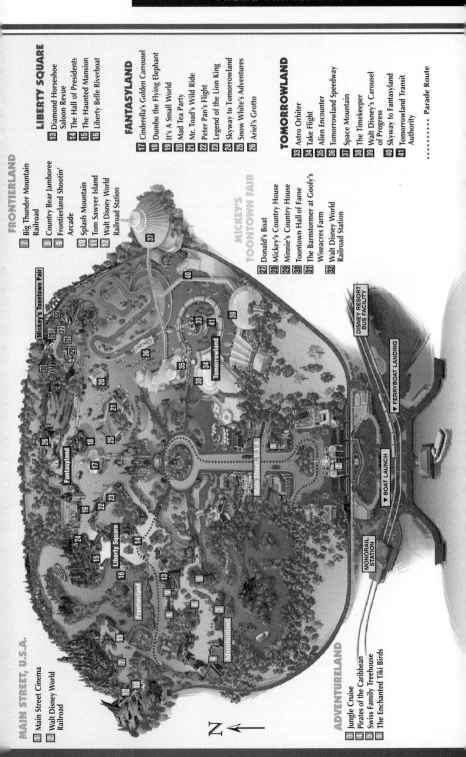

Touring Priorities

DON'T MISS

Splash Mountain*

Space Mountain*

Big Thunder Mountain Railroad*

The Haunted Mansion

Pirates of the Caribbean*

The Timekeeper

The Hall of Presidents**

Peter Pan's Flight*

Alien Encounter*

•CONTINUED ON NEXT PAGE

be less crowded during the afternoon. If you're not in the mood to dally or to fight foot traffic, the horse-pulled trolley cars are a fun way to travel from Town Square to the Hub.

Tomorrowland

Futuristic in a way that would likely go right over Buck Rogers' head, Tomorrowland is a city of the future that never was. Because it's home base for two of the park's most popular attractions—Space Mountain and Alien Encounter—Tomorrowland is best visited first thing after the gates open.

Space Mountain, a must-do for all but those who categorically avoid the fast stuff, is one to head for straight-away. Once the lines reach outside this white structure at the far side of Tomorrowland, they generally don't ease up until the evening. To gauge whether Space Mountain is for you, consider how you feel about roller coasters. This one rockets at speeds of up to 28 miles per hour through a space-age sheath of darkness, shooting stars, and flashing lights. It's a fast and furious 2 minutes 38 seconds of spectacular special effects—an absolute must for the adventurous, and an unforgettable adventure for the suddenly courageous. Space Mountain is also a pretty turbulent ride, however, so riders must be in good health and free from heart conditions, back and neck problems, and other physical limitations (such as pregnancy), as the posted signs warn. If you've just eaten, wait awhile. At the exit, you can play video games or interface with the resident ATM.

If you decide you'd rather observe the rockets' red glare from the vantage point of a train that's doing more like ten miles per hour, the **Tomorrowland Transit Authority** offers a preview to Space Mountain and other attractions on a track that's strictly horizontal. The train is boarded in the heart of Tomorrowland near **Astro Orbiter** (an elevated ride with rockets that's primarily for kids but good fun; it seems to go faster the lower you fly in your Buck Rogers–mobile).

The scariest thing ever to hit the Magic Kingdom, **Alien Encounter** even has scary lines. It's not a motion ride, but rather an intense 20-minute experience born of an interplanetary travel demo gone awry. The story: A company on Planet X has developed something called a teleporter that's capable of beaming people between planets, and is treating you to a demonstration via live broadcast. You are seated in a dimly lit room, with one of these teleporters occupying center stage, when unsettling events begin to occur. A restraint is lowered over your shoulders. Lights scan the crowd, looking for a good subject for teleportation. The chairman of the X-S Tech corporation volunteers to come to Earth, but an alien arrives in his place. There is an explosion. Suddenly, it is completely dark and you hear screams and groans, feel panting on the nape of your neck, and are sprayed with what in this context seems to be alien slime. The verdict: Special effects *are* the experience. Although this attraction is more suspenseful and unsettling than terrifying, if you

scare easily or are simply good at playing along, you'll get some nice chills up your spine.

Just opposite Alien Encounter, **The Time-keeper** is another Tomorrowland attraction that warrants your attention, only this one's a hoot, not a holler. A good bet for early in the day because it's a standing engagement, The Timekeeper is an arresting 20-minute Circle-Vision 360 film amusingly hosted by Audio-Animatronics characters. Basically, a wacky robot, who could leave the attraction and *be* Robin Williams, sends his buddy, a flying robot camera named 9-Eye, back in time on assignment to transmit photos of all she sees for our enjoyment. At the 1900 Paris Exposition, she bumps into H. G. Wells and Jules Verne, one of whom hitches a ride to the future. If you're a "Cheers" fan, you'll probably recognize 9-Eye's voice as that of Rhea Perlman. As for old-fashioned actors, the sort with no Audio-Animatronics stand-ins, you'll see Jeremy Irons playing the role of H. G. Wells and Michel Piccoli as Jules Verne. The bottom line: Pass only if you've been there (to Innsbruck, Austria, say) and done that (bobsledded down a 1,200-meter run at 60 miles per hour).

Right next to The Timekeeper is **Take Flight**, a fanciful 4½-minute journey through the history of air travel (closed for refurbishment spring through fall). Carry-on luggage must be smaller than the entranceway. Around the bend at **Walt Disney's Carousel of Progress**, the stage stays put and you rotate around it

•*CONTINUED FROM PREVIOUS PAGE*

DON'T OVERLOOK

Walt Disney World Railroad; Legend of the Lion King*; Liberty Belle Riverboat; Carousel of Progress; Main Street Cinema; It's A Small World*; Mad Tea Party*; Tomorrowland Transit Authority; Country Bear Jamboree; Diamond Horseshoe Saloon Revue**

DON'T KNOCK YOURSELF OUT

Jungle Cruise*; Cinderella's Golden Carrousel; Mickey's Toontown Fair; Skyway; Take Flight; Swiss Family Treehouse; Snow White's Adventures*; Tom Sawyer Island; Dumbo, the Flying Elephant*; Mr. Toad's Wild Ride; Astro Orbiter; The Enchanted Tiki Birds; Tomorrowland Speedway*

* Long lines; visit in the early A.M., late P.M., or during the parade.
** Pay close attention to performance schedules.

Quiet Nooks

- Rose garden on the right as you face Cinderella Castle

- Cinderella Wishing Well, near the Castle on the pathway to Tomorrowland

- Walt Disney World Railroad

- Main Street Cinema

- Harmony Barber Shop

- Shaded tables behind the shops in Liberty Square

- Liberty Belle Riverboat (unless the characters are on board)

- Rocking chairs on the front porches of Frontierland and Liberty Square shops

- Anywhere but Fantasyland

during the 20-minute show. The attraction fulfills its promise as a warm and fuzzy portrayal of how electricity has altered our lives. Its last (and newest) scene offers a lighthearted glimpse of life in the year 2000. Don't be dismayed by crowds; this place swallows them whole. Next door is **Skyway to Fantasyland**, an airlift that provides a nice vantage, but isn't a big time-saver. Heading north toward Fantasyland, you pass Space Mountain and come upon the rather low-octane **Tomorrowland Speedway**.

Mickey's Toontown Fair

This tiny blip between Tomorrowland and Fantasyland is the park's newest land. In a development that suggests even Mickey's not above the need to keep up with the neighbors, Mickey's Starland was swept off the map in 1996 and replaced with interactive environs akin to Disneyland's Toontown. Now, when you visit the area, you'll find a county fair in progress. The cuteness is in the details (Mickey's ear-bearing crops, Minnie as the local Martha Stewart). Attractions are primarily for kids, but it's still fun to wander. For one-stop character meeting, the **Toontown Hall of Fame** can't be beat (even villains are here shaking hands, perhaps running for office?).

Fantasyland

The danger to the adult entering this, the cheeriest, most magical, and most nostalgic corner of the Magic Kingdom, is that there's a very fine line between rubbing elbows with Cinderella, Peter Pan, and Snow White and being caught in a child thicket. The optimum way to take in Fantasyland is to visit just before and during the daily 3 P.M. parade or in the evening when the parks are open late. Because there is nothing adult about Fantasyland, whimsy is the name of the game.

That said, certain attractions are so artfully executed that they transcend the kiddie genre. Of these, **It's A Small World**—a ten-minute boat ride through the happiest, busiest, and most diversely populated dollhouse on the planet—is surely the most elaborate. A special treat if you've got a sweet tooth, a safe bet if you could use a mood boost. Ride it once and, like it or not, the song is your sound track for the rest of the day. Much more subtle is **Peter Pan's Flight**, an alluring sprinkle of pixie dust in which you can—and do—fly for three minutes above absolutely delightful scenes of Captain Hook and nighttime London in a pirate ship built for two. **Legend of the Lion King**, a 25-minute stage show based on the animated film *The Lion King*, is a knockout mix of puppetry, film clips, and special effects that kids adore but fail to appreciate. It's a rare adult who doesn't savor the sharp sarcasm and wit of Timon the meerkat.

Then there are the purely nostalgic attractions, worth your time only if you're hankering to relive a certain story or amusement ride from your past. Have a thing for carousels in general or **Cinderella's Golden Carrousel** in particular? Go for it. Think you'd get a huge kick out of squeezing your group into an oversize teacup and spinning yourselves silly? Get to the **Mad Tea Party**. Don't skip **Dumbo, the Flying Elephant** if you'll regret it later; but at the same time, don't expect to be wowed by a straightforward kiddie attraction such as **Mr. Toad's Wild Ride**. Although **Snow White's Adventures** has more happy moments than it did in the old days, the twisting journey still feels like a trip through a witch-filled fun house.

Whatever you do, don't miss the gorgeous mosaic murals beneath the open archway of **Cinderella Castle**. No less than a million well-placed pieces of Italian glass tell the whole tale, ugly stepsisters, glass slipper, and all.

Liberty Square

Tucked between Fantasyland and Frontierland, this comparatively small area tends to be relatively peaceful. Brick and clapboard buildings carry the theme—Colonial America—as does the Liberty Tree, a 130-something oak hung with 13 lanterns to recall the original Colonies.

Though Liberty Square has just a few attractions, it still takes more than an hour to take them all in. **The Hall of Presidents** merits attention not just as a well-delivered 20-minute dose of patriotism in which Abraham Lincoln and Bill Clinton speak, but as a chance to observe all 42 chief executives of our country in action. The shifting, swaying, and nodding begins the moment the curtain rises on the amazingly faithful and impeccably dressed group of Audio-Animatronics figures. The pace is slow, but just right for an air-conditioned theater with comfy seats. Don't be intimidated by a big line—this is a *big* theater. The **Liberty Belle Riverboat**—a large, paddle wheel–driven steamboat that makes 17-minute loops around Tom Sawyer Island—is a pleasant distraction, especially on a steamy afternoon. (Beware the daily character cruises running until 3:30 P.M.) Don't ask what **The Haunted Mansion** is doing in Liberty Square. Just note that it's a not-to-be-missed eight-minute experience overrun with clever special effects and ghoulish delights (your typical ballroom of waltzing ghosts, door knockers that knock by themselves, and spirited graveyards).

Entertainment

The character-laden floats in the Remember the Magic Parade take over Main Street at 3 P.M. Also, the Walt Disney World Band performs in Town Square and the Dapper Dans barbershop quartet harmonizes on Main Street.

During busy seasons, when the park is open until 10 P.M. or later, the spectacular Fantasy in the Sky fireworks (200 shells released in six minutes) is presented nightly. And the dazzling SpectroMagic light parade wends its luminous fiber-optic way down Main Street nightly (the best vantage point is the railroad platform; if there are two performances, the later one is always less crowded).

To catch a specific performance, check a guidemap (available at City Hall) for precise days and showtimes.

Frontierland

This land conjures something of the Old West, with a little country charm thrown in for good measure. Although there's more to Frontierland than mountains, it is most notable as the home to two of the Magic Kingdom's biggest (and most addictive) thrills—Splash Mountain and Big Thunder Mountain Railroad.

The first thing to know about **Splash Mountain** is that it's okay to feel anxious just watching the log boats plunge down this ride's big drop—you're looking at the steepest flume in the world (although it appears to be a straight drop, it's actually 52 feet down at a 45-degree angle). Even so, this waterbound ride themed to Disney's *Song of the South* is tamer than it looks from the ground. Steep plunge aside, there are just three smaller dips during the 11-minute trip. If you're like us, the first time around you'll be way too nervous about when "it" is going to happen to fully appreciate the delightful humor, enormously appealing characters, and uplifting "Zip-A-Dee-Doo-Dah" ambience. But coax yourself into riding once and you'll be hooked. If you prefer to get splashed, not drenched, sit in the back of the log. Onlookers should note that a water cannon takes aim at the observation bridge without warning. A note on timing: Both Splash Mountain and Big Thunder Mountain Railroad tend to draw big crowds all day long; your best bet is to shoot for early evening.

Think of **Big Thunder Mountain Railroad** as a thrilling ride on the mild side. As roller coasters go, this one's exciting, but as much for the surrounding scenery—bats, goats, a flooded mining town—your runaway mine train races past as for the ride itself. Big Thunder Mountain Railroad is not nearly so fast or turbulent as Space Mountain, and nothing in its four-minute series of reverberating swoops and jerky turns comes close to Splash Mountain's intimidating plunge. For a bigger thrill, ride it after dark, when you can't see what lies ahead even from the first car.

But Frontierland's appeal extends beyond its two high-profile attractions. The **Country Bear Jamboree**, a 17-minute musical variety show put on by 20 impossibly corny Audio-Animatronics bears, is a fine attraction to hit when you're feeling a little punchy. If your schedule can accommodate an entire hour's worth of song, dancing, and hokeyness, the **Diamond Horseshoe Saloon Revue** delivers. While **Tom Sawyer Island**, a short raft ride away, provides a nice break from the more structured parts of the park, it tends to attract lots of kids.

Adventureland

When you hear the beating of drums and begin to notice palm trees and bougainvillea, you've crossed over into Adventureland, the Magic Kingdom's most exotic locale. Among this land's attractions are the immensely popular Pirates of the Caribbean and Jungle Cruise, best visited during the early morning and evening. The local ATM (near The Enchanted Tiki Birds) is pretty popular, too.

The Enchanted Tiki Birds, a 17-minute affair, showcases Disney's earliest Audio-Animatronics figures—chirping, whistling birds—which are most interesting as a point of comparison to the more recent creations. However, this attraction will be closed for renovation through spring; the updated show will star *Aladdin*'s Iago and *The Lion King*'s Zazu in a fresh script set to new music. Remember **Pirates of the Caribbean** as an elaborate, engaging, not-to-be-missed boat ride in which you watch pirates attack and raid a Caribbean village. A classic attraction, it provides plenty of leering, jeering examples of how wonderfully, frighteningly realistic Disney's Audio-Animatronics can be. The unsavory scenes in this ride are offset by upbeat choruses of "Yo Ho, Yo Ho; a Pirate's Life for Me." Note that the ten-minute Pirates of the Caribbean ride includes a small dip and some loud cannon blasts.

Jungle Cruise is an extremely popular attraction that transports passengers on a steamy ten-minute boat trip through the Nile Valley and the Amazon rain forest. Although the flora is quite beautiful, the lines for this ride can be prohibitively long. Finally, if you feel up to climbing some serious stairs, **Swiss Family Treehouse** is a fascinating replica of the Robinsons' ingenious perch that's worth the effort, even though the tree itself is a product of the prop department's imagination.

Snacker's Guide

For a healthy bite, visit the Liberty Square Market in Liberty Square for fresh fruit, carrot sticks, and baked potatoes; Auntie Gravity's Galactic Goodies in Tomorrowland for fruit, juices, and frozen yogurt; or Aloha Isle in Adventureland for pineapple spears and refreshments.

For a sweet treat, seek out old-fashioned lollipops at the Market House on Main Street; fudge, peanut brittle, marshmallow crispies, and Mint Chocolate Cookie Gems at the Main Street Confectionery; the humongous fresh baked cookies at the Main Street Bake Shop; or strawberry shortcake at the Farmer's Market in Mickey's Toontown Fair.

For a frozen refresher, try the ice cream and strawberry bars from a vendor cart, or choose a flavor at the Plaza Ice Cream Parlor on Main Street.

For a savory pick-me-up, head for the Egg Roll Wagon in Adventureland, the Turkey Leg Wagon in Frontierland, or the cappuccino cart right outside Tony's Town Square at the foot of Main Street.

EPCOT

Epcot's hours are somewhat staggered. Whereas Future World is usually open from 9 A.M. to 9 P.M., World Showcase generally opens later in the morning, at 11 A.M. Epcot's hours are extended during holiday periods and the summer months; call 824-4321 for up-to-the-minute details. One-day park admission is $42.14 for adults (see *Planning Ahead* for ticket options). Prices are subject to change.

Think of Epcot as an extraordinary balancing act. This park is huge—bigger than the Magic Kingdom and the Disney MGM-Studios combined—and it performs two rather ambitious feats simultaneously. While the part of Epcot known as Future World offers a multifaceted look at what lies ahead for humankind, its alter ego, World Showcase, transports guests (at least in spirit) to 11 different countries. This division of labor works well, and it certainly keeps things interesting here in Disney's "experimental prototype community of tomorrow." While the more serious-minded Future World is striving to spark the imagination, illuminate the technological future, and heighten environmental awareness, lively World Showcase is serving forth Oktoberfest, traditional English pub grub, and panoramic views of France, China, and Canada. As Future World is ushering visitors through a 21st-century greenhouse and into the mind of a 12-year-old boy, World Showcase is escorting others along a calm river in Mexico and over a stormy Norwegian sea. Together, the two entities stimulate guests to discover new things about people, places, and, indeed, their own curiosity.

If Epcot boasts a tremendous following among legal voters, it's because it has more of the things adults appreciate—live entertainment; quiet gardens; beers, wines, and frozen drinks; tasteful shops and galleries; international cuisine; sophisticated restaurants; and specialty coffees; and that's just the supplementary stuff. Epcot also woos the older crowd by making Mickey a little more scarce, by splicing enrichment of one form or another into the greater part of its amusements. It appeals to adults on a purely aesthetic level as well: World Showcase, wrapped around a vast lagoon, has a commanding natural and architectural beauty that changes with each border crossing. And Future World more than holds its own with the massive, gleaming silver geosphere of Spaceship Earth. Not surprisingly, we've met a number of Walt Disney World regulars who spend their entire vacations here at Epcot. One couple who confessed as much one afternoon at the Rose & Crown Pub couldn't say exactly what they liked so much about Epcot, although they were enjoying their pints of Guinness.

Epcot has its die-hard Future Worlders and its World Showcase fanatics, but most visitors list favorite pavilions on both sides of the lagoon. Renovations and additions to the Epcot landscape over the past few years make this especially true today. You won't find a "New! Improved!" banner pasted to the Universe of Energy or flying from Test Track, but Disney has made smart changes in Epcot's entertainment mix that have lightened up Future World, livened up World Showcase, and in the process, earned the park a fresh crop of admirers.

We'll describe these new and improved attractions later so that we might first present The Official Six Things We Bet You Didn't Know You Could Do at Epcot List: (1) You can get some terrific gardening tips. (2) You can simultaneously break a sweat and split the 100th annual Rose Bowl Parade right down the middle. (Pedaling against the tide, and seemingly catching floats, bands, majorettes, and horses quite by surprise, we got a Wondercycle up to 15½ miles per hour.) (3) You can drink fresh watermelon juice. (4) You can watch a butterfly open its wings for the first time. If you want, you can be nibbling on a freshly picked spearmint leaf while that orange-barred sulphur butterfly decides when to flee the hatching box. (5) You can "test drive" an electric car. (6) You can tour the world with a steel-drum band, mon. The band cranks out soca, calypso, and reggae rhythms from atop its funky tour bus, and is always looking for extra groupies to jam along with the regulars.

The most important thing to know about Epcot is that it is no small undertaking. Even the choosiest visitor will need two full days to cover the park effectively at a comfortable pace.

Hidden Mickey

A constellation in the overhead star field within Spaceship Earth outlines Mickey in the sky with diamonds.

HOT TIPS

■ On Tuesday and Friday, guests staying at WDW resorts may enter Epcot 1½ hours before the official opening time and get an early crack at selected Future World attractions and pavilions, usually The Living Seas; Honey, I Shrunk the Audience; The Land; Spaceship Earth; and Test Track. Early-entry days and attractions are subject to change.

■ Not coincidentally, Tuesday and Friday tend to be the most crowded days at Epcot.

Since Future World and World Showcase keep different hours, strategically minded guests will do well to follow our lead. In the name of efficiency, we say: Take in a few key Future World pavilions during the hours before World Showcase opens. Explore World Showcase during the early afternoon, when Future World is most congested (one day, begin with the United Kingdom and work your way counterclockwise; the other, start at Mexico and proceed clockwise). Return to Future World to explore a few more pavilions during the relatively uncongested hours of late afternoon and early evening. And finally, revisit World Showcase during the exceptionally pleasant evening hours to experience the beauty of the park at night and the fantastic IllumiNations show.

GUIDING PRINCIPLES: The following section is designed to offer a telling preview for first-time visitors and a timely update for returnees. Structured as a guided walking tour through the 9 themed pavilions of Future World and the 11 countries of World Showcase, it provides a geographical orientation to the layout of the park. Running commentary takes stock of all pavilions (and the attractions located therein) and their place in the adult world, highlighting the essentials, pointing out the redeeming qualities of less compelling attractions, and noting recent additions and renovations to Epcot.

For at-a-glance cues, the Touring Priorities list in the margin ranks the park's best adult bets. Note: This book's evaluations of attractions are based on the quality of the experience and the entertainment value for an adult with average interest in the topic; but if you have a serious fascination with the subject at hand—gardening or farming, say—you should find the attraction and the pavilion (in this case, the Behind the Seeds tour in The Land pavilion) all the more satisfying.

To learn the most efficient strategies for exploring Epcot, look to the Hot Tips in the margins of this section, and the flexible touring plans provided in the *Planning Ahead* chapter. For information about getting to Epcot via Walt Disney World transportation or car, consult the "Getting Around" section of the *Planning Ahead* chapter. For tips and recommendations on dining at Epcot, refer to the "Restaurant Guide" in the *Dining & Entertainment* chapter.

GETTING ORIENTED: It's helpful to think of Epcot as the park with the hourglass figure. In this conception, the gleaming silver ball of Spaceship Earth is the head and northernmost point; the other Future World pavilions, arranged on either side of Spaceship Earth in southward arches, form the outline of Epcot's "upper body"; and the promenade of World Showcase pavilions connects to Future World at Epcot's "waist" and, tracing the lines of a long, full skirt, wraps around

MOROCCO

FRANCE

JAPAN

INTERNATIONAL GATEWAY

THE AMERICAN ADVENTURE

AMERICA GARDENS THEATRE

UNITED KINGDOM

ITALY

WORLD SHOWCASE LAGOON

CANADA

JOURNEY INTO IMAGINATION

THE LAND

SHOWCASE PLAZA

CHINA

INNOVENTIONS WEST SIDE

THE LIVING SEAS

NORWAY

INNOVENTIONS EAST SIDE

MEXICO

SPACESHIP EARTH

To Buses

TEST TRACK

HORIZONS (closed for rehab)

WONDERS OF LIFE

UNIVERSE OF ENERGY

Entrance Plaza

N

Touring Priorities

•CONTINUED ON NEXT PAGE

the World Showcase Lagoon. The American Adventure pavilion, located due south of Spaceship Earth along the bottom hem of the World Showcase skirt, effectively serves as the foot of Epcot.

Visitors should come prepared to do a great deal of walking, as the World Showcase Promenade itself is 1.3 miles around (and the World Showcase visitor with wanderlust will easily log double that distance). Avid walkers and the simply health-conscious will be interested to know that a person typically covers more than two miles in a full day of touring Epcot. Don't be dismayed, though; Epcot is equipped with plenty of pleasant resting spots (see the margins of this section for tips to the whereabouts of said nooks) as well as a key foot-saving alternative. Water taxis link Showcase Plaza at the foot of Future World with Germany and France, located at the farthest corners of World Showcase. Many seniors who choose to tour the smaller theme parks on foot rent a wheelchair or a self-driven Electric Convenience Vehicle (ECV) here at Epcot.

A Walking Tour

Our tour begins at the main entrance. This is where you take care of logistics while the gleaming ball of Spaceship Earth offers a 16-million-pound hint (to you and, on a clear day, to airplane passengers flying along either Florida coast) as to the precise direction of Future World. Epcot's monorail station is right outside the gates here, as is an ATM (the latter is located on the far left just before you enter the park). On the far right side of the entranceway, also outside the gates, you can claim lost articles, exchange currency, and pick up any cumbersome purchases you arranged to have forwarded here during your visit. An important note: If you need to use the ATM or any of these other services mid-visit, remember to have your hand stamped upon exiting the turnstiles so you can reenter the park.

As you close in on the big ball, remember that there are still more services here in its shadows. If you want to avail yourself of storage lockers, pass around Spaceship Earth's right side. Otherwise, keep left. This course will lead you past the stroller and wheelchair rentals and on to Guest Relations. The primary resource for Epcot information, Guest Relations is equipped not only with guidemaps but also with representatives who can provide answers to most anything that's got you confused. If you haven't made lunch or dinner plans for the day and know you'd like to dine here at Epcot, head straightaway for Guest Relations' wall of touch-sensitive TV screens to secure priority seating arrangements. Video attendants "stand by" all morning to book tables. If you'd like to peruse a few menus first, note that Guest Relations has a compilation of current offerings. Also, when the screens are not being used to consign dinner tables, they can call forth encyclopedic information about Epcot. For the really tough questions, do as we do: Follow the teachers to the **Epcot Discovery Center** in the Innoventions building on the west side of the plaza. The staff here is thoroughly steeped in Epcot-ology and the database is, as far as we can tell, bottomless. In the center of the plaza, you'll find the **Tip Board**, an electronic information board listing current waiting times for popular attractions.

Future World

You know you're in Future World when you see a thunderous fountain that acts like it owns the place; something resembling an oversize golf ball that would require a club roughly the size of the Empire State Building; kaleidoscopic fiber-optic patterns in the walkway; abstract gardens that could pass for modern art; and freewheeling water fountains that do swan dives and geyser imitations.

This highly conceptual land makes a striking first impression, and no wonder—it's awash in the sort of grand music that might trumpet the credits of an Academy Award–winning film. And it wears its sleek architecture and futuristic landscaping like a power suit. The nine themed pavilions that comprise Future World collectively document humanity's progress in this world and offer intriguing visions of our technological fate. Such broad concerns as communications, health, and the environment serve as springboards for the attractions here, which make positively stimulating experiences of topics that commonly make boring conversation.

An ongoing tweaking spree has truly invigorated Future World. The croissant-shaped buildings formerly occupied by CommuniCore have a lively young tenant in Innoventions, an area devoted to interactive exhibitions that escort guests to the technological frontier. An updated Spaceship Earth journeys well into the next century of global communication. The Land has a greater raison d'être in the form of an environmental film that takes its cue from *The Lion King*, and in Food Rocks, a nutrition-oriented concert that really swings. And Journey

•CONTINUED FROM PREVIOUS PAGE

DON'T OVERLOOK

The Living Seas; Innoventions; Spaceship Earth*; China; Norway*;
Mexico; Italy; Morocco

DON'T KNOCK YOURSELF OUT

Journey Into Imagination ride*; El Río del Tiempo boat ride

* Long lines; visit in the early A.M., late P.M.
** Pay close attention to performance schedules.

Entertainment

Epcot's ever-growing entertainment slate is always changing. So pick up a guidemap at Guest Relations and consult it often.

In Future World, acrobats and a trash-can percussive unit dressed in custodial wear are popular head-turners. A drum-and-bugle corps performs several times daily at Innoventions Plaza. The Fountain of Nations erupts into a computer-choreographed water ballet every 15 minutes.

In World Showcase, a jamming steel-drum band (with accompanying dancers) and a truly extraordinary flock of birdlike stilt walkers are part of the notable mobile entertainment.

•CONTINUED ON NEXT PAGE

Into Imagination has a runaway hit in Honey, I Shrunk the Audience, a 3-D flick with special effects that are not to be believed. As if that weren't enough, Universe of Energy has been reincarnated as a streamlined, humor-laced version of its former self (hint: "Audio-Animatronics dinosaurs, meet game show–contestant wannabe.") Guests are beating a path to Test Track, a ride on the wild side of automobile testing that replaced World of Motion and put Epcot in an entirely novel spot: atop the thrill seekers' "Must Do" list. Soon to be added to the list: a new attraction at Horizons, which is undergoing a major overhaul. Clearly, Future World's self-improvement kick is no passing phase.

A reminder: This tour is designed to provide a sense of place, not a recommended plan of attack. Future World pavilions are described here as you would encounter them geographically, beginning with Spaceship Earth, the park's northernmost pavilion. Innoventions, which cradles the west (right, as you face World Showcase) and east (left) sides of the central plaza, is next, followed by a counterclockwise exploration of the remaining pavilions, from The Living Seas in Future World's northwestern corner southward to The Land and Journey Into Imagination, and then across the central plaza to the eastern flank of pavilions, beginning with Test Track and proceeding to Wonders of Life and Universe of Energy.

Spaceship Earth

This 180-foot-tall "geosphere" sticks out like a wayward planet come to roost. You may be interested to learn that the silver exterior comes from layers of anodized aluminum and polyethylene, and is composed of 954 triangular panels, not all of equal size or shape (although it takes an awfully keen eye to discern any differences). Or maybe you'd rather hear how the gleaming exterior funnels every raindrop that hits it into World Showcase Lagoon. Strange, but true.

While outward appearances can be deceiving, that is not the case here. Spaceship Earth is visually arresting to the core. The **Spaceship Earth** ride inside the geosphere winds past exquisitely detailed scenes, neatly tracing the evolution of human communication using Audio-Animatronics figures that here, in their element, seem more natural than many sitcom actors. (There is a Benedictine monk asleep at his desk who is so realistic that people hush their companions out of courtesy.) In 14 minutes you've gone from Cro-Magnon grunts all the way to the fabled information superhighway. Narration by Jeremy Irons adds an element of drama. The finale provides a hip, forward-looking finish for Spaceship Earth; take away the lasers and it would still be the ride's biggest head-turner. This attraction—your worst bet first thing in the morning—is least crowded during the hours just prior to park closing.

Outside, in the Global Neighborhood, you can dabble in interactive activities, from viewer's-choice sporting events to video shopping.

Innoventions

You might think of Innoventions as a boarding house for the next generation of lust objects. This is a huge technological showcase of new goodies for home, entertainment, and office. Within the 100,000-square-foot area, you will find an ever-changing array of hands-on exhibits and displays presented by major manufacturers such as IBM, AT&T, General Electric, Motorola, Honeywell, and General Motors. If you are a devout techie or a gadget hound, this is your Consumer Electronics Show. If you are a partial or total technophobe, this is your opportunity to check out things like virtual reality, the Internet, and CD-ROM in a fun, friendly, pressure-free environment. The representatives in each area are knowledgeable and unobtrusive; they're quick to answer any questions you might have about a product or to talk you through a computer program, but they are just as quick to honor your wishes if you'd prefer to be left alone.

Innoventions is a bright (meaning beige stands out, screaming yellow blends in) labyrinth of activity that's difficult to pass through quickly even if you cannot stand video games. (Sega runs quite an "arcade" here, however, with lots of new and proposed video games set out for sampling.) Be aware that this pavilion is housed in two structures, one on the east side of the plaza and the other on the west side. Within each building, exhibit areas are organized by company. What you'll see here is constantly changing, just as Walt Disney envisioned.

•CONTINUED FROM PREVIOUS PAGE

In addition, each pavilion has a cast of performers, any of whom could be appearing during your visit. Among the possibilities: bagpipe players in Canada, a pub pianist in the United Kingdom, belly dancers in Morocco, drummers in Japan, singers in Italy, oompah musicians in Germany, acrobats in China, and a mariachi band in Mexico. The American Adventure features the outstanding Voices of Liberty a cappella group, and revolving stage shows at the America Gardens Theatre.

Epcot's grandest entertainment—a spectacle of fireworks, lasers, symphonic music, and dancing fountains known as IllumiNations—provides an extraordinarily dramatic and memorable finale every night at closing time. IllumiNations is centered around the lagoon and visible from any point on the World Showcase Promenade.

Ears to the Ground

During a visit to Innoventions, we once observed a couple totally consumed with a game that involved piloting a glider. With her husband at the controls, the woman assumed the (seemingly familiar) role of backseat driver: "You've got to get your nose up....Decrease your speed....You're coming down too fast!" It was a fiery landing, but they both walked away from it laughing.

Of course, some exhibits are more compelling than others. For a fun initiation to virtual reality, start with the area occupied by Silicon Graphics, where you can rifle through the riches in a royal Egyptian tomb or grab virtual ski poles and schuss down an Alpine slope. While you're here, redecorate the Oval Office and surf the Internet's World Wide Web. If it's still around, look to the Mandala Virtual Reality station for one of Innoventions' most precious visions: true-blue adults lunging, jumping, and squatting for sunken treasure. There's no room for self-consciousness in this one. Move too subtly and (as your reality-based companions look on helplessly) you're shark food. Want still more? Test your mettle in Motorola's game world or slip away on Enel's virtual tour of St. Peter's Basilica.

For experiences rooted in reality, take an electric car for a simulated test drive at General Motors, go on an interactive shopping spree at Oracle, and (dare we say it?) learn how to build your own home page at one of the pavilion's many Internet-oriented areas. For an almost incurable case of wanton appliance envy, tour Honeywell's incredibly high-tech **House of Innoventions**. At Motorola, allow an Audio-Animatronics figure to introduce you to the next wrinkles in wireless technology. AT&T showcases an array of communications services that's usually worth browsing through. At IBM and Apple, audition personal digital assistants and check out the latest interactive software and computer models.

The keys to an enjoyable experience at Innoventions:

■ Adjust your touring plans if need be, but do visit when you're feeling fresh—this is no place for a zombie.

- Take advantage of the fact that this pavilion is split between two buildings; plan to check out the one on the east side of the plaza one day and explore the one on the west side the next.
- Study the large maps placed on stands just inside both entrances to familiarize yourself with exhibit locations.
- Give the exhibits some time. If you breeze through, you'll miss a lot.
- If you're not sure where to start, begin by looking over people's shoulders.
- Finally, don't be shy. Whether you're highly skeptical or curious about something you see, ask the question.

The Living Seas

The Caribbean is not as far away as you think. If you want to catch a wave, some mammoth lettuce-munching manatees, and a richly stocked coral reef environment (pop.: 5,000) that even a scuba diver would find extraordinary, look no further. This pavilion, dedicated to the study of oceanography and ocean ecology, ranks among Future World's most inspired and compelling areas. During the toasty summer months, it's particularly refreshing to ogle The Living Seas' pièce de résistance, a 5.7-million-gallon tank in which a simulated Caribbean Sea and man-made reef support a glorious array of life, including sharks, dolphins, sea turtles, rays, and crustaceans.

There are two paths to this not-to-be-missed underwater vista, where in addition to colorful sea life you can observe one-person submarines and divers conducting marine experiments. If you're certified in scuba diving or want a little Dolphin 101, take a behind-the-scenes route. For details, see the bottom of page 107.

To immerse yourself thoroughly without getting wet, take the **Caribbean Coral Reef Ride**. This three-pronged journey features a waterlogged film about the relationship between humankind and the seas, a simulated descent to the ocean floor (the elevator-like capsules actually plunge only an inch), and a quick taxi through an underwater viewing tunnel to the main event, **Sea Base Alpha**. Here, you can linger all you like in front of enormous eight-inch-thick windows to the undersea world (be on the lookout for moray eels, barracuda, and puffers). You needn't know a parrot fish from an angelfish to spot the ever-amphibious homo sapiens. Scuba divers enter the tank via a floor-to-ceiling lockout chamber, and can be observed conducting experiments. (Wireless radios allow them to explain their

---

A Flash from the Future?

Guess the technological innovation referred to in the following quote: "The growth of [Technology X] as a medium of mass communication among people around the earth cannot be halted, nor much longer delayed. And eventually every land will want to share in this international audiovisual exchange of ideas, of pleasurable entertainment, and [of] closer neighborliness." Hint: It's not the Internet. Bigger hint: The speaker was Walt Disney. Jumbo hint: It begins with "tele" and ends with "vision."

A Healthy Crop

If you're eating your vegetables (and fruits) at Future World's Garden Grill, Coral Reef, or Sunshine Season Food Fair, odds are good that you're sharing in The Land pavilion's bounty. Some 30 tons of produce are harvested each year from The Land's greenhouses. Talk about fresh local ingredients!

work even before they emerge, dripping, from the chamber.) Exhibits offer insight into marine research methods, additional display tanks, and—unless you encounter those endangered, impossibly animated sea barges known as manatees frequently in your travels—compelling reasons to stick around awhile.

If you hunger for more than oceanic knowledge, every table in the Coral Reef restaurant has an unobstructed view of the main reef environment.

Of course, no seafaring adventure is complete without the opportunity to shout "Land ho!" so it's only right that The Land is the next pavilion.

The Land

This popular six-acre plot, surpassed in size only by Innoventions (or the manatees at The Living Seas), explores themes related to food and farming while planting seeds of environmental consciousness. Underneath this pavilion's dramatic skylighted roof, you'll find a well-balanced slate of attractions, a bountiful food court, and a lazy susan of a restaurant, the Garden Grill, which rotates *very* slowly past several of the ecosystems featured in the pavilion's boat ride. All things considered, The Land merits two green thumbs up as the purveyor of one of Future World's strongest lineups.

The **Celebrate the Land** boat ride is a beautifully informative 13½-minute journey that escorts you through a stormy prairie, a windswept desert, and a South American rain forest en route to experimental greenhouses and an area given over to fish farming. The dripping, squawking rain forest is so realistic you'd need to chomp on a faux fern to convince yourself it's all plastic. The narration is an interesting commentary on the history and future of agriculture. The impressive greenhouses show futuristic technology at work on real crops (many of which are served here at Epcot), with NASA experiments and cucumbers in desert training among the highlights. This popular attraction is best visited in the morning or during the hours just prior to park closing. If you're an avid gardener or Celebrate the Land has you intrigued, we heartily recommend **Behind the Seeds** (for details on this behind-the-scenes tour, see "Future World Unplugged" on page 107).

The Land's newest attraction, *The Circle of Life*, is an entertaining ecological fable featuring Timon and Pumbaa, the wisenheimer meerkat-warthog duo from *The Lion King*, as developers, and Simba as the environmentally sensitive lion. The 20-minute film includes stunning nature footage.

Remember **Food Rocks**—a so-called musical tribute to good nutrition that turns out to be a nutrition-oriented salute to great music—as a satisfying snack. This 15-minute concert performed by endearing Audio-Animatronics lip-synchers is Disney showing its sense of humor. Among the reasons you'll be a groupie: Pita Gabriel, singing "I wanna be your high fiber," and The Refrigerator Police's

arresting refrain, "Every bite you take, every egg you break" (guess who is a milk carton with dark sunglasses?). It's usually possible to get into the next show. But wander around the muraled pre-show area and you'll learn a lot—like what Ethiopian goats have to do with your morning coffee.

Journey Into Imagination

While you'd think that glass buildings would leave very little to the imagination, the glass pyramids that house Journey Into Imagination have quite the opposite effect. Fronted by fountains that seem to have agendas of their own, this pavilion is one of Future World's most whimsical.

The attraction at Journey Into Imagination that earns a solid high five is **Honey, I Shrunk the Audience**. If you had time to visit only a few attractions at Epcot, this spectacle of a 3-D movie should be high on your list. The 25-minute film is so riddled with sensational special effects that the audience is consistently

Knock on Plastic

While they're good enough to fool any lumberjack, every last tree in the Celebrate the Land boat ride's ecosystems is plastic to the core. Disney artists molded the trunks and branches from live specimens, then snapped on polyethylene leaves one at a time. So be sure to see the trees for the forest.

On Pins and Needles

We once observed a couple in their mid-forties so fixated by an exhibit at Image Works that they wouldn't lift their eyes to acknowledge the other's artistry. Standing on either side of a table whose surface was composed of long, soft-edged pins, they ran their hands along the bottom of the table as if playing a harp. As they pushed up the pins to form fleeting patterns, the one-upmanship began. He made a perfect fish. She made a dolphin. He made a school of fish. She made a swooping gull and a fish. We didn't stick around to see the finale.

reduced to a shrieking, squirming, giggling mass. The experience is not rough, but the effects *are* heightened with a little suspense, so we'll say no more. This popular attraction is least congested in the morning.

On the other side of the priority spectrum, ironically enough, is the pavilion's title attraction. The **Journey Into Imagination** ride is a lighthearted 14-minute trip in which an adventurer and his dragon explore the creative process. Better yet, head upstairs to sample the interactive offerings of **Image Works**. (Don't miss the terrific photography display near the entrance.) In Image Works, amuse yourself by trying to conduct the Electronic Philharmonic orchestra. Simply step up to a console whose panels represent instrumental sections and raise and lower your hands over them to control volume. Another highlight is Stepping Tones, a floor endowed with such dazzling sound qualities (step here, it's a fiddle; there, it's a drumroll) you'll wish you'd brought a push broom.

Test Track

Thrill seekers, drop to your knees and rejoice. Behind this pavilion's steely doors lies the longest, fastest ride at Walt Disney World. A certifiable blockbuster, **Test Track** recently opened in the spot formerly occupied by the World of Motion. In this supercharged introduction to automobile testing, computer-controlled ride vehicles barrel up steep hills, zip down straightaways, squeak around heavily banked hairpin turns, and slam on the brakes (not always on the best road conditions). Test Track is more than a thrill ride: It's a realistic run-through of tests performed on real cars at real facilities, known as proving grounds.

During a 20-minute tour of the plant, you see everything from the all-important seat-squirming test to the crucial trials endured by air bags, tires, and the human interface clan (our courageous crash-prone counterparts) to ensure our safety. Then you hop into a six-seater vehicle, fasten your seat belt, and—making note that you've got a video display, but no steering wheel or brake pedal—prepare for an exciting five-minute road trip. As the sporty open-top cars traverse the nearly one-mile track, you experience a rough-and-tumble suspension workout, become indebted to antilock brakes, narrowly avoid a fiery crash, and whiz outside and around the pavilion at speeds of up to 65 miles per hour. Incredible insight into cars is a given; you'll also gain respect for the complex systems contained therein. On the way out, check out the smarty-pants car demo, the automotive boutique, and the General Motors concept cars.

Beyond "visit in early morning for minimal crowds," there's one caution: Riders must be in good health and free from heart conditions, back and neck problems, and other physical limitations.

Wonders of Life

While the 72-foot-tall steel DNA molecule certainly marks the territory of this mostly whimsical pavilion devoted to health and fitness concerns, the sculpture also provides a visual reminder of the uniqueness of this area. Wonders of Life gets credit for introducing three elements to Epcot—a true thrill ride, a health food bar, and (believe it or not) exercise equipment.

First, the main attraction: **Body Wars**, a frenetic five-minute trip through the human body in a flight simulator, could be the fraternal twin of Star Tours, the rocky ride through space located at Disney-MGM Studios, but for a couple of things. It is a year older and a couple of notches rougher than its Studios counterpart. The premise of Body Wars is that you are along for the ride on a routine medical probe to remove a splinter (from the inside) when things get out of hand. Before you know it you are barreling through the human lungs, heart, and brain. Body Wars is a tremendously exciting journey, both visually and physically, that rates among WDW's biggest thrills—but it is also a turbulent ride with a lot of very jerky movements.

On the Horizon

The outer space–minded Horizons pavilion is nothing if not forward thinking. Proof: A complete renovation is planned in the not-too-distant future. Expect to find an exciting new attraction that's in keeping with the fresh enticements at neighboring Future World pavilions. Note that this attraction will probably be closed throughout 1998.

Like Child's Play

As Walt Disney once said, "Laughter is no enemy to learning." And so it is that Future World is blessed with attractions that make great fun of enlightenment. For entertainment so whimsical you're barely conscious of any information intake, consider the following amusements:

■ Cranium Command and Body Wars at Wonders of Life

■ Food Rocks at The Land

■ Honey, I Shrunk the Audience, and Image Works, at Journey Into Imagination

■ Ellen's Energy Adventure at Universe of Energy

Note that if you're especially squeamish, you may find the visual content too much in this context. If you are pregnant, you will not be allowed to board this ride. You should also bypass Body Wars if you've recently eaten, have a back problem or heart condition, are susceptible to motion sickness, or have other physical limitations. While crowds flock to this attraction, it is generally least congested first thing in the morning and during the hours just prior to park closing.

Another Wonders of Life attraction that merits not-to-be-missed status is **Cranium Command**, an utterly tame, utterly delightful 17-minute journey into the mind of a 12-year-old boy. This is an attraction so good Billy Crystal would have a tough time making it funnier. The setup, basically, is that the commander of a specialized corps of brain pilots is issuing assignments, and our pal Buzzy is dealt the unlucky task of piloting an adolescent boy. The show follows a day in this boy's life, with Buzzy calling the shots. Celebrity cameos include George Wendt (Norm from "Cheers") manning the stomach.

For more whimsical fun, explore the challenges of the Sensory Funhouse, located just outside Cranium Command. And don't neglect the stable of Wondercycles, computerized stationary bicycles that let you pedal (headlong into traffic) through the Rose Bowl Parade and Disneyland.

While Wonders of Life ranks among Future World's most lighthearted pavilions, it does have a serious side. This is best evidenced at Frontiers of Medicine, an exhibit in the far-left corner that showcases recent medical advances.

Universe of Energy

B ehind this mirrored facade lies a pavilion on a serious power trip (it draws some of its electricity from photovoltaic cells mounted on the roof). Universe of Energy is notable for its lifelike dinosaurs, some of the largest Audio-Animatronics animals ever created. After a recent update, it also fetches a few nominations for Best Comedy in a Future World Pavilion.

The pavilion is given over entirely to a 45-minute presentation that explores the origins of fossil fuels and muses about alternative energy sources. (A large group is let into the theater every 17 minutes, so don't let the crowd scare you off.) **Ellen's Energy Adventure** boasts some familiar faces. The show is powered by Ellen's sudden yen for knowledge about such things—largely so she can beat her know-it-all friend Judy should they ever land on their favorite game show together. Bill Nye, the Science Guy, offers to educate Ellen, and just so happens to have some rather extensive visual aids handy. As Bill lectures Ellen, arresting visuals are shown on a series of huge screens. (Look for a brief appearance by a caveman you'd swear was a famous sitcom actor.)

When Bill insists they travel back 220 million years to seek greater knowledge, the seating area rotates and splits into six vehicles, which then move into the clammy, sulfur-scented air of the primeval world. Here, you encounter erupting volcanoes, an eerie fog, and prehistoric creatures locked in combat, rearing up suddenly from a tide pool, and gazing down at you like vultures. You also come upon an Audio-Animatronics Ellen, desperately attempting to reason with a snakelike dinosaur. She makes it out of the forest in one piece, and hits the big time on her game show, if only in her dreams. (For those playing along at home, the category is ENERGY; the answer, THE ONE ENERGY SOURCE WE'LL NEVER EXHAUST. We won't give away the question.) This pavilion is best visited in the afternoon, but if the line extends beyond the marquee, try again later.

Future World Unplugged

Insight into the inner workings of Epcot is easier to come by than you might think. The passwords in Future World:

■ **Behind the Seeds:** This one-hour greenhouse tour at The Land ($6) covers much the same terrain as the Celebrate the Land boat ride, but in a much more intimate fashion. Reservations are necessary and must be made in person (at the Green Thumb Emporium on the pavilion's lower level) on the day you wish to participate. Spots fill up quickly, so reserve yours first thing.

■ **DiveQuest:** In addition to offering an informal introduction to marine research and conservation, this 2½-hour program ($140) invites certified scuba divers to suit up for a 30- to 40-minute dive in The Living Seas aquarium. For details, call WDW-TOUR (939-8687).

■ **Dolphin Exploration:** This initiation to dolphins takes place at The Living Seas. Call 939-8687 for further information and cost.

Leave Future World by walking through its central plaza past the fountain that aspires to be Niagara Falls (in an odd case of confused identity or perhaps an attempt at foreshadowing, it's called the Fountain of Nations). As you head south over the walkway that leads to World Showcase, be sure to look to each side: On the right, a spontaneously erupting fountain is delivering a merciless soaking (mostly to children); on the left, note the ATM, and farther down, the resident flock of flamingos, bathing in the canal. Welcome to the flip side of Future World.

World Showcase

Think of World Showcase as a handful of gourmet jelly beans, the sort so flavorful they make your taste buds believe you're actually putting away strawberry cheesecake, champagne punch, and chocolate pudding. You know they're just jelly beans, of course, but you pretend, fully savoring the essence of that piña colada. In the same way, World Showcase cajoles your senses into accepting its 11 international pavilions at face value, enveloping you in such delectable representations of Germany, Japan, Mexico, and more, that you are content to play along.

This parade of nations, a cultural thoroughfare wrapped around a lagoon the size of 85 football fields, is marked by dramatic mood swings. The atmosphere changes markedly with each border crossing, going from positively romantic to utterly serene, toe-tappingly upbeat, patriotic, festive, wistfully Old World, or cheerfully relaxed in a matter of yards.

Of course, the World Showcase pavilions are not simply outstanding mood pieces, but occasions to get uniquely acquainted with the people, history, and beauty of nearly a dozen nations. Each has a strong, unmistakable sense of place that announces itself with painstakingly re-created landmarks and faithful landscaping that ensures bougainvillea in Mexico and lotus blossoms in China. Each contributes its culinary specialties to the apple tart–to–zabaglione smorgasbord that makes World Showcase one of Walt Disney World's hottest meal tickets.

To transport yourself totally, try to supplement the smattering of attractions—panoramic films, theater and dinner shows, boat rides, and the nightly not-to-be-missed fireworks extravaganza known as IllumiNations—with the legions of less structured pursuits. Start by trying to catch one street performance per country. So frequent it's practically ongoing (check your guidemap for exact times), this feast of live entertainment encompasses everything from mariachi bands to acrobatics, belly dancing, and bagpipes—and makes a great accompaniment to a mobile wine tasting. Take time, too, to chitchat with the "locals" in each village (nearly all of whom claim the represented country as their homeland) and to talk with visiting artisans as they demonstrate their crafts. To personalize your journey even more, make a mission of snacking, drinking, shopping, gallery-hopping, or even benchwarming your way around the World.

Structurally, World Showcase is perhaps the most user-friendly area of Walt Disney World's theme parks. You may get tired walking along the 1.3-mile promenade that leads past all pavilions as it encircles the lagoon, but you won't lose your sense of direction. While locations of countries here don't correspond at all to their placement on the planet, the landscape offers a wealth of Eiffel Tower–like clues that *almost* preclude use of a map. Because World Showcase is less attraction-driven (5 of the 11 countries have no attractions, per se), it requires less strategic maneuvering.

If World Showcase came with an instructions booklet, it might say:

■ Touring is a clockwise or a counterclockwise proposition that's best begun as soon as this part of Epcot opens.

International Gateway

Think of this second entrance as Epcot's back door. The turnstiles here provide a direct "in" to World Showcase, depositing guests between the France and United Kingdom pavilions. Because the International Gateway is connected via walkway to the Yacht Club, Beach Club, BoardWalk, Swan, and Dolphin resorts, guests at these lodgings have exceptional access to Epcot. (Water launches also make the trip.) Be aware that:

■ Wheelchairs and camcorders are available for rent at this entrance.

■ If you plan ahead, you can make a quick exit from here after IllumiNations.

■ Nothing in World Showcase opens until 11 A.M., so guests arriving earlier must walk to Future World at the opposite end of the park.

Snacking Around the World

When your stomach's growling, every World Showcase country has a little something to satisfy your craving. Here's an inkling of what we have (happily) sampled.

Near the Canadian border, it's cheddar cheese soup at Le Cellier. In the United Kingdom, we like the stuffed baked potatoes outside the Rose & Crown Pub. In France, we appreciate the Boulangerie

•CONTINUED ON NEXT PAGE

■ Shops are optimally saved for the afternoon, when the throngs from Future World have descended, lengthening lines for movies, rides, and shows.

■ The movies at Canada, France, and China are often better appreciated when spaced out over two days.

■ IllumiNations, a nightly spectacle of fireworks, lasers, and music, is the biggest draw in all of Epcot. The display is visible from most any point along the World Showcase Promenade.

Moving along, this tour describes World Showcase pavilions in the order they're encountered when walking counterclockwise around the lagoon.

Canada

In a marked departure from the real world, a refreshment stand poised a good 50 yards before the border makes it possible to arrive in Canada with Molson in hand. This large pavilion—which merits kudos as the site of an outstanding panoramic film, a classy cafeteria, interesting shops, and the coolest spot in World Showcase—covers an impressive amount of territory in its bid to capture the distinctive beauty and cultural diversity of the Western Hemisphere's largest nation.

An artful ode to the Indians of Canada's Northwest (towering totem poles and a trading post) leads to an architectural tribute to French Canada (the Hôtel du Canada here is a hybrid of Ottawa's Château Laurier and Quebec's Château Frontenac).

From here, follow the sounds of rushing water to find the cooling sprays of a miniaturized Niagara Falls that's tucked neatly into the face of a Canadian Rocky and usually blessed with a rainbow. A stunning feature film, a visual anthem of sorts appropriately called *O Canada!*, is shown in all its Circle-Vision 360 glory within the mountain itself. Filmed with nine cameras mounted on a 400-pound rig that crews suspended from a B-25 bomber, among other aircraft, the 17-minute movie places you smack in the middle of most all things Canadian, including a hockey game, a flock of Canadian geese taking flight, enormous reindeer herds, and the Royal Canadian Mounted Police. Because it's a standing engagement, it's best viewed earlier in the day, when the standing's still good. Whatever you do, don't miss it. As you leave, check out the bountiful greenery inspired by the famous Butchart Gardens in Victoria, British Columbia—while not as cool as the falls out back, they're still a great place to lay claim to a bench, especially when the Caledonia Bagpipe Band or the pavilion's troupe of Canadian folk dancers is performing.

United Kingdom

This cheery neighborhood, which reveals its identity via the bright-red phone booths dotting its cobblestoned streets, is clearly a fine place for a bit of shopping or making new friends over a pint of ale. What's less obvious: the knotted herb garden tucked behind the thatched-roof cottage (note the spearmint plants); the butterfly hatchery on the hill behind it; and the courtyard at the rear of the pavilion, where you'll find a traditional English hedge maze and a Mary Poppins topiary. A table at the Rose & Crown Pub is the best perspective from which to view this pavilion, because the Tudor, Georgian, and Victorian structures seem all the more real from the window of a friendly English pub.

Architectural enlightenment is a great excuse to dally in the fine shops. You can cover 300 years of building styles just by walking from the slate floor of The Tea Caddy (a replica of the thatched-roof cottage of Shakespeare's wife, Anne Hathaway) straight through to the carpeted room with the Waterford crystal chandelier, which signals your arrival at the Neoclassical period and the shop known as The Queen's Table. Note how the building that houses The Magic of Wales widens from foundation to roof; this is because property tax in the 1600s was based on square footage at ground level.

Because the United Kingdom has no queue-driven attractions, it is easily explored any time of day.

France

A footbridge from the United Kingdom leads across a picturesque canal to one of the most romantic areas of World Showcase. Petite streets and Eiffel Tower aside, you're looking at Paris during the Belle Epoque ("beautiful age") of the late 19th century. The one-time Parisian institution Les Halles is recreated here, as is a one-ninth-scale Eiffel Tower that would be infinitely more evocative were it not so obviously perched atop a building (note that the model here is brown, to reflect the Eiffel Tower's original color). Luxurious boutiques, bustling sidewalk cafés, talented mimes, and, of course, pastries that

•CONTINUED FROM PREVIOUS PAGE

Pâtisserie's fine snacking sensibility, particularly the pastry known as the Marvelous. In Morocco, we go for the baklava. Japan's Matsu No Ma sates when we're in a sushi frame of mind. The American Adventure's Liberty Inn provides—what else?—apple pie, french fries, and cola. La Cucina Italiana stands by with scrumptious Italian specialties. Germany comes through with killer soft pretzels, potato salad, and bratwurst at Sommerfest. China squeaks by with egg rolls at the Lotus Blossom Café. Norway (specifically Kringla Bakeri og Kafé) satisfies sweet and savory instincts, most notably with open-face sandwiches and *vaflers* (heart-shaped waffles) made on the spot and topped with fresh preserves. And Mexico surprises with fresh watermelon juice alongside the requisite chips and salsa at the lagoonside Cantina de San Angel. In other words: No set dining plans? No problem.

Quiet Nooks

A greater character presence in Epcot brings occasional breaks in the calm, but there's always a peaceful spot to be found.

- Fountain View Espresso and Bakery in Future World

- Plaza de los Amigos inside Mexico's pyramid

- Stave Church Gallery in Norway

- Benches near reflecting pools in China

- Lagoonside benches near the gondola in Italy

- Garden alongside The American Adventure

- Bijutsu-kan Gallery, hillside gardens, and Matsu No Ma in Japan

- Tucked-away garden with benches in France

- Gardens at rear of United Kingdom pavilion and Rose & Crown Pub

- Waterfall and mountain setting in Canada

announce their presence *par avion* are among the big draws here, as is the wine-tasting counter at the nicely stocked La Maison du Vin. Beckoning, too, is one of the most peaceful spots in all of Epcot—a quiet park on the canal side of the pavilion that might have leapt off the canvas of Georges Seurat's *Sunday Afternoon on the Island of La Grande Jatte*.

But the biggest lure here is certainly the breathtaking 18-minute film *Impressions de France*, which puts its five 21- by 27-foot screens to terrific use in a tour de France that ranges from Alpine skiing to foothills of buttery pastries. If you know France, you'll love it; if you don't, you'll want to. The superb score, featuring French classical composers, could stand on its own. *Impressions de France* is least congested during the morning and early-evening hours. A few key words to help you communicate with the locals: Say *bonjour* (bohn-ZHOOR) for good day, *merci beaucoup* (mehr-see boh-KOO) for thank you very much, and *au revoir* (OH re-VWAR) for goodbye.

Morocco

This enchanting area—arguably the most meticulously crafted of all the represented nations—also happens to be the loudest World Showcase pavilion. The authenticity has something to do with the fact that nine tons of tile were handmade, handcut, and handlaid by Moroccan artisans into the mosaics seen here. The prayer tower at the entrance takes after the famous Koutoubia Minaret in Marrakesh, and sets the scene for the energetic Moroccan musicians and dancers who perform in the courtyard. The Bab Boujouloud gate, patterned after one that stands in the city of Fez, leads to the Medina (or old part of the city), a tangled array of narrow passageways where basketry, hand-knotted Berber carpets, leather goods, and brass items are among the wares for sale.

Walk through the bazaar, whether or not you feel like shopping, so you can get a feel for the Medina and try out your Arabic. Hello is *salam alekoum* (sah-LAHM wah-LAY-koom), thank you is *shokran* (SHOWK-ran), and goodbye is *b'slama* (b'-SLEM-ah). The Medina also brings you to the entrance of Marrakesh restaurant, notable for its North African menu, its belly dancers, and the fact that it's about the only full-service restaurant in World Showcase where you can frequently get a table without securing priority seating. Make a point of checking out the extraordinary tilework and costumes displayed at the Gallery of Arts and History, and be on the lookout for visiting artisans demonstrating their crafts. It may interest you to learn that the gardens of this pavilion are irrigated by an ancient working waterwheel located on the promenade. Morocco is easily toured any time of day.

Japan

As quietly inviting as Morocco is vibrantly enticing, Japan is a pavilion of considerable beauty and serenity. Its most prominent landmarks are the red *torii* gate (a popular good-luck symbol) that stands close to the lagoon, and the five-tiered pagoda, created in the mold of an eighth-century shrine located in Nara.

Note that each level of the pagoda represents one of the elements that, according to Buddhist teachings, produced everything in the universe (from bottom to top: earth, water, fire, wind, and sky).

The most compelling features of this pavilion—restaurants aside—are the entertainment (the Matsuriza drummers and the indescribable stilt birds), the elaborate detail of its manicured gardens (note the differently patterned fences, the bamboo "scarecrow" contraption in the stream), and the consistently strong art exhibits at the small Bijutsu-kan Gallery. Japan also claims one of the largest shops in all of Epcot. The Mitsukoshi Department Store, housed in a structure reminiscent of a section of the Gosho Imperial Palace, which was originally constructed in Kyoto in 794 A.D., counts bonsai, kimonos, and dolls among its many offerings. This pavilion is easily toured any time of day. Note that good morning in Japanese is *ohayo gozaimasu* (oh-hi-yoh goh-zy-ee-mahs), thank you is *arigato gozaimasu* (ah-ree-gah-toh goh-zy-ee-mahs), and good evening is *konban wa* (kohn-bahn wah).

Tired of Walking?

Water taxis in the lagoon link Showcase Plaza at the foot of Future World with Germany and France, located at the farthest corners of World Showcase. Convenient—but keep in mind that it's often quicker to walk.

Where the Art Is

Exhibits change periodically, but here's an indication of what you can expect to see.

■ Mexico's "Reign of Glory" exhibit features pre-Columbian pieces (some are on loan from the Smithsonian).

■ Norway's tiny Stave Church Gallery contains exhibits tracing the history of the once-commonplace churches.

■ Japan's Bijutsu-kan Gallery displays traditional Japanese art and carvings.

■ Morocco's Gallery of Arts and History showcases intricate tilework and costumes.

■ China's House of Whispering Willows displays ancient Chinese art and artifacts.

The American Adventure

The centerpiece pavilion of World Showcase is so devoted to Americana it can bring out the Norman Rockwell in you even when you're cranky. Housed in a Colonial-style manse that combines elements of Independence Hall, the Old State House in Boston, Monticello, and various structures in Colonial Williamsburg, it's dressed for the part. The 26-minute show inside—an evocative multimedia presentation about American history—is among Disney's best, both for its astonishingly detailed sets and sophisticated Audio-Animatronics figures, and for its ability to rouse goose bumps from unsuspecting patriots. Ben Franklin and Mark Twain lead what's been called "a hundred-yard dash capturing the spirit of the country at specific moments in time."

A talented a cappella vocal group called the Voices of Liberty sometimes entertains in the lobby before the show begins. (So talented are these singers that they are consistently able to get most every person in the place singing "God Bless America.") The wait for The American Adventure can be long because the show itself is lengthy, so stop by for curtain times and plan accordingly. This pavilion also features a fast-food restaurant and the lagoonside **America Gardens Theatre**, where you may very well find worthwhile entertainment. An interesting aside: The garden alongside The American Adventure acknowledges the days before red, white, and blue by showcasing plants used traditionally by Native Americans for food and medicinal purposes.

Italy

This little Italy is defined by an abiding you-are-there ambience and meticulous authenticity that extends from the gondolas tied to striped moorings at the pavilion's very own Venetian island to the homemade (before your eyes) fettuccine and spaghetti at its popular L'Originale Alfredo di Roma Ristorante.

Look to the very top of the scaled-down Venetian campanile dominating the romantic piazza here, and you'll see an angel covered in gold leaf that was molded into a spitting image of the one atop the bell tower in the real St. Mark's Square in Venice. The Doge's Palace here is so faithfully rendered that its facade resembles the marbled pattern of the original. Adding to the effect are tall, slender stands of Italian cypress, replicas of Venetian statues, an abundance of potted flowers, and delightfully fragrant olive and citrus trees.

This pavilion is among the most romantic and evocative areas in all of World Showcase. It has no major attractions per se, but between its memorable street

performers (especially the amazing Living Statues) and the strolling musicians who perform during dinner at Alfredo's, it has all the entertainment it needs. Among the interesting shopping options is a gem of a gourmet food shop, called La Cucina Italiana, that also stocks fine Italian wines. This pavilion is easily visited at any time of day. When in Italy, note that good day is *buon giorno* (boo-on JOR-no), thank you is *grazie* (GRAHT-see-eh), and goodbye is *arrivederci* (ah-ree-veh-DAIR-chee).

Germany

In a word: oompah. Arguably the most festive country in all of World Showcase, Germany is immediately recognizable by its fairy-tale architecture. To the rear of the central cobblestoned square (which is named for Saint George), you'll see a giant cuckoo clock, complete with Hummel figurines that emerge on the hour. Immediately past this clock lies the Biergarten, the vast restaurant and entertainment hall that—thanks to lively lunch and dinner shows primed with German beer, sausages, yodelers, and folk dancers—serves as the pinnacle of this pavilion's entertainment. For a more impromptu beer or piece of Black Forest cake, there's an outdoor counter called Sommerfest; a strolling accordionist and trio frequently usher the festive Bavarian atmosphere of Biergarten out into the square.

Germany also scores with tempting shops, an ATM, and the Weinkeller, which offers wine-tasting opportunities. In Glas und Porzellan, it's usually possible to watch a Goebel artist demonstrating the elaborate process by which Hummel figurines are created. Outside, note the miniature 1930s German village, complete with castle, farmhouse, monastery, and a railroad that weaves throughout. Germany is easily toured at any time of day. When in Germany, good day is *guten Tag* (GOOT-en-tahkh), thank you very much is *danke schön* (DAHN-kuh shurn), and goodbye is *auf Wiedersehen* (owf VEE-der-zay-in).

For the Lovebirds...

Epcot's World Showcase has some great romantic spots, namely:

■ El Río del Tiempo boat ride and the San Angel Inn in Mexico

■ The lovely courtyard at the rear of the United Kingdom

■ Italy's piazza and gondola landing

■ Every inch of France

Several walking tours offer great insight into one of Disney's more enlightened creations.

■ **Hidden Treasures of World Showcase:** The instructor stops just short of turning pavilions inside out to illuminate their scrupulous detailing and eye-fooling design.

■ **Gardens of the World:** A horticulturist leads guests to the beautifully distinctive gardens here. Discover the lengths to which Disney has gone to create authentic-looking landscapes and find out how to apply clever techniques at home.

Tours last two to five hours and cost about $25 to $65 (not including the required Epcot admission). Schedules vary; reservations are necessary. Call WDW-TOUR (939-8687).

China

This at once serene and exciting pavilion is marked by a dramatic half-scale replica of Beijing's Temple of Heaven set behind stands of whistling bamboo and quiet reflecting pools, where you'll often see an egret posturing on a rock and almost always see floating lotus blossoms. Traditional Chinese music wafts over the sound system. In addition to its arresting gardens, the pavilion features the House of Whispering Willows, an ever-changing exhibit of ancient Chinese art and artifacts from well-known collections that's always worth a look. Live entertainment here is invariably stirring, whether it's a demonstration by the Red Panda Acrobats or a rare performance of the Chinese Lion Dance.

But the main reason to visit China is the Circle-Vision 360 film shown inside the Temple of Heaven, which is right up there with the extraordinary films presented at Canada and France. Basically, you stand, and *Wonders of China* whisks you on an incredible 19-minute, blink-and-you've-missed-the-Great-Wall journey that visits Inner Mongolia, Beijing's Forbidden City, and Shanghai, and provides fascinating glimpses of the people of China. Pay special attention to the fleeting scene of mist-enshrouded Huangshan Mountain if you can; the film crew and 40 laborers had to haul the 600-pound camera nearly a mile uphill for those three seconds of footage. When in China, hello is *ni hao* (nee HOW), thank you is *xiexie* (shay-shay), and goodbye is *zai jian* (SIGH jee-ahn).

Norway

This 11th addition to the World Showcase landscape is immediately intriguing. A curious array of buildings ring the pavilion's cobblestoned square, including a reproduction of a wooden stave church (an endangered species of sorts, with just 30 remaining in Norway) and a replica of the 14th-century Akershus Castle that still stands in Oslo's harbor. Beside a grassy-roofed, thick-logged structure that harks back to Setesdal, there's a statue of a Norwegian running champion, living legend Grete Waitz. This Land of the Midnight Sun has added some twists to the World Showcase lineup—among them, the promise of troll encounters and Norwegian handicrafts of the gorgeous hand-knit sweater variety.

The stave church houses a gallery of artifacts recalling the history of these charming benchmarks of Norwegian culture (don't skip it, if only to see the inside of this teensy church). But Norway really scores with **Maelstrom**, a trip in dragon-headed boats through Viking territory that is good fun, if not a veri-fiable thrill ride. An inspired and technologically sophisticated voyage that sur-prises you with a troll here, a backward plunge there, a sudden waterfall here, a storm there, Maelstrom doesn't throw big punches; it just keeps you guessing. The ten-minute trip lets you out at a quaint Norwegian village, then finishes up with a brief film on the essence of Norway. This attraction is least crowded in the evening. When in Norway, hello is *god dag* (goo DAHG), thank you is *takk* (TOCK), and goodbye is *adjø* (ahd-YUR).

Mexico

There's no mistaking this pavilion's identity. A wild thicket of tropical foliage leads past squawking (sometimes shrieking) macaws to a great pyramid. Inside, you wend your way through a brief but consistently engaging cultural exhibit to the main event. What you see next—a thoroughly romantic vision of a quaint Mexican village at twilight—is among the most wondrously escapist visions in World Showcase. True to form, there are stands selling col-orful sombreros, baskets, pottery, and piñatas (the shop off to the left is your source for higher-quality Mexican handicrafts). In the rear of the plaza, note the dimly lit San Angel Inn and, behind it, the river and smoking volcano. Here too, you'll find the embarkation point for **El Río del Tiempo**, a pleasant six-minute boat trip through Mexican history that might be described as a sub-dued south-of-the-border It's A Small World. If you encounter long lines early in the day, skip it, and check back later. Note, too, that the mariachi band that performs inside and outside of this imposing pavilion is quite good—particu-larly when you have a margarita in your hand. When in Mexico, hello is *hola* (OH-lah), thank you very much is *muchas gracias* (MOO-chahs GRAH-see-ahs), and goodbye is *adios* (ah-dee-OHS).

Drinking Around the World

We've never actually completed such a circuit (nor would we recom-mend your doing so), but there's Samuel Adams lager at The American Adventure, and at least one good imported excuse to bend the ol' elbow in each World Showcase country. Namely: Molson and more from Le Cellier or the Refreshment Port in Canada; shandies, Guinness, black and tans, Tennent's, and beyond from the Rose & Crown Pub in the United Kingdom; a bottle of Kronenbourg from the Boulangerie Pâtisserie or a glass of wine from La Maison du Vin in France; a glass of hot mint tea (poured from three feet above) at Marrakesh in Morocco; Kirin beer or sake specialty drinks at Matsu No Ma in Japan; wine in Italy, although until tastings become available, you'll have to drink it with a meal or dessert at Alfredo's; Beck's beer and H. Schmitt Söhne wine at Germany's Sommerfest; Chinese wine and beer at the Lotus Blossom Café; Ringnes drafts from Kringla Bakeri og Kafé in Nor-way; and what else but margaritas in Mexico's Cantina de San Angel.

DISNEY-MGM STUDIOS

Like an actress who is just right for the part, Disney-MGM Studios is perfectly cast as the vivacious, movie-obsessed theme park that is seemingly incapable of keeping a secret. Since its 1989 debut, this park has worked hard to make the transition from entertaining sidekick to leading lady, and it has succeeded.

Disney-MGM Studios holds its own at Walt Disney World not merely by offering ticket holders a rose-colored reminiscence of 1930s Hollywood, but by resurrecting decades of Tinseltown magic as innovative rides, stage performances, and theater shows, and by baring all manner of backstage secrets. The park immerses guests in showbiz to the point that they can momentarily forget there *is* life beyond television and motion pictures.

You'd do well to think of the Studios as the adult's Magic Kingdom. The place is magical, but in a more meaningful and sophisticated way; it is marked by a whimsicality far more ageless than that which pervades the Magic Kingdom itself. Sure, it has a Beauty and the Beast stage show and a 3-D movie featuring the Muppets, but these hardly constitute a satellite Fantasyland. In fact, at times the Studios seems to have even been scripted for a mature crowd, carefully crafted with a wink of the eye by (and for) grownups to elicit knowing laughs and no-holds-barred nostalgia.

Certainly, The Great Movie Ride has greater meaning to an audience steeped in the films of James Cagney, Judy Garland, and Humphrey Bogart. Another case in point: the 50's Prime Time Café, a nostalgia-fest of a restaurant that harks back to the era of "Father Knows Best" and "I Love Lucy" with a montage of black-and-white television clips, pot roast, Formica tables, fussbudgety moms, and vinyl sofas. It's packed with inside jokes the younger crowd just wouldn't get. Meanwhile, over at the frightful Twilight Zone Tower of Terror, any adult with an inkling of Rod Serling's legacy will appreciate Disney's superbly rendered fifth dimension despite the approaching doom (*two* 13-story plummets down an elevator shaft). Even the Studios' most child-oriented attraction, Voyage of The Little Mermaid, packs a few lines that whoosh right over kids' heads (sea witch to love-struck mermaid about to be stripped of her voice in exchange for a pair of feet: "Don't underestimate the importance of body language").

The Studios also speaks to adults by offering an intimate brush with Disney's creative and technical prowess, a chance to penetrate and even take part in the magic. The park is so brimming with behind-the-scenes glimpses that a photo of Walt himself sketching a certain fawn nets but quick glances as folks enter The Magic of Disney Animation to meet the next Mickey Mouse–wannabe in its formative stages. Other tours allow you to prowl the catwalks of a television production studio, to feel the power of special effects in a catastrophe-laced demo complete with flash flood, and to learn the gymnastic logistics behind daring film stunts. Audience participation plays a bigger part in attractions here, making experiences dynamic and—if you or a companion are chosen to, say, test your ear for making sound effects on a cartoon sound track—uniquely personal.

While the Studios remains the most manageable of Walt Disney World's major theme parks, it has more than doubled its repertoire over the years. The most dramatic addition, the Tower of Terror, looms over the park's ostensible

HOT TIPS

■ On Wednesday and Sunday, guests staying at WDW resorts may enter the Disney-MGM Studios 1½ hours before the official opening time and get an early crack at selected attractions, such as the Tower of Terror, The Great Movie Ride, and Star Tours. Early-entry days and attractions are subject to change.

■ Not coincidentally, Wednesday and Sunday tend to be the most crowded days here at the Studios.

landmark, a specially endowed water tank commonly known as the "Earffel Tower." Additional expansion is in the works. Expect the much anticipated nighttime show known as Fantasmic!, a magic-infused restaurant à la David Copperfield, and a thrill ride to appear behind Tower of Terror in the near future.

Certain attractions here, such as The Hunchback of Notre Dame show, sometimes don't open until an hour or more after the curtains officially rise. This fact underlines the importance of pausing to align your schedule with the showtimes and crowd patterns listed on the Tip Board. The board will also alert you to any celebrities who will be appearing during your visit. The most strategic spot to take a catnap: a sofa at the Catwalk Bar, which puts you far above the madding crowd with access to such things as frozen drinks and shrimp cocktail. For more cues to pleasantly removed refuges, note the restful and shady nooks described in the margins of this section.

GUIDING PRINCIPLES: The following walking tour is designed to offer a basic overview for first-time visitors and a timely update for returnees. The running commentary highlights the adult essentials, pointing out redeeming qualities of less-than-vital attractions and spotlighting recent additions to the park. For visitors with a limited amount of time, the Touring Priorities list contained in this section ranks the park's best adult bets.

The size of the Disney-MGM Studios makes it possible to experience most everything there is to see and do here in a leisurely day, but only if you're efficient. For additional touring tactics, consult the Hot Tips located in the margins of this section and the flexible touring plans in the *Planning Ahead* chapter. For information on how to get to the Studios via WDW transportation or by car, see the "Getting Around" section of the *Planning Ahead* chapter. To find out about the unique shops and merchandise found at the Disney-MGM Studios, see the "Shopping" section of the *Diversions* chapter. For restaurant recommendations, look to the evaluative "Restaurant Guide" located in the *Dining & Entertainment* chapter.

GETTING ORIENTED: Disney-MGM Studios is about half the size of Epcot, and easily navigated despite the fact that it has no distinctive shape or main artery. You enter the park—and 1930s Tinseltown—via Hollywood Boulevard, a bustling shopping venue. The first major intersection you come to is Sunset Boulevard, an equally starry-eyed venue that branches off to the right of Hollywood Boulevard; this shopping and entertainment strip ends in a cul-de-sac right at the foot of the park's tallest landmark, the 199-foot Tower of Terror.

Hollywood Boulevard ends where The Great Movie Ride begins—at a replica of Mann's (formerly Grauman's) Chinese Theatre. This ornate building is the

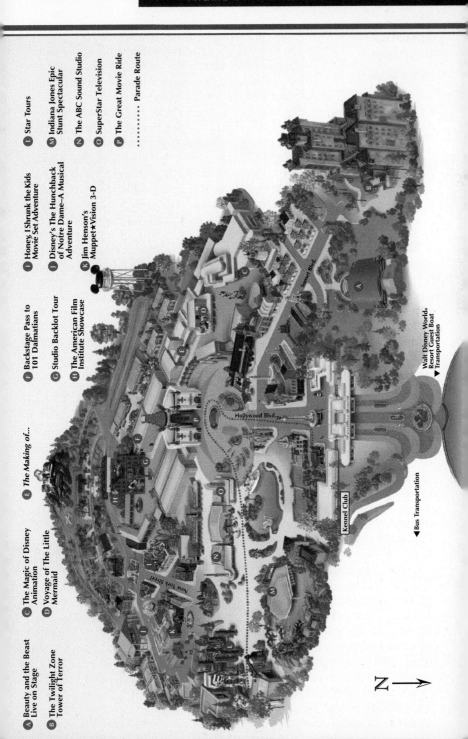

A Beauty and the Beast Live on Stage

B The Twilight Zone Tower of Terror

C The Magic of Disney Animation

D Voyage of The Little Mermaid

E The Making of...

F Backstage Pass to 101 Dalmatians

G Studio Backlot Tour

H The American Film Institute Showcase

I Honey, I Shrunk the Kids Movie Set Adventure

J Disney's The Hunchback of Notre Dame–A Musical Adventure

K Jim Henson's Muppet★Vision 3-D

L Star Tours

M Indiana Jones Epic Stunt Spectacular

N The ABC Sound Studio

O SuperStar Television

P The Great Movie Ride

•••••••••• Parade Route

Sunset Blvd.

Hollywood Blvd.

New York Street

Kennel Club

Walt Disney World Resort Guest Boat ▼Transportation

▼Bus Transportation

N →

Touring Priorities

DON'T MISS

Tower of Terror*

Star Tours

Jim Henson's
Muppet*Vision 3-D

The Great Movie Ride

Beauty and the Beast
Live on Stage**

The Hunchback of
Notre Dame show**

•CONTINUED ON NEXT PAGE

most centrally located landmark at the Studios, and the plaza fronting it, called Hollywood Plaza, is the site of a Hidden Mickey. (From above, garden plots in this plaza form his eyes and nose, the theater entrance is his mouth, and Echo Lake and the building that houses the Hollywood Brown Derby serve as ears.)

If you stand in Hollywood Plaza facing Disney's Chinese Theater, you'll see an archway off to your right; this leads to Mickey Avenue, an area with more of a backstage feel to it, where tours of working animation and television studios are among the attractions. If you make a left off Hollywood Boulevard and proceed clockwise past Echo Lake, you are on course for such attractions as The ABC Sound Studio, SuperStar Television, Indiana Jones Epic Stunt Spectacular, and Star Tours. Just past Star Tours lies one last entertainment pocket. Jim Henson's Muppet*Vision 3-D theater is the main draw here, together with a facade of a Manhattan block called New York Street. Walk left past the skyscraper end of New York Street and you're on a quick track back to Hollywood Plaza and the Chinese Theater.

A Walking Tour

Just inside the gates, you may be too distracted by the bright Art Deco looks of Hollywood Boulevard to notice a building on your left—but this is the site of Guest Relations, where you can go for information as well as first aid. Stop here or at Crossroads of the World (the gift stand smack in the center of the entrance plaza) to pick up a guidemap. To your immediate right, check out Oscar's Super Service, which has a 1949 Chevrolet tow truck parked out front. This is one of several striking and utterly unscratched classic automobiles you'll notice along the streets of the park. (We're not sure how they got through the turnstiles.) Also remember Oscar's as the spot for storage lockers and wheelchair rentals; the lost and found, along with package pickup, is right next door. If you'd like to witness the taping of a television

show, inquire at the production window adjacent to Oscar's to see what, if anything, is being filmed during your visit and to obtain tickets (free, and available on a first-come, first-served basis). Note that the Studios' sole ATM is just outside the turnstiles here.

Hollywood Boulevard

One look at this main drag and you have a hunch you're not in Central Florida anymore. The strip oozes star quality with a Mae West sort of subtlety. Movie tunes from Hollywood's Golden Age waft through the air. Palm trees make like Fred and Ginger in the tropical breeze. Streamlined storefronts with neon and chrome Art Deco flourishes line the boulevard like would-be movie sets hoping to get noticed. Don't be surprised if you encounter budding starlets sparring with their agents, paparazzi angling for shots, or a starry-eyed soul who wants *your* autograph.

Note that the shops along Hollywood Boulevard typically stay open about a half hour after the rest of the park has closed. (Consult the "Shopping" section in the *Diversions* chapter for specifics on our favorite shops; wares generally include a sampling of movie memorabilia, plenty of Disney character merchandise that's a cut above T-shirts, and a healthy supply of amazing fudge.)

However you get there, it's important to stop at the corner of Hollywood and Sunset boulevards to check the **Tip Board** (a trusty blackboard that lists current waiting times for popular attractions). Until 1 P.M., this is also the place to make priority seating arrangements for any of the Studios' full-service restaurants. Lest you ignore breakfast, the Starring Rolls Bakery is constantly auditioning coffee drinkers and croissant and cinnamon roll eaters a few steps away.

Sunset Boulevard

This newest Studios block is a broad, colorful avenue every bit as glamorous as Hollywood Boulevard. It has the same high-cheekbone style and its own stock of towering palms, evocative facades, and tempting shops. It also has stage presence, in the form of the 1,500-seat Theatre of the Stars amphitheater, where

•CONTINUED FROM PREVIOUS PAGE

DON'T OVERLOOK

The Magic of Disney Animation; Indiana Jones Epic Stunt Spectacular**;
The Making of...; The ABC Sound Studio; SuperStar Television;
Studio Backlot Tour

DON'T KNOCK YOURSELF OUT

Voyage of The Little Mermaid*; Backstage Pass to 101 Dalmatians;
Honey, I Shrunk the Kids Movie Set Adventure

 * Long lines; visit in the early A.M., late P.M., or during the parade.
** Pay close attention to performance schedules.

Quiet Nooks

- Starring Rolls Bakery
- Catwalk Bar
- Tune-In Lounge
- Sunset Ranch Market
- Shaded benches around Echo Park
- Brownstone stoops on New York Street
- Benches in Washington Square, at the far end of New York Street

Ears to the Ground

A middle-aged woman removed her eyeglasses but insisted on keeping her Mouseketeer hat intact as she prepared to board a Tower of Terror elevator bound for The Twilight Zone and a pair of 13-story plummets down an elevator shaft. "I've got a bobby pin in it," she said confidently to the attendant. Better make that an industrial-strength bobby pin.

you can see live performances of *Beauty and the Beast*. Sunset Boulevard begins innocently enough, with a friendly old-fashioned farmers' market, and a shop called Once Upon A Time that's housed in a replica of the Carthay Circle Theatre where *Snow White* premiered. But none other than the white-knuckle Tower of Terror looms at the end of the road.

Somehow, **Beauty and the Beast Live on Stage**, a production that was the raison d'être behind the Broadway musical, manages to remain oblivious to its eerie neighbor. The show is 20 not-to-be-missed minutes of rich musicality, delightful costuming and choreography, and uplifting entertainment. While a canopy keeps the sun's heat at bay, we still try to aim for an evening performance during the summer months; note that this show generally opens shortly after the park does.

Then there's **The Twilight Zone Tower of Terror**, a don't-miss attraction. Because few of us have a natural yen to drop 13 stories down a dark elevator shaft, this one requires some bravery. It helps to know what to expect.

Basically, "guests" enter the mysteriously abandoned Hollywood Tower Hotel and are invited into a library, where even the cobwebs appear to be circa 1939. Here, Rod Serling appears on a black-and-white television set to brief you (stormy night, Halloween 1939, lightning strikes, guests disappear from hotel elevator) and welcome you to tonight's episode of "The Twilight Zone": "If you'll just step this way into the boiler room, this is where you'll board our service elevators." You reach a boarding area—Last Call for Chickening Out— and file into an elevator (look at the diagram above the doors to avoid, say, the front row). Once you are seated and the safety bars are secured, the doors shut and the elevator ascends. You're soon so entranced with astonishing special effects—apparitions that appear in a corridor that vaporizes into a dark, star-filled sky, and a gigantic eye straight from the fifth dimension—that dread becomes (almost) secondary. When the elevator moves over into a second, pitch-black shaft, anything can happen, since Disney's Imagineers deviously transformed this ride from a two-screamer into a five-screamer. The bottom falls out more than once, and not subtly: Two 13-story plummets are scripted. One thing's for certain: Your cue to strike a great casual pose—a scream resembling a yawn, perhaps—is when you reach the top of the shaft. You want to look good in the group picture, which is taken as a panorama of the park suddenly gives way to a drop. The big plunges are incredibly fast downward pulls with surprisingly smooth landings. It's small comfort, perhaps, but the really hairy part is over faster than many vocal cords can respond.

A few notes: The jitters tend to stay with you for a bit after the 12-minute drama has ended. If you have back or neck problems, a heart condition, or are pregnant, we suggest that you pass on the Tower of Terror. And *don't* try it on a full stomach.

Animation Courtyard & Mickey Avenue

A djacent to Sunset Boulevard and Hollywood Boulevard is the section of the park that takes you under the sea with a diminutive mermaid and into working animation and television production studios. Passing under an archway located off Hollywood Plaza, you see Animation Plaza immediately in front of you, with Mickey Avenue to your left.

A few words about timing: First, note that The Magic of Disney Animation sometimes does not open until late morning (check the Tip Board and guidemap). And know that the three tours here—The Magic of Disney Animation, the Studio Backlot Tour, and Backstage Pass to 101 Dalmatians—are most exciting on weekdays before 5 P.M., because glimpses of Disney's magic makers at work stop when they call it a day.

Tower of Terror Tip

Impending threat of two multistory plunges in darkness not terrifying enough for you? Disorient yourself further by looking UP into the towering void before the shaft opens to a window on the park.

Exact Replicas

- Chinese Theater—Mann's Chinese Theatre in Hollywood

- Once Upon A Time storefront—Carthay Circle Theatre in Hollywood, where Disney's *Snow White* premiered

- Mickey's of Hollywood storefront—Frederick's of Hollywood

- Jim Henson's Muppet*Vision 3-D theater—the theater from "The Muppet Show"

- Hollywood Brown Derby—Brown Derby of 1930s Hollywood

A walking tour through working animation studios, **The Magic of Disney Animation** is a chance to learn the facts of life as they relate to Mickey Mouse and to see Disney's next animated film as a work in progress. Changes are in the works here, given the current expansion of the animation facility, and the attraction will be closed through spring for refurbishment. When it reopens, we're sorry to report that it will be without the uproarious commentary of Robin Williams and Walter Cronkite. Nonetheless, the tour does offer the chance to see Disney animators work their magic. You don't spend the whole 45 minutes peering over shoulders, however. After touring the animation studios while viewing snippets from a future movie release (perhaps *Mulan*, *Tarzan*, *A Bug's Life*, or *Fantasia 2000*), you gather round an actual artist, who reveals still more secrets of animation. Finally, you are led into a theater and treated to a finale of Disney classics.

If you think you'd enjoy a behind-the-scenes look at moviemaking of the "lights, camera, action" sort, take two: The Studio Backlot Tour and Backstage Pass to 101 Dalmatians complement each other well. The **Studio Backlot Tour** is a two-pronged gig that begins with an entertaining six-minute demo of how a realistic sea storm or naval battle might be filmed (two guests are asked to don yellow raincoats and brave the elements). The second segment, a 35-minute tram ride, starts calmly enough; but sit on the right side to stay dry. You visit the wardrobe area (2.25 million bodies clothed); the lights, camera, and props departments; and the backlot neighborhood of facades where you can see "The Golden Girls" house, or at least its exterior. Then suddenly there you are in a special-effects zone called Catastrophe Canyon, which specializes in nature's wrath: violent downpours, fiery explosions, flash floods. Just as you're thinking that New York City would seem hospitable compared to this, there it is, a realistic-looking Manhattan block made mostly of fiberglass and Styrofoam. The Studio Backlot Tour can accommodate about 200 people per tram; lines here tend to be shorter in the late afternoon (ask the attendant for an e.t.a., and if it's more than 30 minutes, check back later). The tour exits through the **American Film Institute Showcase**, a revolving display of props and partial sets that also features interactive elements related to film lore and legends.

A matter of yards away, **Backstage Pass to 101 Dalmatians** beckons with inside stuff on the (inherently challenging) process of making this megapooch live-action Disney film. The 25-minute walking tour steals through prop- and set-filled rooms and a special-effects shop, as well as along a soundproof catwalk that overlooks soundstages (where you may see live takes, if sets are "hot"). En route, you find out how the real and Audio-Animatronics puppies interacted on the set, how some of the more memorable scenes were achieved,

and just how many trainers were saying "Stay" and "Sit" during filming. You also get a gander at Cruella de Vil's $500,000 car, her mansion, and her decadent costumes, created just for the movie.

For an elaborate look at production, see the film *The Making of...* (fill in the blank with a recent Disney feature). The attraction headlines live-action movies, periodically swapping in a current release. It typically introduces the directors and producers, who explain the ins and outs of creating a given film, and shows the actors on location. (A past film, *The Making of Evita*, showed clips of Madonna recording music.) Haven't seen the movie yet? You'll enjoy this behind-the-scenes glimpse anyway.

If you can get near **Voyage of The Little Mermaid**—and at this 15-minute musical adapted from the hit movie, that's no easy task—don't hesitate. It's not the story line that's so compelling. It's the upbeat music, the amazing puppetry,

Snacker's Guide

For a healthy nibble, seek out the Sunset Ranch Market on Sunset Boulevard for carrot sticks and fruit, or try the small fruit stand located between Hollywood Boulevard and Echo Lake. For a savory bite, try the mini or foot-long hot dogs or the turkey legs at Rosie's Red Hot Dogs on Sunset Boulevard. If you need a sweet fix, consider the cookies at Starring Rolls Bakery on Sunset Boulevard, and the fudge and wonderfully addictive Mint Chocolate Cookie Gems at Hollywood Boulevard's Sweet Success. For a frozen treat, try Catalina Eddie's Frozen Yogurt on Sunset Boulevard or the ice cream at Dinosaur Gertie's on Echo Lake.

the occasion to watch children ogle this real, live mermaid *whose tail is moving*, and the mist-infused feeling that you are underwater. Voyage of The Little Mermaid seems to start the day with a 30-minute wait; your best bet is the first show in the morning. Check the guidemap for showtimes.

Echo Lake Area

Heading back through the archway into Hollywood Plaza, you come upon **The Great Movie Ride**. This drive-through theater of sorts is a classic in its own right and the best ticket we know to a quick video rental decision your next time out. Housed in an artful replica of Mann's Chinese Theatre, this not-to-be-missed 22-minute attraction is bursting with Audio-Animatronics figures that bring motion-picture legends and moments from almost every genre astonishingly to life. It's "Chim Chim Cher-ee" meets "Here's looking at you, kid," cigarette-puffing Clint Eastwood meets broom-brandishing Wicked Witch of the West, *Alien* meets *Singin' in the Rain*, and then some—be prepared for surprises. The ride has meticulous detailing and astonishing realism. Notice, for example, how Julie Andrews' throat vibrates as she sings. If you think of it, look for the Hidden Mickey in the window above the bank in the gangster scene. The Great Movie Ride draws large crowds all day long. However, with queues that wind past some ruby slipper–caliber props and a screening of famous movie scenes, it is also one of the most entertaining waits in Walt Disney World. (Note: It takes about 25 minutes to reach the ride vehicles when the line extends to the theater entrance.)

Heading through Hollywood Plaza toward Echo Lake, the next attraction you encounter is **SuperStar Television**. Remember it as one that simply goes for the laugh and gets it. Good fun whether you're in the limelight or in the audience, the 30-minute variety show merges live action with original film clips to slip audience volunteers into scenes from classic television programs. Most stars are chosen by a casting director in the pre-show area, others in the 1,000-seat theater (situate yourself toward the front to increase your odds). One of the more choice adult roles up for grabs: the Al Borland part opposite Tim "the Tool Man" Taylor in a scene from "Home

Improvement" (raise your hand if the emcee asks for a guy who's handy). Although the experience changes with the cast, SuperStar Television always weighs in somewhere between a good chuckle and a muffled guffaw. This attraction can be enjoyed any time of day; note that changes may be in the works.

Right next to SuperStar Television is the **The ABC Sound Studio**, an updated 15-minute affair in which recruits attempt to create the whimsical sound effects for a couple of short cartoons. In its new incarnation, guest volunteers are responsible for every boink, bonk, and whistle. Even the most diligent end up making some off notes, but that's part of the fun. Interestingly, many of the sound-effects gizmos used and displayed here are the creations of Jimmy Macdonald, Disney's man of 20,000 gadgets.

Note that the Soundsations booths (located in the small interactive area called SoundWorks, just outside the theater) here are among the neatest things in Walt Disney World. These inconspicuous rooms feature 3-D audio effects so realistic you will swear someone is cutting your hair, placing a newspaper hat on your head, or whispering in your ear. You *have* to try it.

If you are an action-movie connoisseur, it's worth risking life and limb to catch a showing of the **Indiana Jones Epic Stunt Spectacular**. Arrive a good 40 minutes before showtime to snare a seat toward the front of this 2,000-seat amphitheater. The half-hour performance steals its thunder from *Raiders of the Lost Ark* and begins with the selection of a few fearless "extras" (they're put to use during a scene involving a sword fight in Cairo). Nimble stuntpeople perform one death-defying caper after another, leaping between buildings, dodging snipers and boulders, and eluding fiery explosions. You feel the heat of the flames, you fear for the Harrison Ford look-alike. Tricks of the trade are revealed, and you're *still* impressed. The Indiana Jones Epic Stunt Spectacular nearly always plays to capacity audiences, so your best bet for getting a great seat (not to mention staying cool) is the first or last show of the day. Keep in mind that seating begins 30 minutes prior to each show.

As exciting as the Indiana Jones Epic Stunt Spectacular is, the attraction just around the corner packs even more punch. At **Star Tours**, you don't sit in an amphitheater, you strap yourself into a flight simulator. You don't live vicariously through professional stuntpeople; you experience the extraordinary sensation of barreling through space at the speed of light for yourself. The premise: Enterprising droids R2D2 and C-3PO are working for a galactic travel agency whose fleet of spacecraft makes regular trips to the Moon of Endor. As luck

Hidden Mickey

In The Great Movie Ride, look at the window above the bank in the gangster scene.

Just Add Tap Shoes

One of the niftiest things at the Studios is a certain lamppost (yes, lamppost) on New York Street back by the Backlot Theater. It's not just any street fixture, mind you; this one has a (fiberglass) umbrella sticking out from it and a few well-placed sprinkler heads. Simply grab hold of the umbrella's handle and you'll have all the precipitation you need to pretend you're Gene Kelly in *Singin' in the Rain*.

would have it, you draw a rookie pilot who gives new meaning to reckless abandon. Soon you're spiraling through deep space, dodging lasers and giant ice crystals. Be prepared for an intense five-minute ride that encompasses a lot of bucking, tilting, and other jerky, disorienting movements.

Star Tours is an incredible experience—one of those don't-miss-unless-you-have-a-very-good-reason attractions. (Among the very good reasons: just ate, heart condition, pregnancy, back problems, suscepti-ble to motion sickness, other physical limitations.) This ride is also a good test of how you'll fare on its Epcot equivalent, Body Wars, a thrilling journey through the human body with visuals that are some-times even quicker to trigger a yen for Dramamine. Star Tours is frequently mobbed; shortest lines are generally in the morning, with waits of about 30 min-utes the remainder of the day.

New York Street

Moving along, you arrive at the Studios' back corner. This is a glimpse of Manhattan as it used to look, with a few alterations having to do with the Empire State Build-ing's dimensions and the size of the puppet population.

You're here for one thing: the fabulously entertaining, special effects–laden presentation of **Jim Henson's Muppet*Vision 3-D**. Miss it and you've deprived your sense of humor. So head straight for the Muppet theater and fill up on a 25-minute stream of amusing Muppet antics that push the creative envelope of 3-D movies with such effects as a cannon blast through the screen, some bub-ble magic, and a floating banana cream pie. (Yes, the curmudgeons from "The Muppet Show" are in attendance, in their familiar balcony spot, wry and cyni-cal as ever. And yes, we've actually seen a 45-year-old man lift his 3-D glasses several times during a showing.)

Okay, we lied. There's another reason you're here. As you leave the Mup-pets, veer right to reach the Backlot Theater. Here, beneath the blissful shade of a canopy, you'll slip away to 15th-century Paris for **Disney's The Hunchback of Notre Dame—A Musical Adventure**, a 32-minute reprise of the Disney ani-mated feature. In this rendition, gypsies imaginatively reenact the tale of the world's most famous bell ringer, Quasimodo, and his selfless acts in the name of love. If not for the music, vibrant sets, and artful staging, go for the comical gargoyles (Victor, Hugo, and Laverne) who act as Quasimodo's collective con-science. Special effects are first-rate: Esmeralda arrives in a puff of smoke and a cauldron of fire pours from a balcony. Note that shows start late morning.

From the Backlot Theater, walk straight toward New York Street, where you can take in the skyline or sit down on a stoop. A sign in the window of our favorite

brownstone cautions NO SOLICITING, but it says nothing about stoop trespassing. So we take a seat, do some people-watching, or simply gaze at the Empire State Building. Disney apparently used a technique called forced perspective to make the 4-story version here appear to have 104 floors. (We can't help but muse about what would happen if the fashion industry applied this forced perspective principle to petite clothing.) If passersby ask you for directions, it's good to know that the **Honey, I Shrunk the Kids Movie Set Adventure** playground is behind one of the facades here. And if they want to know where to find the Toy Story Pizza Planet arcade, tell them it's right across from the Muppet theater.

Entertainment

Disney's Tinseltown sticks close to its Hollywood heritage in its roster of live entertainment. Because the marquee is ever changing, it's essential to consult a guidemap. You are sure to run into budding starlets, gossip columnists, and the like along Hollywood Boulevard. On any given day, there may be a visiting celebrity about. At 2 P.M., a 14-minute stream of off-the-wall characters from the animated film *Hercules* pays tribute to that mythological hunk and brings ancient Greece to the Studios' parade route. During seasons when the park is open late, the ten-minute Sorcery in the Sky, one of Disney's best fireworks shows, lights up the horizon behind the Chinese Theater, complete with music from classic films, including Disney's *Fantasia*. Last but hardly least: Fantasmic!—Disneyland's 25-minute pyrotechnic dazzler—will premiere this fall in a new lagoon-endowed theater behind Tower of Terror. Expect lasers, dancing fountains, and amazing special effects synchronized to classic Disney tunes.

DISNEY'S ANIMAL KINGDOM

So strong is this park's sense of purpose that it's as if the animals of the world put their antlers and antennae together and created it themselves—to celebrate their aardvarks-to-zebras diversity, remind us of their prehistoric heritage, and rally support for wildlife conservation efforts. Not that Disney's creative hand isn't greatly evident in this park, five times the size of the Magic Kingdom (and easily the company's biggest ticket item to date). In fact, when Animal Kingdom opens in May, it won't merely expand the dimensions of a Walt Disney World vacation. It will usher the theme park genre into wholly uncharted territory.

How so? This park is something of an African wildlife preserve, an interactive natural history museum, and a conservation-minded retreat rolled into one. The natural world predominates. And not just on the surface. Endangered species breeding programs coexist with blockbuster attractions. Sophisticated Audio-Animatronics dinosaurs share the marquee with more than 1,000 animals (some 200 species), whose habitat needs dictate much of the landscape. Dinosaur fossils are abundant; plastic coffee stirrers and Styrofoam, conspicuously absent.

Animal Kingdom's biggest attraction, Kilimanjaro Safaris, delivers the high adventure of the African classic, with a bonus: the chance to race across the savanna, chasing ivory poachers. Enter Disney's Africa and you can essentially put a check mark next to that travel fantasy. The transportive powers of elephants and other signature African creatures roaming en masse are not to be denied. And you haven't gotten acquainted with lions and cheetahs until you've been mere yards away, with no visible separation between you and them. While the safari is perhaps the best example of the inventive realism and evocative entertainment style that define the park's most adult attractions, it's hardly the last word.

The thematic center of Animal Kingdom is—bongo drumroll, please—The Tree of Life, a 14-story monument to creatures large and small, with more than 300 carvings. Call it the animal version of "I claim this land in the name of...."

GUIDING PRINCIPLES: The pages that follow are designed to provide a thorough initiation to this new addition to Disney's theme park circuit. The fact is, even folks who could find their way from Space Mountain to Pirates of the Caribbean with bags over their heads will be starting from square one when this WDW frontier opens to homo sapiens in May. Structured as a guided walking tour through the three themed "lands" that comprise the park, this section offers a geographic orientation to Animal Kingdom while also taking stock of attractions as they relate to adults.

For at-a-glance recommendations, the Touring Priorities list in the margin on page 136 ranks the park's best adult bets. Note: This edition's evaluations of Animal Kingdom attractions are based on pre-opening appraisals; know that subtle tweaking by Imagineers may heighten certain experiences beyond expectations. To learn the most efficient touring strategies, consult the Hot Tips in the margins of this section and the flexible tour plan provided in the *Planning Ahead* chapter. For details on how to get to Animal Kingdom via Walt Disney World transportation or by car, turn to the "Getting Around" section of the *Planning Ahead* chapter. For brief descriptions of shops worth perusing in this corner of the World, see the "Shopping" section of the *Diversions* chapter. And finally, to find out the park's best bets for dining, refer to the evaluative "Restaurant Guide" in the *Dining & Entertainment* chapter.

GETTING ORIENTED: Although greenery reigns in Animal Kingdom, resigning concrete, and indeed most architecture, to garnish status, successful penetration of this particular jungle requires no compasses, scythes, or snakebite kits. (Do work on your Tarzan call, however.) The park is set up as a series of themed lands decidedly unlike any you've encountered in the Magic Kingdom. To see the forest through the trees, look up: Like the icons of its Worldly siblings, Animal Kingdom's Tree of Life serves as an instant beacon for the momentarily disoriented. It also anchors the park's most central land, Safari Village.

The layout of Animal Kingdom might be compared to the silhouette of a simple flower. Acting as the stem is the lush expanse of The Oasis. The character area, off to the immediate left (west), is a low-lying leaf. Safari Village (the land that serves as the park's hub), encircled by Discovery River, is the flower's center. And extending from the center like petals are bridges leading northwest to Africa, the park's largest land, and sharply southeast to the primeval area known as DinoLand U.S.A. By the end of 1998, a third petal will unfold with the introduction of Asia, on the right-hand side of Safari Village, due northwest of DinoLand U.S.A. In several years, a fourth petal will extend southwest of Safari Village to a new land.

It's true that Disney's Animal Kingdom is more than double the size of Epcot. But thanks to the considerable roaming room designated for residents only, it takes no more legwork to circumnavigate this park than to explore Future World and World Showcase. As anyone who's been to Epcot can attest, this is still a good amount of walking—so follow our efficient touring plan and take advantage of the many pleasant resting spots throughout the park. For respite in the form of a

HOT TIPS

■ Expect Animal Kingdom's stature as Disney's newest and biggest park to translate into tremendous attendance, and attempt to visit during a less crowded time of year (see "When to Go" in *Planning Ahead*).

■ Since operating hours were not set at press time, be sure to call 824-4321 for schedules and to find out if there is a designated early-entry day for this park.

■ Weekends are expected to be the most crowded days at Animal Kingdom.

scenic overview, remember the Discovery River Boats, which call regularly at Safari Village and at Upcountry Landing, a dock near Africa. Seniors who opt to tour the smaller parks on foot may prefer to rent a wheelchair or a self-driven Electric Convenience Vehicle (ECV) here at Animal Kingdom.

A Walking Tour

Our tour begins much like any other intrepid adventure, assuming that intrepid adventurers have inexplicably omitted mention of the turnstiles that must be traversed en route from urbane Central Florida to the Great Unknown. No matter. You're about to be enveloped by **The Oasis**, a lush canopy of nature that serves as the Animal Kingdom's inviting foyer. Several paths (pick one, any one) lead north to Safari Village and the looming Tree of Life. Before you proceed further into the fragrant tangle of tropical trees and flowers, where you're bound to be distracted by waterfall-laden streams and glimpses of flamingos, deer, tree kangaroos, iguanas, and giant anteaters, *stop!* Tell yourself it's all a mirage and pause long enough to pick up a guidemap at Guest Relations. You don't have to cool your jets for any other practicalities, unless you're picking up some wheels for the day, renting a video camera, visiting the lost and found, or picking up a package.

As in the rest of the park, Disney has endowed The Oasis with borders infinitely more discreet than turnstiles, creating the illusion that you've somehow entered that rare animals-are-drawn-to-me realm inhabited by Audubon and Snow White. It's tempting to linger, but this is better done later in the day, when there's no rush to beat the masses to Animal Kingdom's biggest thrill rides, Kilimanjaro Safaris and Countdown to Extinction.

Emerging from the northern reaches of The Oasis, you arrive at a bridge to the island of Safari Village and receive your cue to gasp—a panoramic view of Animal Kingdom's central land, the moatlike Discovery River, the soaring Tree of Life, and the glorious balance of the park before you. Whether you gasp or launch into a tale about the time you stood at just such an overlook and outsmarted a lion, you should also take a minute to glance at the **Tip Board**, a blackboard listing current waiting times for popular attractions.

Safari Village

Exotic in a neither-here-nor-there-but-certainly-not-North-American sense, Safari Village is awash in the sort of vivid color paintbrushes dream about imparting. Meticulously carved and painted building facades and smatterings

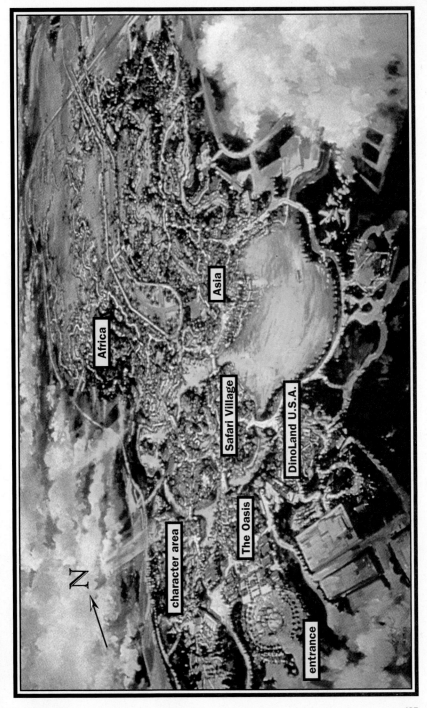

Touring Priorities

of African and Caribbean folk art add to the eye-catching allure of environs intended to replicate a village in the Tropics. Notable as the land that serves as the gateway to all other Animal Kingdom lands, it's also the park's core dining and shopping zone (for humans, at least; the animals steer clear of fast food).

The biggest attraction in Safari Village—quite obviously **The Tree of Life**—is as awe-inspiring on close inspection as it is from afar. The man-made, banyan-like tree looms 140 feet over the Animal Kingdom as it's central icon. Even dung beetles have their place on this arboreal masterpiece, whose 50-foot-wide trunk and windblown limbs contain nose-to-nose carvings of every animal Disney artists could fit. Certainly, Mickey's lineage is represented. The carvings are an elaborate tribute to the richness and diversity of animal life on earth. To get a better look at them, do your best imitation of a dachshund that thinks it's a giraffe. Also, be especially nice to anyone carrying binoculars—there's a lot to be seen. Don't neglect to check out the red kangaroos, ring-tailed lemurs, white storks, and other wildlife exhibits near the base of the tree and elsewhere in Safari Village.

Before you leave The Tree of Life, consider the possible advantages of starting small. If you can bear six minutes of larger-than-life insects creeping and crawling into your personal space, plan to see a later showing of *It's Tough to Be a Bug*, a 3-D film shown in a 450-seat auditorium (where else but inside the tree). You may suddenly cease to be fazed by any creature with fewer than six legs.

For a dose of serenity with a few surprises thrown in as reminders that you're cruising in Disney (and hence Audio-Animatronics) territory, embark on a **Discovery River Boats** voyage. The fire-breathing dragon lurking in the river foreshadows the introduction of Animal Kingdom's fifth land, still several years away. Whether you board here in Safari Village or at Upcountry Landing near Africa (boats launch approximately every ten minutes), you're privy to a thorough overview of the park, as the coolly refreshing trip closely follows the shores of Safari Village, Africa, DinoLand U.S.A., and what's soon to be Asia.

If you want to convene with animals more accustomed to standing still for pictures, the trail heading left (west) of

Safari Village goes to a character area, where nothing but a touch of humility stands between you and shaking hands with the biggest britches from *The Lion King*, *The Jungle Book*, and other Disney films. If you decide to take this detour, do it outside the park's prime migration periods (opening and closing) and note that you may encounter more than you bargained for—namely, alfresco frolicking and singing by characters from *The Lion King*. Shows and character appearances are scattered throughout the day.

DinoLand U.S.A.

As you pass underneath the immense brachiosaurus skeleton and into what appears to be a kitschy park created around a remote archaeological dig site, picture this: armadillos, having suavely inherited the earth, filing under a human skeleton at the entrance to HumanLand U.S.A. theme park. Kind of a nifty perspective, eh? Anyway, this wryly wrought, thought-provoking land feels decidedly removed from Walt Disney World, like a little-known curiosity off Route 66. Attractions feature intimate rendezvous with winners (suave armadillos) as well as sore losers of the Cretaceous period's Survival of the Meteorproof. The biggie, sure to elicit lots of white lies ("I didn't even flinch") and skepticism ("Yeah, right"): **Countdown to Extinction**, an exciting time-travel journey fraught with errant asteroids and frightening run-ins with Disney's largest and most realistic Audio-Animatronics figures yet.

A five-minute thrill attraction sure to earn raves, Countdown to Extinction is found inside the Dino Institute, a staid building that reveals nothing of the fast, jarring, and heart-pounding ride ahead. Of course, there's a larger mission that has nothing to do with any personal desire for an adrenaline rush and everything to do with selfless intentions to save the last of the iguanodons. (Don't worry, we'll explain.) Basically, you have it on good authority that if you shoot 65 million years back in time, pronto, there's a chance you can rescue the iguanodons from the meteor showers thought to have sealed their fate and ended the Cretaceous period. So you strap yourself into the vehicle, and think about what you'll say to the 16-foot-tall creatures when you get there. Need a lift? You *are* a vegetarian, right?

And so it is that you find yourself in this perilous race against time, ducking meteors and attempting to blink away encroaching nonvegetarian dinosaurs as your vehicle rages out of control. Just when you think you've spied some friendly faces in the crowd, you notice the nostril-flaring carnotaurus hot on your tail. This would be the climax. What happens next, alas, is for us to know and for you to find out. Countdown to Extinction is not to be

The Better to See Them With

Have a pair of binoculars? The 14-story Tree of Life is reason to tote them along—unless you like craning your neck. There are over 300 animals carved into the tree, and you want to be able to see the ones at the top.

Quiet Nooks

missed (unless, of course, you have dinophobia, are pregnant, suffer from back or neck problems, or have a heart condition).

The winding **Cretaceous Trail** nearby offers a much tamer inroad to this bygone era—and a bit of shade to boot. Along this pathway, you'll discover frogs, turtles, lizards, and other animals whose ancestors were dinosaurs' compatriots. And believe it or not, some of the plants are the sorts once favored by iguanodons. Searching for dinosaur clues, you'll also see the evolution of a dig site as you pass several in various stages.

Because it's rare that you get a chance to compare shoe sizes with a dinosaur, traipse over an arch made of dinosaur bones (Olden Gate Bridge), and unearth the fossils of a woolly mammoth, **The Boneyard** is worth a passing glance, even if it is a playground. So cross your arms as if you were supervising the dig. And as you watch for a park curator to come around with an interesting animal in tow, listen up as diggers uncover clues to how the woolly mammoth died (hint: it wasn't Professor Plum in the conservatory with the lead pipe).

Africa

If imitation is the sincerest form of flattery, then Africa has got to be blushing. In creating this largest section of the park, bigger than the Magic Kingdom, Disney seems to have stopped just shy of moving mountains (Kilimanjaro is conspicuously missing). The artfully reconstructed African savanna and woodland aren't merely stunning to behold. They're designed to satisfy the habitat specifications of each meerkat, zebra, and elephant. Countless trips to the continent, exhaustive planning, and some slick adaptations have enabled Disney to mesh the intimacy of a zoo with the aura of a safari.

Disney's Africa is truly a land of opportunities. Among them: treading just yards from cavorting gorillas, observing rhinos, gazelles, and hippos en masse, exchanging glances with a passing giraffe, getting up to speed on wildlife protection and conservation efforts, and chasing renegade ivory poachers.

Of course, you don't cross the bridge from Safari Village and find yourself suddenly surrounded by gorillas and elephants. You acclimate to the continent in the atmospheric village of **Harambe**, patterned after coastal communities in East Africa. Harambe is important as the best spot for food, drink, and shopping during your stay in Africa. It's also the gateway to the land's several exceptional attractions.

Kilimanjaro Safaris, Disney's enticing variation on the classic African travel adventure, is the one to beat a path to straightaway. The guided trip through a simulated Serengeti escorts you within boasting distance of many of the world's most beloved animals—so close you'll begin to wonder which of the 32

people in your open-air gawkmobile (as we've loosely dubbed the roofed, rugged transportation of choice) has unsuppressible animal magnetism. As the vehicle bumps along the dust-caked road, you'll observe large herds on the move; watch for elephants, gazelles, rhinos, baboons, and lions. Such animals as giraffes and zebras may draw quite near. Your guide will fill you in on less familiar species; for a preview, steal quick glances at the species identification cheat sheet on the seatback in front of you. These animals have room to roam and thus better things to do than stare back at you—graze, frolic, yawn, pick fights, tend their young, head for the water hole, and socialize, for starters.

As we see it, this not-to-be-missed safari has five advantages over the real thing, proximity aside. (1) This African landscape was designed to provide good vantage points of animals' stomping grounds. (2) The rocky road is for effect only; the prime photo junctures are smooth. (3) Creature comforts

Coming Attractions

Late this year, Animal Kingdom's fourth land (and second continent) is expected to debut. With Asia comes a rough-and-tumble raft ride and a self-guided wildlife discovery trail through a replica of a Southeast Asian rain forest. An amphitheater will offer a variety of animal shows. Asia is located northeast of Safari Village, beside Africa, and can be glimpsed in its formative stages on a Discovery River Boats cruise. The fire-breathing dragon in these waters marks the territory of Animal Kingdom's fifth land, slated to open several years from now southwest of Safari Village.

Did you know...

■ The carvings on The Tree of Life represent only about 300 of the 1.4 million existing species.

■ Disney has established the Disney Wildlife Conservation Fund to help nonprofit organizations protect and study endangered and threatened animals and their habitats.

■ Most of the animals at Animal Kingdom were born in other zoological parks throughout the country. Many of the animals are registered in special breeding programs called SSPs (Species Survival Programs).

■ Walt Disney World recently eliminated most of its insecticide use, replacing chemicals with millions of harmless predatory insects—many of which are bred at The Land pavilion at Epcot.

(i.e., favorite vegetation for four-footed snackers) are strategically located to provide up-close encounters with the animals. (4) Just because giraffes and other harmless species can come near enough to read the words on your T-shirt (doubtful, given the literacy rate), that doesn't necessarily mean the cheetahs or lions can. Virtually undetectable separations ensure that predatory types maintain a safe distance from people. So you needn't sweat it when a fierce-looking cat licks its chops while staring rather precisely in your direction. (5) Adventure is built into the experience. In addition to being a virtual who's who of animal crackers, Kilimanjaro Safaris is an unpredictable ride in which close calls are as endemic as close encounters.

Throughout the 25-minute journey, you hear reports from a bush pilot flying overhead. Suddenly your guide breaks from the planned route and you embark on a furious chase for ivory poachers in the area. As you track the renegades over a rickety bridge, it begins to bow under, nearly spooning you and your safariing friends into the open mouths of genuine, snap-happy crocodiles. The vehicle careens as it speeds through a narrow, water-filled canyon. You wind up at the Ranger Station, where in addition to the poachers' fate you learn that you're a good distance from your starting point in Harambe. Fortunately, we know of a great self-guided path that leads back to the village.

Also accessible from Harambe, **Gorilla Falls Exploration Trail** segues from the research lab context of the Ranger Station to the enchanting environs of a free-flight aviary and an aquarium filled with exotic fish. A little farther down, you'll come upon a clear stream dammed with glass—the site of a synchronized swimming demonstration by hippos. Okay, so maybe it's not synchronized. But the buoyant beasts don't have to wear nose plugs to be amusing to observe in their underwater glory. Even so, we know what you're thinking: "Are we there yet? Where are the gorillas?" Rest assured, the chest thumpers are close at hand.

There's more to see before you reach the gorilla sanctuary, however, namely a scenic overlook of the savanna and an ensemble of warthogs and meerkats extemporaneously demonstrating their fine chemistry. After walking over a suspension bridge, you arrive in the gorilla valley, and begin turning your head U.S. Open–style to take in the appreciable antics of the family brood and the bachelor brood now flanking you. What does it feel like to walk alongside these expressive creatures with only a "bamboo" fence standing between you and their *Planet of the Apes* physiques? Privileged.

Back in Harambe, you'll find the depot for the **Wildlife Express to Conservation Station**, a narrated train tour that chugs quietly behind the scenes of Africa, providing a reverse perspective of Kilimanjaro Safaris along with insights to the park's inner workings. For those in a hurry to take a load off their feet, it offers a leisurely lift to and from **Conservation Station**, the attraction that serves as Animal Kingdom's ideological cornerstone. The park's center for wildlife preservation efforts and veterinary care (potential baby animals alert!), it acts as a sweeper of sorts, crystallizing the environmental themes presented in the other areas of the park, and encouraging active support of wildlife programs while the safari's still fresh.

If EcoWeb, a WWW computer link to international conservation organizations, is the most practical of Conservation Station's hands-on exhibits, the Animal Cams are the ones David Letterman would doubtless make a beeline for; in the latter, you zoom, tilt, and pan any of some 20 cameras set up to surreptitiously monitor activity in animals' "backstage" areas. (And you thought they didn't study their lines.) Another highlight is Song of the Rainforest, a binaural booth that lets you vicariously experience the drama of the Amazon with nothing more than a simple headset. The interactive video displays of Planet Watch (Endangered Animals 101) and Eco Heroes (Meet the Conservationist) are potential points of interest. Animal Health & Care, a walking tour through the park's working veterinary facilities, can be fascinating, depending on what's happening the day you visit. Overcome by an urgent need to make some tails wag? Follow the tykes to The Affection Section, where you can scratch some tame ones behind the ears.

Entertainment

A small lineup of stage shows supplements the inherently entertaining antics of the animals. Performances are held throughout the day in DinoLand U.S.A.'s 1,500-seat, covered Theater in the Wild. The park's repertoire will grow, soon after the park's official opening, to include bird and other animal shows in the Caravan Stage amphitheater. The theater, which is located in the area that will become Asia later this year, is slated to have half the capacity of Theater in the Wild. Pick up a guidemap at Guest Relations for schedules of these shows and any other featured entertainment.

A Disney Institute vacation can lend insight into how topiaries are made.

Diversions: Sports, Shopping & Other Pursuits

It's a cool April morning and you are posing for a picture with an eight-pound largemouth bass. You've caught so many fish over the past two hours you're wondering if given more time, you couldn't hook them all. You'd signed on for this guided catch-and-release fishing trip around Seven Seas Lagoon expecting a relaxing morning on the water and a few polite nibbles, but here you are, no more than a few hundred yards from Disney's posh Grand Floridian resort, catching bass that require muscle. And this is not an isolated occurrence. Though fishing may not be the first sport that comes to mind when you think of the Royal Mousedom (that would be golf), in angling circles Walt Disney World is fondly known as the theme park metropolis with world-class bass fishing. In lay terms that means big fish (and a lot of them) showing a great time to even the most inexperienced angler who drops them a line.

. . .

It is nearing 10 P.M. on a January night, and a group of sophisticated shoppers are fawning over such things as shortbread baked in the image of Mickey Mouse's shorts. One of them wants Mickey-shaped pasta, while another has a $100 Mickeyfied teakettle under one arm. A third is off playing credit card bingo with Disney-characterized Christmas ornaments and office accoutrements. If the shops at the Downtown Disney Marketplace don't close their

Unless otherwise noted, all phone numbers are in area code 407.

doors soon, these purchases are not going to fit through them. We've made a startling discovery about the shopping scene at Walt Disney World: It can throw unsuspecting adults into a frenzy. The bottom line: Shops here are loaded with nicely evolved character goods and lots more merchandise (labels such as Waterford and Liz Claiborne, for example) that's simply way beyond kid stuff.

. . .

It is the evening of your first day at the Disney Institute, and you've already learned the ropes of rock climbing, tried your hand—and voice—at animation, and overcome your insecurities about wine. You suspect that you've received somewhere in the neighborhood of ten times the Recommended Daily Allowance of stimulation, and wouldn't mind repeating the feat tomorrow. You want to try that healthy cooking program your rock-climbing partner was raving about, catch the afternoon lecture, anchor a television news show, and schedule some quality time at the spa. Tomorrow's another day, and at this invigorating experiential resort devoted to hands-on discovery, another grand buffet of temptations.

Here's the point: The World beyond the major theme parks offers a slew of terrific diversions that, interspersed between park visits, help establish perfect symmetry in a well-rounded Walt Disney World vacation. Once you get over the shock of finding such activities here in the first place, you're still pinching yourself because the quality of the experiences is so astonishingly good. In other words, even more world-class playgrounds for adults (thoroughly described on the following pages) exist within the world-class playground that is Walt Disney World.

We're just hinting at the possibilities when we mention golf courses widely considered among the country's best; state-of-the-art tennis facilities, health clubs, and spas; and the spectators' dream known as Disney's Wide World of Sports—all perfect examples of Disney's ability to dazzle in the most unexpected arenas. On the shopping front, tantalizing new shops (including a collection of character-defying options at Downtown Disney West Side) are popping up propertywide. Defying the term *diversion* is the Disney Institute, a vacation realm unto itself. Add the last word in water parks, including the world's tallest water slide and one of the largest wave pools, and the list is still incomplete. For a full inventory of distractions (the categories: sports, shopping, and other pursuits) so compelling you'll wonder why anyone bothers with those theme parks, read on.

SPORTS

O kay, sports fans, it's time for our play-by-play guide to Walt Disney World. First and foremost, you can play some of the finest golf courses in the country. There are 99 holes here (available in increments of 9 or 18), and you can take your pick from five designer-name par 72s that both individually and together have earned hosannas from *Golf Magazine* and *Golf Digest*. And as we can personally attest, you need not possess a smidgen of ability in order to enjoy yourself. Whatever your skill or mood, there's a course in Walt Disney World's diverse lineup to suit; each venue is a unique challenge, and opportunities abound to test your mettle on fairways that have humbled the pros.

You can also play some serious (or casual) tennis on the most advanced surface that exists—right here at Disney's Racquet Club or The Villas at the Disney Institute. You can angle for largemouth bass weighing eight pounds or more (waterways here are teeming with trophy-scale bass). You can rent boats and bikes galore. And last but not least, you can swim yourself into a waterlogged prune. In other words, you are not lacking for sporting opportunities. All of these playful options plus a few more, including health clubs, jogging, spas, and spectator sports (what can we say, it's a big World out there), are fully detailed in the sections that follow. Of course, you can also choose to play couch potato, although after you know your options, it will doubtless require some willpower.

Golf

D isney's 99-hole "Magic Linksdom"—second only to the Mouse in drawing power—is renowned for the challenge, variety, and fairness of its courses. Walt Disney World has become a familiar name on *Golf Magazine*'s biennial list of the best golf resorts in the country. *Golf Digest* has tabbed four of the World's five par-72 courses as outstanding ("plan your next vacation around it") or very good ("worth getting off the interstate to play"). And noted golf writer Glen Waggoner is hardly alone in giving Mickey Mouse's backyard the nod as America's greatest golfing haven. In Waggoner's words, "Some other places have an individual course that is superior to any in Walt Disney World's lineup, but no other resort in the entire country has five courses this good." Solidifying this reputation are several tournaments: the PGA Tour's Walt Disney World/Oldsmobile Golf Classic, with over a quarter century behind it; the LPGA HealthSouth Inaugural, which debuted here

In the Rough

"There's a lot of wildlife around the Palm course's property," says a former Disney pro. "People have seen deer, otters, turkeys, bobcats, and even panthers. The other day, someone said he saw a couple of bald eagles."

Golf Rates

The following greens fees were in effect at press time for the WDW golf courses. Prices do not include tax and they are subject to change.

PALM, MAGNOLIA, LAKE BUENA VISTA

	PEAK 1/19–4/26	NONPEAK 4/27–1/18
Day Visitor	$115	$100*
Resort Guest	$100	$90*
Twilight**	$57	$50*

OSPREY RIDGE, EAGLE PINES

	PEAK 1/19–4/26	NONPEAK 4/27–1/18
Day Visitor	$135	$120*
Resort Guest	$120	$105*
Twilight**	$68	$60*

* Summer discounts (May 24 through August 31) lower rates for all WDW courses to $45 as of 9 A.M. for WDW resort guests, 10 A.M. for day visitors.

** Twilight rates begin at 3 P.M. during much of the year, starting up to an hour earlier in certain seasons.

in January 1995; and the Dave Pelz World Putting Championship, which began in December 1996.

Depending upon the tee box chosen, the immaculately kept Disney courses provide challenging or relaxed play; while the layouts are quite distinct in their design, they are all constructed to be especially forgiving for the mid-handicap player. Of the original three Joe Lee–designed courses, the Palm and the Magnolia get the most attention, but the Lake Buena Vista is a popular layout that more than holds its own. Tucked into a corner of the Magnolia is Oak Trail, a par-36 walking course especially suited to beginners. Rounding out the mix are the two challenging venues added in 1992—the Tom Fazio–designed Osprey Ridge and the Pete Dye–designed Eagle Pines.

KNOW BEFORE YOU GO: WDW's peak golfing season extends from January through April. During this period it is especially important to secure reservations well in advance for play in the morning and early afternoon (though starting times after 2 P.M. are usually available at the last minute). Tee times are extremely difficult if not impossible to get during the LPGA HealthSouth tournament (January); during the third and fourth weeks of January, when some 30,000 truly serious golfers descend on the area for the PGA of America's Merchandise Show; and during the WDW/Oldsmobile Golf Classic (October). The Citrus Bowl (January) and Daytona 500 (February) also have proven capable of filling the courses rather quickly, and also beware when a Super Bowl is scheduled anywhere in Florida. During such busy periods, the advance reservations and guaranteed tee times afforded by golf packages can be absolutely indispensable (call 934-7639 for package details).

Rates: Greens fees for the 18-hole courses vary according to when you visit (peak versus nonpeak seasons), which course you play (Osprey Ridge and Eagle Pines are more expensive, but only during peak season), and your guest status (WDW resort guests and Magic Kingdom Club members get a break). A detailed breakdown of rates is provided at left. Basically, though, you can count on paying $90 to $135 per round, including the required cart. The most dramatic savings can be had by teeing off in the late afternoon, when twilight rates afford savings of 50% or more. At Oak Trail, a nine-hole walking course, play is $24 for one round or $32 for two. From May 1 through October 31, season badges ($50) provide substantial savings by allowing golfers to pay just $35 to $50 per round (depending on the season) for unlimited play after 10 A.M., including cart; badges are also good for admission to the Walt Disney World/Oldsmobile Golf Classic.

Reservations: Anyone buying a golf package may reserve tee times up to 90 days ahead. Golfers who book lodging at any on-property resort can secure tee times up to 60 days in advance of their check-in date. For everyone else, the window of opportunity is 30 days in advance when booked with a credit card, or 7 days without a credit card guarantee. The practical effect of these rules is that it's very difficult, if not impossible, for guests staying outside WDW borders to obtain prime tee times during the busiest weeks. Also note that four golfers are assigned to each starting time, so singles and pairs may very well be matched up. To book tee times call WDW-GOLF (939-4653).

Transportation: Complimentary taxi service to the Palm, Magnolia, Osprey Ridge, Eagle Pines, and Lake Buena Vista courses is available from any WDW resort. The taxis work on a voucher system.

Dress: Proper golf attire is required on all courses. Shirts must have collars, and if shorts are worn they must be Bermuda length.

A New Lease on Mini Golf

Leave it to Disney to create a pair of 18-hole miniature golf courses that eschew the typical tackiness for clever designs, both fanciful and devious. The *Fantasia*-themed Fantasia Gardens complex—located adjacent to the Swan, Dolphin, and BoardWalk resorts—even has a course worthy of serious golfers. Cost per round on either course is $9. Hours are 10 A.M. to midnight, with some seasonal variations.

■ **Fantasia Fairways** (play time: about 1½ hours) is ruled by daunting doglegs, sand traps, water traps, par 3s, and par 4s. Astute players may notice shrunken signature holes from famous links. The toughest tee: number 12, a par 4 with such fierce banking that all balls are destined to hit water. At press time, only one person had made par.

■ At **Fantasia Gardens** (play time: about an hour), whimsical tees offer odes to *Fantasia*. En route, balls hit chimes and xylophone stairs, and spur water spouts and fife playing, not to mention hippo dancing.

Tee Time

Want to increase your chances of getting on one of the courses? Heed the following:

■ Try to play on Monday or Tuesday

■ Tee off in late afternoon

■ Come in the summer (when special rates are available)

Equipment rental: Good-quality gear, including Callaway clubs ($40 for graphite shaft, $30 for steel), range balls ($5 a bucket), and Footjoy shoes ($6), is available for rent at all WDW pro shops.

INSTRUCTION: Players looking to discover or improve their game have several options: one-on-one instruction, swing analysis sessions, and playing lessons. At the Walt Disney World Golf Studio, based at the Palm and Magnolia, PGA professionals offer 45-minute sessions that concentrate on improving players' swings through video analysis; cost is $75. Nine-hole playing lessons, in which a PGA pro provides on-course instruction, delve into strategy, club selection, and short game skills, as well as the psychological side of golf; cost is $150. Private lessons are available for $50 per half hour. Reservations are required for all lessons; call WDW-GOLF (939-4653).

The Bonnet Creek Golf Club, based at Eagle Pines and Osprey Ridge, has a new draw in the Callaway Golf Experience, a state-of-the-art machine that allows golfers to compare different clubs and balls, as well as evaluate their swings. Call 888-223-7842 for more information or reservations (up to one month ahead); the 45-minute session is free.

The Disney Institute offers a first-rate golf instruction program at the Lake Buena Vista course. The multi-day immersion comprises two parts that may be taken separately: "Golf: The Game" emphasizes form, with video swing analysis; "In-Depth Golf" provides targeted advice for long-term improvement. Private lessons are available for $60; call 827-4455 for reservations. (Specifics are subject to change; for details on the Disney Institute, turn to page 172.)

TOURNAMENTS: The Walt Disney World/Oldsmobile Golf Classic, which draws top PGA Tour players every fall, is among the most celebrated events on Disney's sports calendar. The tournament has been a major magnet for golf fans since 1971 when, two months after Walt Disney World opened its gates, Jack Nicklaus won the inaugural event. Because the Classic is one of the last regular PGA Tour stops of the year (it's usually held in October; this year, 22–25), exciting competition is a given; pros are looking to vault themselves into the Tour Championship or secure their spots on the top 125 money list.

Venues for the four-day tournament have traditionally been the Palm, Magnolia, and Lake Buena Vista courses. During the first three days of the competition, the pros play each course once. After 54 holes, the field narrows to the low 70 pros, who compete for a cut of the tourney's $1.5 million purse in the final round, played on the Magnolia. Tickets are available on-site each day of the tournament, with one-day admission ranging from $5 for the first three rounds to $10 for the final round. Gallery badges for all four rounds are $20. Practice rounds (held several days before the tournament) are open to spectators at no cost. For more information, call 939-4653.

Those who are willing to pay big dues (starting at $5,150 for a one-year membership) can play the Classic alongside the pros. In exchange for their sponsorship, card-carrying members of the Classic Club play side by side with a different competing pro each day for the first three rounds of the tournament. Some memberships include lodging during the tournament, reduced greens fees on Disney courses for a year, and admission to the theme parks for a week. For additional details, call 939-4653.

The LPGA HealthSouth Inaugural is not the first-time event its title suggests. Rather, it's a circa-1995 event that draws its name from the fact that it is the first full-field event of the year (this year, January 17–19). The "new year's resolution" timing all but ensures a constellation of star players. The tourney is contested on the Lake Buena Vista course over three days, with a two-day pro-am preceding the event. For more information, call 939-4653.

The Dave Pelz World Putting Championship, still in its toddler years, allows amateurs to compete with pros, champions, and some celebrities for a $250,000 prize. The two-day tournament, held in December, is played on Eagle Pines and Osprey Ridge. Call 800-824-8899 for further information.

The Courses

PALM: This prickly yet picturesque course (located just west of the Polynesian resort, with the Magnolia to its immediate north) is marked by tight wooded fairways, a wealth of water hazards, and elevated greens and tees, which bear Joe Lee's unmistakable signature and make for challenging club selections. The par-72 Palm plays shorter and tighter than its mate, the Magnolia, and measures 5,398 yards from the front tees, 6,461 from the middle, and 6,957 from the back. The palm-dotted venue hosts the Walt Disney World/Oldsmobile Golf Classic, along with its fellow Lee designs (the Magnolia and the Lake Buena Vista courses). Of the holes garnering the most locker room curses (numbers 6, 10, and 18), the sixth, a 412-yard par 4, is the most notorious. There's a lake on the left, woods and swamp on the right, and more water between you and the two-tier green. The course—whose greens were rebuilt in 1993 from the drainage basin up—opened in 1971 with the Magnolia and the Magic Kingdom itself. Facilities shared by the Palm and the Magnolia include two driving ranges, two putting greens, and a pro shop. The Walt Disney World Golf Studio is also based here. Course record: 61 (Mark Lye, 1984).

Slope Scope

The slope ratings for the five Disney courses are: Osprey Ridge, 135; Magnolia, 133; Palm, 133; Eagle Pines, 131; Lake Buena Vista, 128. By way of comparison, an average slope rating is around 115. The famously challenging links at Pebble Beach check in at 139; the formidable TPC Stadium course at Ponte Vedra, at 135.

The Ten Most Humbling Holes

Cumulative toughest-playing Classic holes since 1983:

1. Palm No. 18
2. Palm No. 6
3. Palm No. 10
4. Lake Buena Vista No. 18
5. Magnolia No. 18
6. Palm No. 4
7. Magnolia No. 17
8. Magnolia No. 5
9. Lake Buena Vista No. 11
10. Magnolia No. 15

MAGNOLIA: Like the Palm, the Magnolia opened with the Magic Kingdom in 1971. It received a major face-lift in 1992. Course designer Joe Lee realigned teeing areas, recontoured greens, and replaced their original playing surface with a "faster" grass, among other things. The Magnolia features abundant water and sand, but what really sets it apart—aside from the 1,500 magnolia trees in its permanent gallery and the mouse-eared bunker beside the sixth green—is exceptional length, vast greens, and a flaw-exposing layout requiring precision and careful course management. Meandering over 175 acres of wetlands and gently rolling terrain, the par-72 course measures 5,232 yards from the front tees, 6,642 from the middle set, and 7,190 from the back markers. Among the signature holes is number 17, a long par-4 dogleg left that dares long hitters to bite off the edge of a lake, then avoid more water to the right of the green. It is the Magnolia that has final say in the outcome of the WDW/Oldsmobile Golf Classic, and it takes full advantage with a final hole that rates among the tournament's testiest. Among facilities shared by the Magnolia and the Palm are two driving ranges, two putting greens, and a pro shop. The WDW Golf Studio is also based here. Course record: 61 (Payne Stewart, 1990).

OAK TRAIL: This nine-hole par-36 walking course ensconced in a 45-acre corner of the Magnolia is worth noting as an unintimidating venue for beginners, yet it's no cream puff for better players. The 2,913-yard layout unleashes plenty of challenges—including two fine par 5s—and boasts especially well-maintained greens.

OSPREY RIDGE: Tom Fazio has taken his signature mounding along fairways and around greens to monumental heights here—most dramatically with a namesake ridge that meanders through the property and elevates some greens as high as 25 feet above the basic grade. The designer counts Osprey Ridge among his best efforts, and the sentiment is echoed in the course's considerable popularity among experienced golfers. The long par-72 layout winds through a beautifully remote and thickly forested part of the property near Fort Wilderness; it has a deceptively gentle start, then raises the stakes en route to its three great finishing holes. Along the way, players will confront the signature par-3 third hole, with its elevated tee, and the fierce 14th, a long par 4 with a carry over water. Osprey Ridge plays to 5,402 yards from the front tees, 6,680 from the middle, and 7,101 from the back. Facilities shared by Osprey Ridge and Eagle Pines include a driving range, a putting green, a pro shop, and a restaurant and lounge. Course record: 65 (Daniel Young, 1992).

EAGLE PINES: The subtle contours of this low-lying links provide a decided contrast to the dramatic landscaping of its companion course, Osprey Ridge, which also plays from the Bonnet Creek Golf Club. Designed by Pete Dye on a (successful) mission to create a unique challenge for players of all levels, Eagle Pines features target fairways, expansive waste areas, and roughs lined with pine needles. True to its rustic environs (it's located on the outskirts of Fort Wilderness), the course is sufficiently nestled in foliage and marshlands to summon comparisons to a nature preserve. Although water comes into play on 16 holes, the overall impression is one of great variety, from short par 4s to far sterner challenges—this is one course that lives up to the cliché of making you use every club in the bag. The course measures 4,838 yards from the front tees, 6,309 from the middle, and 6,772 yards from the back markers. Facilities shared by Eagle Pines and Osprey Ridge include a driving range, a putting green, a pro shop, and a restaurant and lounge. Course record: 60 (Bart Bryant, 1993).

LAKE BUENA VISTA: This Joe Lee design is a Rodney Dangerfield of sorts. The shortest of the five 18-hole courses, it features a good amount of water, and its fairways, hemmed in by stands of pine and oak, are Disney golf's tightest. Lake Buena Vista honors its reputation as a friendly course perfect for beginners. But it is also well equipped to challenge more skilled players (at least those who don't mind the wear and tear inflicted by duffers). As golf writer Glen Waggoner puts it, Lake Buena Vista may be the weakest link in the Disney chain, but it's still head and shoulders above the number two venue at most other golf resorts. The course's toughest holes—the second and ninth—are counted among the ten most humbling tests in the history of the WDW/Oldsmobile Golf Classic. But perhaps no one has greater respect for the course than Calvin Peete, who during the 1982 Classic blitzed the Palm in a record-breaking 66 strokes, only to give it all back—and more—on little ol' Lake Buena Vista. The course plays to 5,176 yards from the front tees, 6,268 from the middle, and 6,829 from the rearmost markers. Facilities at Lake Buena Vista include a driving range and a practice green. The course is immediately adjacent to the Disney Institute, and is therefore the base for its golf instruction programs, described on page 148. Course record: 61 (Bob Tway, 1989).

Celebrate Your Options

Famed designers Robert Trent Jones Sr. and Robert Trent Jones Jr. teamed up for the first time to create the new course that recently opened in WDW's town of Celebration, Florida. Fees for the par-72 course range from $45 to $95, depending on the time of day and year; call 566-4653.

Try the Beat the Pro
program at Disney's
Racquet Club. Win two
out of three sets and
the match is free. Lose
and you pay the full
private-instruction rate.

Tennis

E ven if you can't quite picture Mickey with a mid-size racquet in his hand, Walt Disney World can still serve up plenty of tennis action for players of any caliber. There are a total of 25 courts scattered around the World, including four at the Dolphin hotel, which shares them with the Swan. You'll find a pair of hard-surface courts at the Yacht Club and Beach Club, two more at Fort Wilderness (watch out for swinging toddlers), and a nice, quiet trio (the courts, not the players) at Old Key West. The Grand Floridian's duo boasts clay surfaces; ditto the pair at BoardWalk and the foursome at The Villas at the Disney Institute. Courts lighted for night play are available at each resort; this is a big deal, given the daytime heat during much of the year.

For quality court time, the most important three words that serious tennis buffs need remember when planning a visit are: Disney's Racquet Club. The Villas at the Disney Institute also rates consideration, though its hydrogrid clay courts are available almost exclusively to guests participating in Disney Institute programs.

Disney's Racquet Club

Disney's Racquet Club should please even the pickiest players. The six courts, lighted for night play, are state-of-the-art hydrogrid clay, with a subterranean irrigation system that keeps them evenly watered without sprinklers. The pro shop is chock full of high-quality equipment and tennis fashions, from Wilson's popular Hammer series racquets to those cushy Thorlo socks everyone covets.

KNOW BEFORE YOU GO: Disney's Racquet Club is located just beyond the Contemporary resort's north wing. Courts are at their busiest during June and July, when tennis camps can take over from 10 A.M. to 4 P.M. Two courts are open to guests at these times, but they are first-come, first-served (so to speak). February, March, and April also tend to be busy, especially around holidays and spring break. January, October, and November should be considered prime time to play. Courts and pro shop are open from 9 A.M. to 8 P.M.; summer hours are 8 A.M. to 9 P.M.

Rates: Court rentals are $15 per hour. Racquets can be rented for $5. Ball machine rental is $12.50 per half hour. Locker room facilities are available at no charge.

Reservations: Courts may be reserved up to 30 days in advance. Call 824-3578. Need a partner? Just ask for the "Tennis Anyone?" sign-up sheet.

Dress: It's hot down here, so we recommend cool, loose-fitting tennis whites. As for showing up in any footwear other than flat-bottom tennis shoes, note that cross-trainers and running shoes tear up clay courts something awful. The pro shop staff will politely, but firmly, recommend you purchase the proper shoes on the spot.

INSTRUCTION: Disney's Racquet Club offers private instruction from USTA pros for all levels of play: Lessons cover everything from strokes to strategy and cost $50 per hour; group skill clinics are $40; and playing lessons are $45 per hour. Video analysis can be added to one-hour lessons for $10 more. The Grand Floridian offers 45-minute lessons for $40; call 824-3578. Note, too, that the Disney

Institute features a top-notch instruction program developed in conjunction with Peter Burwash International. Private lessons are also available for $50 for one person or $75 for two; call 827-4455 for reservations (for details on the Disney Institute, see page 172).

TOURNAMENTS: Private tournaments may be arranged through the pro shop at a cost of $50 per hour. Disney's Wide World of Sports—with an array of courts, fields, arenas, and pools big enough to host everything this side of the Olympics—is the site of the U.S. Men's Clay Court Championships this April. Eleven state-of-the-art clay courts complete with stadium are among the facility's assets (see page 160 for more information on this vast complex).

Fishing

Drop a line, it's promptly answered. That's typical fishing at Walt Disney World. Bay Lake, which adjoins man-made Seven Seas Lagoon, was stocked with 70,000 largemouth bass in the mid-1960s. A restrictive fishing policy allowed the fish to swell in both numbers and size. Even today angling is permitted on Bay Lake and Seven Seas Lagoon strictly in the context of guided expeditions, so the fish have gotten only so wise to plastic worm tricks. Bass pro Bob Decker, a longtime WDW fishing guide who has pursued his sport in lakes and tournaments all over Florida, gives Bay Lake his hard-earned vote

Tennis Tips

■ Court fees are $15 per hour at the Racquet Club, Grand Floridian, and Dolphin. Use of courts at The Villas at the Disney Institute is included in a $15 one-day health club pass. All other courts are free.

■ The courts at the Dolphin are illuminated all night long.

■ Really want to improve your game? The exhaustive tennis program offered at the Disney Institute doesn't disappoint.

■ New tennis balls cost about $5 per can on-property. Bring plenty from home.

The World's Most Striking Feature

Walt Disney World lies squarely within a band of Central Florida known as the Lightning Capital of the World. Prime striking season runs from May through September, peaking during July and August, when Mother Nature unleashes about 40 thunderstorms over just 62 days, according to National Weather Service figures. Most of these storms come and go rather quickly.

To protect yourself, seek shelter (the type with four walls and a roof) the moment you see a storm developing, and wait a good 15 minutes after the last rumble before resuming outdoor activity. Trees and umbrellas do not provide safe refuge. For a weather report, call 824-4104.

for the best bass fishing in Florida. On these waters you're not just likely to catch fish; you're apt to catch largemouth bass weighing eight pounds or more (Decker has seen some so-called bucket mouths that tipped the scale at over 12 pounds). And it's not uncommon for a group to catch 15 to 20 fish over a couple of hours, or for a first-timer to reel in half a dozen good-size bass.

While the guided fishing trips that comb the picturesque waters of Bay Lake and Seven Seas Lagoon generally net the biggest catches, there's more to the WDW fishing scene. Additional guided expeditions lead anglers to a few of Disney's more scenic waterways. And those who prefer to go it alone have some tempting options in the canals of Fort Wilderness and the stocked fishing hole at Dixie Landings.

The official policy is catch-and-release, and no license is required for fishing on Walt Disney World waterways. Disney's guides know their territory well, keep track of where the fish are biting, and serve in whatever capacity guests prefer—from straight chauffeurs to casting coaches and even all-out facilitators.

Guided Fishing Trips

FORT WILDERNESS: Guided expeditions offering first-rate bass fishing depart from the Fort Wilderness marina at 8 A.M., 11:30 A.M., and 3 P.M. for two-hour adventures on Bay Lake and Seven Seas Lagoon. Trips are made on pontoon-style boats, equipped with trolling motors, and can accommodate up to five people. The fee per boatload is about $150 for two hours ($50 for one additional hour) and includes guide, gear, and refreshments (coffee and pastries in the morning, soft drinks in the afternoon). Guides will pick up guests at the Contemporary, Grand Floridian, Polynesian, and Wilderness Lodge marinas. Reservations must be made at least 24 hours in advance and may be made up to two weeks ahead. Call 824-2621.

DOWNTOWN DISNEY MARKETPLACE: Guided fishing excursions plying the 35-acre Buena Vista Lagoon and adjacent waterways depart twice daily from the marina here—at 6:30 A.M. and 9 A.M. On the 6:30 A.M. trips, anglers have the lagoon and the largemouth bass therein all to themselves (after 10 A.M., rental boats can infringe on prime fishing territory). The cost for up to five people, including guide, gear, and refreshments, is $137 for two hours ($50

for one additional hour) or $68.50 per person. Guides will pick up guests at Port Orleans, Dixie Landings, and Old Key West. Reservations must be made at least 24 hours in advance, and can be made up to two weeks ahead; call 828-2461 or 828-2204.

DIXIE LANDINGS: The two-hour fishing trip that escorts anglers on the bass-infused Sassagoula River and Buena Vista Lagoon at 6:30 A.M. daily is sold by the seat rather than by the boat. The trip accommodates up to five people; includes guide, gear, and refreshments; and costs $50 per person. Parties of three or fewer will come out ahead; bigger groups will pay less to fish on Bay Lake. Reservations must be made 24 hours in advance, and can be made up to two weeks ahead; call 934-5409.

YACHT CLUB AND BEACH CLUB: The daily fishing excursions departing at 7 A.M. and 10 A.M. from the Yacht Club and Beach Club marina (824-2621) tour Crescent Lake and nearby canals. Cost for up to five people, including guide, gear, and refreshments, is $140 for two hours. Reservations must be made 24 hours in advance and can be made up to 30 days ahead.

Fishing on Your Own

Individuals who prefer to fish solo may do so on the myriad canals of Fort Wilderness, BoardWalk, and The Villas at the Disney Institute, and off the dock at the Marketplace—catch-and-release only, of course. Poles may be rented for about $8 per hour at the Marketplace and BoardWalk, and $2 per hour at the Fort Wilderness Bike Barn (the latter also rents rods and reels for $4 per hour or $8 per day; bait costs $3.50). While it's also possible to toss in a line right from the shores of Fort Wilderness, canoes allow anglers to slip into some peaceful and often fruitful channels. Canoes may be rented from the Fort Wilderness Bike Barn. Call 824-2742. Note: The canals can be unbearably steamy during the warmer months.

Dixie Landings has a pond called the Ol' Fishin' Hole that's stocked with catfish, bass, and bluegill. Strictly catch-and-release, the quiet fishing spot features a small dock among tall reeds where, from 9 A.M. to 3 P.M. every day, fishing is returned to its cane-pole-and-worm roots. Pole rental is $3.50 per hour, including worms. Call 934-5409.

Fishing Tips

Although the fishing is good here year-round, it's most pleasant from November through May, when temperatures are cooler. As for strategy, one local recommends going with plastic worms, the red shad–colored ones in particular. To stack your odds, he suggests shiners (about $10 for a dozen; ask for them when you make reservations). Also, top-water baits work well in spring and fall.

Running Around the World

Despite pleasant terrain that looks like it's been spread with a rolling pin, Walt Disney World can be a rough place to pursue the world's most mobile form of exercise. From late spring through early fall, comfortable running conditions are fleeting, with early birds getting the best shot at an enjoyable run. In cooler seasons, joggers have greater freedom to explore the many compelling options here.

Inquire about maps of the jogging trails and footpaths accessible from each WDW resort at the hotel's Guest Services desk. Courses range from one mile to just over three. Dixie Landings, Old Key West, and Fort Wilderness offer some of the most extensive and scenic venues.

Boating

Guests looking to cruise, paddle, or even create a small wake on the pristine lakes and waterways of Walt Disney World have nothing short of the largest fleet of pleasure boats in the country at their disposal. Resort marinas stand by with sailboats, pontoon boats, canopy boats, canoes, speedboats, and pedal boats, all of which are available for rental on a first-come, first-served basis.

On the World's most expansive boating forum, the 650-acre body of water comprising Bay Lake and the adjoining Seven Seas Lagoon, watercraft from the Contemporary, Wilderness Lodge, and Fort Wilderness marinas converge with boats lighting out from the Polynesian and Grand Floridian. Other areas are more contained. Craft rented at the Caribbean Beach cruise around 45-acre Barefoot Bay. As boats on brief loan from the Downtown Disney Marketplace roam 35-acre Buena Vista Lagoon, small flotillas of rental craft drift in from the upriver marinas of Old Key West, Port Orleans, and Dixie Landings. Meanwhile, watercraft from the Yacht Club and Beach Club, and the Swan and Dolphin, make ripples on 25-acre Crescent Lake, and pedal boaters ply the World's newest cruising zone—the 15-acre Lago Dorado at Coronado Springs.

All the marinas are open from 10 A.M. until early evening (closing hours vary). No privately owned boats are permitted on WDW waterways. Renters must present either a WDW resort ID card, or a valid driver's license or passport. Some rentals carry other restrictions (described below).

CANOEING: Paddling among the narrow channels of Fort Wilderness during the cooler and more peaceful morning hours, canoers pass through both forest and meadows, encountering solitary anglers and quacking contingents along the way. Fishing and canoeing are an irresistible combination for many, with fishing gear available for rent right alongside the canoes (which run $6 per hour or $10 per day) at the Fort Wilderness Bike Barn. Canoes may also be rented at Caribbean Beach, Port Orleans, Dixie Landings, and The Villas at the Disney Institute. Use of these watercraft is restricted to WDW canals.

CRUISING: For groups interested in taking a leisurely sunning, sightseeing, or party excursion on the water, motorized canopy boats and pontoon boats are the only way to go. Sixteen-foot canopy boats accommodating up to eight adults (about $20 per half hour) and 20-foot pontoon boats holding ten adults (about $22 per half hour) are available for rent at most marinas.

PEDAL BOATING: For those who prefer pedal-pushing to paddling, pedal boats (accommodating two pedaling passengers and two free-loaders) are available for about $6 per half hour or $10 per hour at most marinas. Rentals are restricted to Disney resort guests at the Caribbean Beach, Port Orleans, Dixie Landings, Swan and Dolphin, Coronado Springs, and Yacht Club and Beach Club marinas, and at Fort Wilderness' Bike Barn. The Swan and Dol-

phin, and the Yacht Club and Beach Club, also rent Hydro Bikes (singles, $8 per half hour; doubles, about $16 per half hour), which resemble upright bicycles affixed to pontoons.

SAILING: Bay Lake and Seven Seas Lagoon offer pretty reliable winds and unparalleled running room. Sailing conditions are generally best in March and April. A variety of sailboats may be rented at the Grand Floridian, Polynesian, Contemporary, Wilderness Lodge, and Fort Wilderness marinas. Rental costs range from $11 to $19 per hour. Among the options are Aquafins (two passengers maximum), Capris (good beginner boats holding up to six), and catamarans accommodating two and three people (experience required).

Getting Above It All

If the notion of flying like a kite above Bay Lake with a panorama of the Magic Kingdom appeals to you, factor in a contoured chair (called a Sky Rider) that allows you to sit in a reclined position and you have an idea of the parasailing experience as it exists at Walt Disney World.

The flight lasts seven to ten minutes, and the landing is quite soft, thanks to the parachute and the two-person crew's skillful handling (as one reels in the cord, the other slows the boat just so).

Parasailing excursions are offered at the Contemporary marina, with none other than Mark McCulloh, the man who invented the sport, running the show. The cost is about $60 per person, and reservations are required (call 824-1000, ext. 3586).

Which Way to the Beach?

WDW resort guests need not set out for the coast to find pretty strands to sunbathe on and get sand between their toes. Between the resorts fronting Bay Lake (the Contemporary, Wilderness Lodge, and Fort Wilderness) and those alongside Seven Seas Lagoon (the Grand Floridian and Polynesian), there are over five miles of white-sand beaches. And that doesn't include the powdery white stretches at the Caribbean Beach, Yacht Club and Beach Club, and Swan and Dolphin resorts. The beach fronting the Polynesian's Moorea guest building is among the more secluded shores. All resort beaches are reserved exclusively for guests staying at those properties.

SPEEDBOATING: Among the most enjoyable and popular ways to cool off at Walt Disney World is the legion of mini speedboats called Water Sprites. While the boats max out at a paltry ten miles per hour, their small hulls ride a choppy surface as if they were galloping steeds. The Downtown Disney Marketplace offers one of the more uncrowded arenas in Buena Vista Lagoon. (An additional boon: Riders must be 14 to rent Water Sprites here; elsewhere the minimum age is 12.) While Water Sprites ostensibly seat two, adult boaters will reach greater speeds going solo (and creating tiny wakes for one another). Water Sprites are restricted to lakes only, and are available for about $16 per half hour at the Grand Floridian, Polynesian, Contemporary, Wilderness Lodge, Yacht Club and Beach Club, Fort Wilderness, Caribbean Beach, and Marketplace marinas. At the Contemporary, jet-powered boats called Seariders may be rented for $30 per hour. Accommodating up to three people, the boats can achieve speeds of up to 30 miles per hour; riders must be 18 to rent.

WATERSKIING: Enthusiasts interested in hitching a ride around Bay Lake and Seven Seas Lagoon will pay $82 per hour for a boat and driver. Cost is by the boatload, and up to five skiers can be accommodated at a time, with a two-person minimum. Trips are available exclusively at the Contemporary, Polynesian, Grand Floridian, Wilderness Lodge, and Fort Wilderness marinas. Reservations must be made at least 48 hours in advance and can be made up to two weeks ahead (phone 824-2621 between 8 A.M. and 4 P.M.).

Swimming

As if it weren't enough to have an inside track to three water parks (see "Other Pursuits" in the latter part of this chapter), WDW resorts are themselves bursting at the seams with watery playgrounds. With no fewer than 56 pools spread throughout Disney's hotel grounds, guests at each resort can be assured of access to at least one pool. However, it is important to note that due to a policy initiated to prevent overcrowding, WDW hotel pools are open only to guests staying at that resort; pool-hopping is permitted strictly between sister resorts (the Yacht Club and Beach Club, Port Orleans and Dixie Landings, All-Star Sports and All-Star Music, and the Swan and Dolphin).

As a general rule, the hotels with multiple pools afford the most pleasant swimming for adults. This is because one pool is tailored (most often via a delightfully rendered theme) to attract the splashy crowd, thereby freeing up the other(s) for swimmers in search of calmer waters. The Yacht Club and Beach Club offer the best of both worlds: two secluded pools with whirlpools, and an extraordinary mini water park called Stormalong Bay that sprawls over three acres and features current pools, jets, and a sand-bottomed wading lagoon. The Swan and Dolphin also do things right: A grotto pool filled with waterfalls and alcoves is punctuated by whirlpools and complemented by two rectangular pools.

Among resorts with one swimming hole, the Grand Floridian's pool is vast, unthemed, and open 24 hours; the Wilderness Lodge's, atmospheric yet smallish; and Port Orleans', fun if generally overrun with children (although there's the added option of swimming next door at Dixie Landings). Featuring two pools apiece are the Contemporary, Polynesian, Fort Wilderness, All-Star Sports, and All-Star Music resorts. (Note: Both value-rated All-Star resorts are marked exceptions to the two-pools-means-at-least-one-quiet-pool rule.) BoardWalk boasts three pools; Coronado Springs and Old Key West have four pools apiece; Dixie Landings and The Villas at the Disney Institute each have six; and the Caribbean Beach resort has seven. Each of the Hotel Plaza Blvd. resorts checks in with one pool. Lap swimmers will be happiest with the spacious rectangular pool at the Swan and Dolphin.

Biking Around the World

While Fort Wilderness is certainly prime territory for leisurely cycling, the World is filled with picturesque roads that wind, relatively untrafficked, within some of its most sprawling and scenic resorts.

Bikes are available for rental (about $3 an hour or $12 per day, with some variation among locations) in precisely the spots where guests will want to ride: Fort Wilderness, Wilderness Lodge, Old Key West, Port Orleans, Dixie Landings, Caribbean Beach, BoardWalk, The Villas at the Disney Institute, and Coronado Springs.

■ Schedules vary,
depending on the time
of year. Call for details
(363-6600).

■ Wear comfortable
shoes—there's a lot of
ground to cover.

■ WDW resort guests
may take buses from
Blizzard Beach.

■ Tailgating in the park-
ing lot is not permitted.
(Parking is free.)

■ Bring an umbrella if
you plan to attend an
outdoor contest (keep
in mind summer after-
noon showers), and
know that games can
be canceled due to
inclement weather.

■ Want to be a part of
the action? Volunteer to
work at an event. Call
the number above.

Health Clubs

Not all fitness centers located within the WDW resorts are reserved strictly for guests staying at the hotel that houses them. Contemporary Fitness Center (824-1823), Grand Floridian Spa & Health Club (843-2247), Muscles & Bustles at BoardWalk (939-2370), and the Sports & Fitness Center at the Disney Institute (827-4455) are accessible to all WDW guests; and Body By Jake at the Dolphin (934-4264) is open to anyone.

The bare-bones facility at the Swan (free for resort guests) is fine for on-the-road maintenance. Better equipped—with Nautilus, more current and varied cardiovascular machines, and such extras as a sauna—are the Contemporary Fitness Center ($8.50 per day, $16 for length of stay); R.E.S.T. at Old Key West (free for guests); Muscles & Bustles at Board-Walk ($7 per day, $12 for length of stay for resort guests; $10 per day, $20 length of stay for others); and La Vida health club at Coronado Springs (about $6 per day, $12 length of stay).

The best of the lot distinguish themselves by offering exceptionally pleasant environs and the likes of per-sonal trainers and Cybex machines. Ship Shape at the Yacht Club and Beach Club ($7.50 per day, $12 for length of stay) has a whirlpool, steam room, and sauna; Body By Jake at the Dolphin ($8 per day, $16 for length of stay) offers aerobics and Polaris equipment; and the Grand Floridian Spa & Health Club ($6 per day, $12 per length of stay) comes complete with spa frills. On a level all its own is the immense, incredibly endowed Sports & Fitness Center at the Disney Institute (free to guests; otherwise $15 per day, $35 for length of stay), which could be a Cybex warehouse if not for its airy setting.

Disney's Wide World of Sports

Should your definition of paradise include slam dunks, screeching fast-balls, and the intoxicating aroma of steamed weenies, welcome to nir-vana. Disney's Wide World of Sports, which sprawls over 200 acres, is one agile place. Capable of hosting a dozen events at once, the immense facility has an archery-to-wrestling lineup that makes channel surfing in a sports bar seem positively passive. As the new spring training ground for Major League Baseball's Atlanta Braves, the home of the Harlem Globetrotters and the Amateur Athletic Union (AAU), and a veritable turntable of tournaments, it's the biggest thing to hit the Florida sports scene since the Orlando Magic.

Despite its enormity, the complex somehow comes off as almost quaint. Its old-time Floridian architecture harks back to a simpler era. It recaptures the essence of a neighborhood ballpark, beckoning friends and families to spend a lazy afternoon together.

Wide World of Sports, located near the junction of I-4 and U.S. 192, has an armory of box seats and bleachers to accommodate all manner of spectators. There's a 7,500-seat baseball stadium; 5,000-seat field house that hosts basketball, wrestling, and volleyball; a track-and-field complex; 11 clay tennis courts; four multipurpose fields for football, soccer, lacrosse, and more; and five sand courts.

The $8 general admission ticket allows you the freedom to take in a number of non-premium events—that is, competitions that are worth watching, but not quite major league. Tickets for all premium events, such as Atlanta Braves games, the U.S. Men's Clay Court Championships, and the NFL Quarterback Challenge, are available through TicketMaster (839-3900) and include license to roam the complex. Premium tickets can also be purchased at the Wide World of Sports ticket office on the day of the event. Prices vary.

If an afternoon of cheering (pom-poms optional) and rooting for the next-best-thing-to-the-home-team leaves you with a Nate Newton–style appetite, head straight for the Official All-Star Café. The burgers are good, the atmosphere's festive, and as far as restaurants go, it's the only game in town. More than 30 vendors offer a variety of stadium-style snacks for those dining in their seats or on the run.

Spa Envy?

It doesn't matter where (among WDW resorts) you're staying. If you indulge in a spa treatment at the Grand Floridian Spa (843-2247) or The Spa at the Disney Institute (827-4455), you may use the adjoining fitness center at no additional charge. This is no small plus, given the facilities' extensiveness and usual cost to day guests. Offerings at the Grand Floridian Spa (which has a room where a couple can be pampered together) include massages, facials, and body treatments. At the Disney Institute's spa, possibilities extend from massage therapy to aromatherapy, seaweed skin treatments, and beauty packages.

Further temptation: Licensed therapists also offer massages at the Contemporary, Yacht Club and Beach Club, BoardWalk, Old Key West, Swan, Dolphin, and Coronado Springs resorts. The going rate's about $37 per half hour. Just call the chosen resort's health club to make an appointment.

Did you know...

SHOPPING

There's more to the shopping scene at Walt Disney World than Mouseketeer hats, Mickey Mouse watches, and sweatshirts ad infinitum. Indeed, Disney character merchandise has reached a level of taste and sophistication that will amaze even the most demanding souvenir hunter. The options range from dark chocolate molded in the image of a certain mouse's face to exclusive pieces of Disneyana created by world-class design houses, including Waterford, Goebel, and Lladró. For adults looking to find a grownup forget-me-not, the pickings have never been better. There are henley T-shirts, sweatshirts, and denim shirts playfully adorned with tasteful character appliqués. Silk ties, hair accessories, and dress socks feature surprisingly subtle Mickey Mouse designs. And product lines earmarked for executives and gourmands have deftly infused the World's most recognizable silhouette into the likes of black leather portfolios, fine writing implements, and sugar bowls and creamers.

Although much of the commerce here revolves around Disneyana, most shops offer character merchandise within the context of a broader theme (jewelry or books, for instance). Others, such as a certain shop in the Magic Kingdom, eschew the stuff altogether, offering such unlikely items as beer steins and crystal instead. Yes, that's right, crystal. In the Magic Kingdom. A bit bizarre, granted. But the fact that such a possibility exists on this prime piece of "Please, Daddy, please!" real estate serves as a nice elbow-in-the-ribs allusion to what fills shelves and racks in more adult corners of the World. When we say that Epcot's World Showcase is no United Nations of Kmarts, no international convention of Disney paraphernalia, we mean (1) merchandise eloquently represents each of the 11 nations; (2) we'd trust the folks who stock some of the shops here to choose a gift for our mothers; and (3) the place is a dangerous buying spree waiting to happen. Then there's the Downtown Disney Marketplace, an attractive enclave of boutiques and restaurants on the shores of Buena Vista Lagoon that (from 9:30 A.M. to 11 P.M. daily, until midnight in some busy seasons) offers the best one-stop

shopping in the World. And it's not just because it boasts the biggest hoard of Disney merchandise on the planet: The whirlwind shopping potential of the Marketplace extends to animation cels, books, designer clothing, environmentally themed goods, fine jewelry, and gourmet gifts (and that's just from *A* to *G*). The sort of place that inspires shoppers to drag companions by the arm to see this great thing or that, the Marketplace is loaded.

Because it wouldn't be right to send you out into the World without an itemized shopping list, we've pulled together a diverse selection of the best shops in the World. While particular items may not be in the store when you are, comparable goods should be available.

In Downtown Disney
Standouts

THE ART OF DISNEY (Marketplace): Skip this showroom brimming with limited-edition art pieces, collectibles, and animation cels, and you've missed out on some of the most spectacular ogling to be had at Walt Disney World (Disney characters masterfully rendered by the likes of Lladró and Armani). This is one of four such shops in the World (the Magic Kingdom, Epcot, and Disney-MGM Studios each have one); displays vary among galleries.

CHRISTMAS CHALET (Marketplace): Rather than tick off the many delightful trimmings—both traditional and with Disney characters—proffered at this trove of decorative items, ornaments, and collectibles, we'll cut to the chase: Just add eggnog.

GOURMET PANTRY (Marketplace): This Marketplace institution stocks a full line of Gourmet Mickey cookware, including sleek, Mickeyfied Michael Graves designs (pieces in the collection range from salt and pepper shakers to a limited-edition silver teakettle for $100). It is also positively crammed with delectables;

More Than a Marketplace

In addition to the World's best shopping, the Downtown Disney Marketplace offers restaurants, lounges, a marina, special events, interactive fountains, a walkway to Pleasure Island, and a bigger agenda than ever before. Having already linked arms with Pleasure Island as part of the Downtown Disney entertainment district, the Marketplace has a new, just as spirited, neighbor: Downtown Disney West Side. Together, the three "neighborhoods" (and the horde of clubs, shops, and restaurants that comprise them) are collectively known as Downtown Disney—an ever-expanding district zoned exclusively for entertainment. See our "Nightlife Guide" in the *Dining & Entertainment* chapter for further details on the clubs and restaurants located here.

The Best of the West

While Mickey Mouse has not been banished from Downtown Disney West Side, he's hardly the community's number one pitchman. Rather than invent new ways to display Mr. Mouse, the shops here specialize in merchandise with a more adult appeal (e.g., cigars and classic guitars). Startifacts is the place for movie and political memorabilia. Celebrity Eyeworks can set you up with designer sunglasses just like those worn by big-screen celebs. The Guitar Gallery is the source for vintage guitars. The Virgin Megastore (described at right) is CD central. Sosa Family Cigars offers premium smokes and rolling demonstrations.

while many sweets and savories are meant for instant gratification, others (Mickey-shaped pasta and Mickey Shorts Bread) make good souvenirs.

TEAM MICKEY'S ATHLETIC CLUB (Marketplace): This recently expanded shop specializes in sport-specific Disney character apparel and gear that run the gamut from Goofy golf club covers to Tigger thong leotards.

2R'S READING AND RITING (Marketplace): In this terrific book nook, you'll find plenty of best-sellers, children's books, and Disney tomes; gifts such as Cross pens and Disney's Executive Collection desk accessories, which take Mickey to his sophisticated heights; and a ready supply of both artful and adorable stationery, notepads, and greeting cards. Plus cappuccino.

VIRGIN MEGASTORE (West Side): An enormity clearly built on the premise that music makes the world go round, this high-fidelity hot spot delivers a selection to make Cecilia Bartoli and Blues Traveler fans alike dizzy with delight. Besides chance upon chance to don headphones and listen to the latest releases in every genre (more than 300 listening stations in all), offerings also include 20 video/laser disc booths for movie viewing, a house deejay, and a small snack lounge for those who browse through mealtime. There's one thing you won't need headphones for—catching the periodic live performances on the elevated stage outside the main entrance.

WORLD OF DISNEY (Marketplace): The most comprehensive collection of Disney character merchandise available anywhere, and a shoppers' concierge desk equipped to locate any item in stock, make this emporium an unbeatable venue for one-stop souvenir sprees. Pick up a map inside to make your way through the maze of displays, ranging from limited-edition watches to stuffed animals, from intimate apparel to office accessories, and from frames to photo albums. Each room is themed, replete with colorful murals and whimsical character sculptures. One area, presided over by Disney villains, is overflowing with sophisticated stuff: watches, jewelry, and some great decorative accessories for the home. The most eye-catching room's travel theme is evident in the totes, packs, and hats sold there, not to mention the character-piloted contraptions hung from the high ceilings. Avid cooks will savor the goods in the "Enchanted Dining Room." While conspicuous characters are the rule storewide, there is also a lot of great Mickey Mouse innuendo to be found.

Good Bets

EUROSPAIN (Marketplace): Crystal keepsakes (engraved on-site), porcelain figurines, and decorative masks are among the possibilities at this bastion of breakables.

HARRINGTON BAY CLOTHIERS (Marketplace): Mickey makes himself very scarce at this upscale spot—a reliable resource for men's sportswear and accessories, branded by the likes of Tommy Hilfiger, Polo by Ralph Lauren, and Nautica.

PLANET HOLLYWOOD (Pleasure Island): If there are no *Star Wars* vehicles strung from the rafters at this shop, it's because the place is filled to the hilt with the restaurant's logo clothing. Note that a new superstore—with more of the same—recently opened in the Disney-MGM Studios on Sunset Boulevard.

RESORTWEAR UNLIMITED (Marketplace): With classic separates from such labels as Liz Claiborne and Adrienne Vittadini, a swimwear selection that's among WDW's largest, and a choice stash of accessories (shoes, handbags, and jewelry), this spot is equipped to plug most any hole in a woman's travel wardrobe. It also has a cosmetics counter.

SUMMER SANDS (Marketplace): A beach fix minus the high tide, it's a gift shop tribute to coastal Florida with a smattering of bathing suits, cover-ups, and hats.

Shopping Tips

■ Not enough time in the day? The Downtown Disney Marketplace keeps long hours—9:30 A.M. to 11 P.M. daily, sometimes leaving its doors open until midnight during busy seasons.

■ Short on cash? Stop by the ATM on the West Side, in the Marketplace (in Guest Services, next to Cap'n Jack's), or at Pleasure Island (near Rock 'n' Roll Beach Club).

■ Valet parking is available for the three sections of Downtown Disney from 5:30 P.M. to 2 A.M. Cost is $5. The service is complimentary to guests with disabilities.

■ When shopping in the theme parks, note that you can arrange to have purchases sent to a location near the park gates for later pickup. WDW resort guests can also have purchases delivered back to their hotel at no charge. For either service, just ask the salesperson.

Carved in Stone

Some guests let people walk all over them—for posterity's sake. Actually, they allow fellow guests to step on a hexagonal brick bearing their name, one of the many forming a walkway at the entrance to the Magic Kingdom and around Seven Seas Lagoon. The ten-inch bricks—engraved with Mickey Mouse and up to three lines of text, including name(s), city, and state or country—are carefully numbered and mapped for easy location. Special designs are available to commemorate weddings and anniversaries. The bricks may be purchased for $110 at the Magic Kingdom entrance or by calling 800-272-6201 anytime.

In The Parks

Magic Kingdom Standouts

BRIAR PATCH (Frontierland): The specialties of the house are countrified gifts and merchandise that sweetly portrays Winnie the Pooh (and cohorts) and characters from Disney's *Song of the South.*

CRYSTAL ARTS (Main Street): This shop offers cut-glass bowls and vases, and clear-glass mugs and steins similar to those found at Eurospain in the Downtown Disney Marketplace. Items can be engraved on-site, and guests have the opportunity to observe an engraver or glassblower at work.

MAIN STREET GALLERY (Main Street): One of four WDW showrooms featuring limited-edition art pieces, collectibles, and animation cels (an extraordinary eyeful that should not be missed). Displays are different at each gallery; the other venues are found at the Downtown Disney Marketplace, Epcot, and the Disney-MGM Studios.

DISNEY CLOTHIERS (Main Street): Souvenir clothing earns big style points here, as various Disney characters appear on silk scarves, ties, and leather goods, and are appliquéd on collared shirts, denim shirts, sweaters, jackets, and nightshirts. Selection is small but choice.

EMPORIUM (Main Street): The Magic Kingdom's largest gift shop offers an array of Walt Disney World logo and character merchandise (including lots of stuffed animals, T-shirts, sweatshirts, and hats) whose variety is eclipsed only by that found at the Marketplace.

MAIN STREET ATHLETIC CLUB (Main Street): A nifty stash of sports-related character apparel. If you want to score some unique team-logo items or some great gear sporting classic characters in action, don't pass.

MAIN STREET CONFECTIONERY (Main Street): The sweet-toothed fall in line for delicious peanut brittle, fudge, and marshmallow crispies made on the premises. For milk chocolate golf balls and an amazing find called Chocolate Mint Cookie Gems, this is the source.

MARKET HOUSE (Main Street): Brass lanterns, oak floors, and a hand-crank telephone provide the backdrop for a selection of old-fashioned snacks.

SIR MICKEY'S (Fantasyland): Perhaps it's the proximity to Cinderella Castle that gives this new shop its comparatively highbrow tastes. Expect character clothing and accessories with decidedly adult leanings.

UPTOWN JEWELERS (Main Street): If you're shopping for a character watch or good-quality souvenir charms, earrings, and pendants, this elegant catchall is the place. The full line of Mickey-suggestive Cross writing implements is represented. There is also a large selection of ceramic character figurines.

THE YANKEE TRADER (Liberty Square): A front porch with a rocking chair sets the tone for this cozy niche chock full of country kitchenware.

YE OLDE CHRISTMAS SHOPPE (Liberty Square): Similar to the Christmas Chalet at the Downtown Disney Marketplace, this locale is a fine resource for traditional and character holiday decorations.

The Mouse Delivers

■ Prowling the property, but can't find the Disney object of your obsession? Ask a park employee, and if that must-have Donald Duck screen saver or Tinker Bell tea set exists, they should be able to find out where it's sold.

■ Have a sudden, not-to-be-denied yearning for a certain music box, watch, or tie that you saw in a shop during your visit? Call WDW Mail Order at 363-6200.

■ Still have unfulfilled Disneyana cravings? Call 800-237-5751 for the Disney Catalog, call 818-265-4660 to find the nearest Disney Store, or browse through The Disney Store's offerings on-line at *http://www.disneystore.com*.

Souvenirs with Animal Magnetism

When it's time to shop in Animal Kingdom, beat a path to Safari Village, where most of the major stores are located. At press time, the shelves were still bare, but our scouting report suggests certain standouts: Disney Outfitters in Safari Village for its upscale clothing, watches, and jewelry (note the soaring totem poles in the central room); Mombasa Marketplace in Harambe for its safari and ethnic gear; and Chester and Hester's in DinoLand U.S.A., a "roadside tourist trap" selling mostly wacky dino stuff.

Epcot Standouts

THE AMERICAN ADVENTURE (World Showcase): Heritage Manor Gifts waxes patriotic with Americana in the expected colors. Highlights include decorative throws, quilted items, and political campaign buttons.

THE ART OF DISNEY EPCOT GALLERY (Innoventions, Future World): Epcot's repository for Disney animation cels and limited-edition art pieces and collectibles is the newest of WDW's four such showrooms.

CANADA (World Showcase): An array of Canadian handicrafts and Indian artifacts puts the Northwest Mercantile on the essential shopping circuit.

CENTORIUM (Innoventions, Future World): Epcot's best address for character merchandise also stocks futuristic gizmos that fairly beg for attention.

CHINA (World Showcase): Yong Feng Shangdian is so huge it's almost a province; and the montage of paper fans, Chinese prints, silk robes, antiques, vases, and tea sets is truly something to behold.

FRANCE (World Showcase): Spellbinding boutiques offer things beautiful and French. Our favorites are Plume et Palette (oil paintings upstairs, crystal and collectibles downstairs); La Maison du Vin (wine, cookbooks, and hand-painted dishes); and La Signature (Christian Dior and Guerlain cosmetics and fragrance boutique).

GERMANY (World Showcase): Shops here are simply irresistible. Volkskunst (bursting with cuckoo clocks, nutcrackers, and wood carvings) is joined by Der Teddybär (a delightful toy shop); Weinkeller (with about 250 bottlings from the vintage German vintner H. Schmitt Söhne); Kunstarbeit in Kristall (beer steins and Austrian crystal) and Glas und Porzellan (a boutique with Goebel's M. I. Hummel figurines, where an artist demonstrates the process by which the rosy-cheeked creations are painted and finished).

GREEN THUMB EMPORIUM (The Land, Future World): Do not be misled. While this great shop is flush with seeds, kits, and garden-themed knickknacks, gardening prowess is not sold here. Repeat: No green thumbs change hands.

ITALY (World Showcase): When in this multishop pavilion, we gravitate toward La Cucina Italiana for cannoli and vino, Delizie Italiane for fine chocolates, and Il Bel Cristallo for the brilliant array of Venetian glass.

JAPAN (World Showcase): In the vast emporium known as the Mitsukoshi Department Store, kimono-clad dolls (priced from $3.50 to $3,000) merit special attention, as do kimonos, origami kits, and bonsai.

MEXICO (World Showcase): While the vibrant piñatas presented in the central plaza are great for effect, the ceramics and other handicrafts at adjacent Artesanías Mexicanas tend to be marked by a more enduring appeal.

MOROCCO (World Showcase): At least half the fun of shopping in this pavilion's maze of Berber bangles, basketry, clothing, and hand-knotted carpets is never knowing just what awaits around the bend. Carpet-making demonstrations are ongoing.

NORWAY (World Showcase): The Puffin's Roost is undoubtedly Central Florida's best source for trolls and gorgeous, often hand-knit, Norwegian ski sweaters (bargains when compared to flights to Oslo). Exquisite miniature wood carvings and handcrafted jewelry add to the interesting, if eclectic, mix.

UNITED KINGDOM (World Showcase): Some of Epcot's finest shops lie within this pavilion's borders. There's The Toy Soldier (where Winnie the Pooh, Paddington Bear, and Peter Rabbit star); The Crown & Crest (a British free-for-all complete with fragrances, pub glasses, and dartboards); Pringle of Scotland (a bounty of cashmeres and all things plaid); The Queen's Table (with Royal Doulton collectibles from $5 to $12,500); and The Magic of Wales (featuring handcrafted gifts from the land of Diana). And of course, there's a prime spot for tea lovers—The Tea Caddy.

Disney-MGM Studios Standouts

ANIMATION GALLERY: One of four WDW venues showcasing limited-edition art pieces, collectibles, and animation cels. The difference here: the chance to watch an artist painting and to buy the resulting artwork right on the spot.

ELLEN'S BUY THE BOOK: This cozy purveyor of cappuccino and page-turners resembles the set of its namesake bookstore on the TV show (logo T-shirts and coffee accessories aside). Look for occasional book signings.

Bonsai to Go

When we tell you the Mitsukoshi Department Store in Japan has a bounty of beautiful, reasonably priced bonsai for sale, we mean the collection approximates a miniature forest. Even better: You can leave your purchase with a salesperson for shipping, and let the teensy tree-of-choice meet you back at the home front.

Talk About an Eclectic Mix...

The unique array of merchandise found in shops at the Studios is best quantified by example. At last check, you could fill the following unlikely shopping list:

■ A watch that belonged to James Dean

■ Limited-edition Disney animation cel

■ Tom Hanks' costume from *Forrest Gump*

■ Musical snow globe that tinkles "When You Wish Upon a Star"

■ *Star Trek* T-shirt

■ Grumpy serving dish

■ "I Love Lucy" silk tie

■ Plastic "quacking" whistle (with neck cord)

■ Mickey golf shirt

■ Autographed photo of Walt Disney

■ Elvis key chain

KEYSTONE CLOTHIERS: Characters turn up on smartly styled women's fashions (such as appliquéd nightshirts and chambray shirts, plus jewelry) as well as silk character ties and boxers.

MOUSE ABOUT TOWN: A well-heeled wardrobe of subtly mouse-infused polo shirts, jackets, button-down shirts, and sweatshirts in the sort of deep, dark colors a man-about-town would also appreciate. Some of the apparel holds appeal for women as well.

ONCE UPON A TIME: There was a little shop that offered one of the classiest souvenir collections the World over—musical snow globes featuring artfully rendered Disney characters, wooden and ceramic character figurines, and (at last look) extraordinary Pinocchio and Mickey marionettes, and a fine Grumpy serving dish. It seemed sure to live happily ever after. The End.

SID CAHUENGA'S ONE-OF-A-KIND: Celebrity encounters abound in this den of movie and television memorabilia. There are scads of autographed photos, original movie posters, and much belated premiere invitations to Disney animated films. There's also ample opportunity to snap up hand-me-downs direct from the stars, so when someone compliments your handbag, you can say, "Yeah, Mae West liked it, too." Closet contents turn over too frequently to allow for specifics, but we suspect a certain custom-made pink suit with matching platform boots ($500; courtesy of Sonny Bono) might stick around awhile.

SALE

SUNSET CLUB COUTURE: This purveyor of jewelry and limited-edition timepieces has the sort of incomparable selection that makes collectors' eyes widen. Consider gold pocket watches with conspicuous ears; marcasite pieces with stylized Mickey designs; and custom-made watches with tremendous face value (namely, your choice of characters, drawn and then sealed onto the watch's face).

SWEET SUCCESS: Compelling reasons for an intermission include fresh-made chocolates, fudge, candies, and marshmallow crispies.

OTHER PURSUITS

You're at Walt Disney World, but you're not in the mood for a theme park, don't feel much like swatting a little yellow ball or sitting by the pool, and have already shopped (and dropped). You're up for something, but lacking inspiration. What do you do? Don't despair. Disney's got this one covered.

To spark or indulge your creative side, the Disney Institute stands by with a boundless supply of horizon-stretching and mind-bending experiences. The ultimate Disney learning adventure, the Disney Institute invites you to make

your own magic in hands-on programs specially designed to jump-start a stalled imagination. You have access to state-of-the-art facilities of a sort you've never before had a chance to lay eyes on, and your pick of programs from rock climbing to radio broadcasting—and that doesn't even hint at the potential for a full-day spa indulgence.

If you'd like to select from the aquatic side of the adventure menu, Disney has channeled its usual creative flair, and no less than 4.3 million gallons of H_2O, into three parks that are to water what Liberace was to music. There's River Country, an old-fashioned swimming hole with several water slides and a Huckleberry Finn sense of fun; Typhoon Lagoon, where tsunamis are a house specialty; and Blizzard Beach, with all the trappings of a ski resort, including a ski jump–style centerpiece, the world's tallest water slide.

Or perhaps you'd prefer something more nature-oriented. For a lot of greenery and recreation, there's Fort Wilderness, Disney's most unassuming attraction. Its 700 acres of woodland are rife with picturesque trails and canals, and lots of ways (including biking, canoeing, fishing, and horseback riding) to enjoy them. For glorious foliage, a litany of unusual animal encounters, and blissful peace and quiet, the zoological park called Discovery Island is the natural distraction of choice.

Did you know...

Norman Rockwall—the 26-foot-tall cornerstone of the Disney Institute's rock-climbing program—was molded from rocks found in the California and Nevada deserts.

All in a Day's Adventure

One-day packages are a terrific way to get a taste of this enticing place. The $79 rate includes your choice of (available) programs, use of the Sports & Fitness Center, and entry to that evening's performance or film screening (no overnight stay). Half-day programs are also available. Spa treatments may be bought separately. Reservations can be made up to two weeks ahead by calling 827-4800. For efficiency's sake, try to slot in a culinary session around mealtime.

For an evening Disney Institute foray, consider the dinner-and-show combo (about $27 per person), which includes a three-course meal at Seasons and tickets for the evening entertainment. Call WDW-DINE (939-3463) to make reservations.

Disney Institute

Insatiable souls looking to take home fresh perspective, newfound skills, and fascinating experiences as souvenirs can go to town at this innovative vacation resort. With a wide variety of participatory programs that immerse guests in everything from animation to gardening, rock climbing, culinary arts, and photography, the Disney Institute is uniquely configured to provide fun and meaningful dabbling for grownup vacationers. Designed for adults and families with older children (seven years and up), the resort gives guests free rein to explore whatever programs in the eclectic, ever-evolving mix most interest them. Each day, they can choose several sessions; an instructor-guest ratio of 1 to 15 ensures personal attention.

As an indication of the possibilities, consider: You might experiment with food and wine pairing, make your radio debut, create topiaries, or become the anchor or roving reporter for the Disney Institute's television news team (news programs are broadcast on a closed-circuit channel). Or you might work alongside Disney animators (brainstorming story ideas, sketching characters, coloring cels, or mixing sound) to produce animated shorts. Complementing (and facilitating) such programs is an artists-in-residence program that brings noted talents in arts (music, film, theater, dance, and the spoken word) to the Disney Institute to interact with guests and do some cross-cultivating of their own. As an example of how this works, imagine members of the (visiting) Pilobolus modern dance troupe bringing guests into play in freshly choreographed dances; practicing in open rehearsals; staging an evening recital in the Disney Institute's

Performance Center; and in their spare time, learning how to make soufflés, paint a faux finish, or improve their golf game right along with the rest.

If there's one thing we've learned about this invigorating lakeside retreat, it's that the Disney Institute is a complex entity that can be tough to grasp, sight unseen. The detailed information that follows should answer most of your questions, but we also acknowledge the truth of a statement made at the Disney Institute's 1996 dedication: "The Disney Institute is like a present. You don't know what it is until you open it."

BIG DRAWS: In an atmosphere akin to summer camp for adults, the Institute delivers inspiring, even mesmerizing, experiences while making extraordinary fun of learning. The most adult-oriented environs in the World.

WORTH NOTING: The Disney Institute is near Downtown Disney, and couldn't be closer to the Lake Buena Vista golf course. Designed by noted architect Tom Beeby, the lakeside resort takes after a small town. Guest buildings are clustered in neighborhoods just slightly removed from the village center, where most of the primary structures and facilities are located. The self-contained community also boasts sophisticated program studios, an intimate recital hall called the Performance Center, an outdoor amphitheater, a state-of-the-art cinema, and closed-circuit television and radio stations. The Welcome Center is the site of check-in, program services, the wonderful Dabblers gift shop, and the Seasons Dining Room and Terrace Lounge. Completing the picture are impressive recreational facilities, including a rock-climbing wall. Use of the immense Sports & Fitness Center is complimentary to Disney Institute guests (see next page for details). The Spa at the Disney Institute, described on page 175, is a

Disney Institute Tips

■ Don't miss the evening entertainment, even if it runs contrary to your usual tastes. From the intimate atmosphere to the laid-back candor of the artists-in-residence performing, the evening lineup's generally as good for the soul as the day programs.

■ Trade stories with Disney Institute instructors and fellow guests over breakfast, lunch, or dinner at the Community Table in Seasons Dining Room (a boon for singles).

■ If you intend to keep a busy schedule, buy a meal plan because you'll want to eat most of your meals in Seasons Dining Room. Another trick: Take cooking programs at lunchtime or dinnertime.

■ Arrive with a not-so-jammed suitcase, as you'll be making lots of nifty things that you'll want to bring home with you.

■ Take time to read the inspiring inscriptions framing the signs at each studio door.

Fit to Be Tried

We can't gush enough about the vast Sports & Fitness Center—complimentary to Disney Institute guests, and so incredibly equipped it has to be seen to be believed. The comprehensive lineup of state-of-the-art Cybex equipment has things die-hard fitness enthusiasts have never before laid eyes on—including machinery that tests muscular agility and range of motion. The knowledgeable instructors standing by to offer workout assists include such sports notables as Super Bowl alum Kenny Blair. There's also a wealth of cardiovascular machines, aerobics and stretching classes, water exercise, and more. An unintimidating approach caters to all fitness levels. We dare the most wishy-washy exercisers to resist.

peaceful retreat. Four state-of-the-art hydrogrid clay tennis courts are available at no cost when not in use for programs. Swimming pools; whirlpools; a lakeside jogging loop; volleyball courts; and canoe, bike, and electric cart rentals round out the options.

Core programs: Of course, the crux of a Disney Institute vacation is not the sophisticated playground, but the fascinating experiences that occur within this compelling context. The continually evolving roster of offerings comprises many programs; each one- to four-hour session falls into one of eight subject areas (including Disney Day Camp, which we'll ignore). Wherever you turn, you're in the hands of an expert determined to make your stay—with fun, insight, and a made-it-yourself memento or two documenting new skills and broken barriers. Because it's a design-your-own vacation, you can make your personal renaissance as narrowly or broadly focused as you please.

The following listing merely hints at the possibilities within each area. In Communication Arts and Entertainment, you can create your own home page on the World Wide Web, star in a radio drama, and hone your photography skills. Disney Discoveries invites you behind the scenes to learn Disney's storytelling techniques and wax creative as an Imagineer. The enormously popular Animation programs bring two-dimensional characters to life as you paint cels, create storyboards, lend your voice to a character, and experiment with clay and computer animation. Programs in Home, Gardens, and the Great Outdoors explore the realms of topiaries and flower baskets as well as birds and alligators, and also resolve the mysteries of faux marble finishes and WDW architecture. Culinary Arts is a natural favorite, with lip-smacking lessons that reveal the subtle tricks of healthy cooking and put a cork on wine anxiety. Performing Arts and Film programs—open rehearsals, presentations, and workshops in dance, theater, and beyond—offer forums for interaction with artists-in-residence. Also, an initiation to rock climbing, and exceptional golf and (Peter Burwash–driven) tennis programs, are the stars of the diverse Sports and Fitness area.

Entertainment: By day, artists-in-residence offer interludes to the usual programs with book signings, lectures, workshops, and recitals. At night, they provide entertainment that's every bit as engaging as the core programs. Big names and up-and-comers take to the stage and perform newly choreographed numbers, sing songs as yet unreleased, and otherwise embrace the

Disney Institute's laid-back style as an excuse to experiment and play loose with their material. Films are screened at the cinema; the Performance Center hosts intimate recitals and jam sessions; and anything from gospel music to performance art might happen at the amphitheater. Something's on tap every night, and whatever it is, it's generally not to be missed.

Where to eat: All meals are served in Seasons Dining Room (lunch seatings at Seasons Terrace Lounge are an option). Reflections Coffee & Pastries is a good bet for a light bite. Dabblers gift shop stocks snacks and limited groceries.

Where to drink: Seasons Terrace Lounge (offering beer, wine, and specialty drinks) supplements the myriad options at nearby Downtown Disney.

KNOW BEFORE YOU GO: Two Disney Institute programs per day can be reserved up to 90 days in advance; once you are here, computer terminals (comparable to ATMs, and accessed with your resort ID) and program concierges make it easy to change your schedule at whim, given availability. While it's possible to take up to four courses per day, we recommend settling for two so you have sufficient air in your schedule to chat with instructors and artists-in-residence; and enjoy the fitness center, spa, and entertainment.

Rates: Programs and accommodations are entwined. Rates are based on double occupancy and a minimum three-night stay, and include accommodations at The Villas at the Disney Institute, unlimited program participation (excluding spa treatments), taxes, and baggage gratuities, plus a one-day theme park ticket. Single rates are available for the Bungalows. An optional meal plan is offered. Spa packages are an option.

Rates for Bungalows (with one bedroom and separate sitting room) start at $499 for three nights, $653 for four nights, and $1,111 for seven nights. Starting rates for one-bedroom Town Houses with fully equipped kitchens are $573 for

Aah, Spa

While serious pampering is a treat anywhere, it's particularly divine in the invigorating context of the Disney Institute. The spa, easily the resort's most luxurious and peaceful haven, tempts with an array of indulgences bound to render that million-bucks feeling. Offerings include aromatherapy and sports massages, seaweed wraps, facials (including one for men designed to relieve razor burns), hand and foot treatments, and themed packages.

Use of the spa is limited to guests purchasing treatments. Expect to pay $15 to $40 for hand and foot pampering, about $70 for a 50-minute aromatherapy massage. Be sure to show up early, as requested, to enjoy the whirlpool, steam room, sauna, and lounge (in men's and women's locker rooms). Reservations are necessary, and can be made by calling 827-4455.

For head-to-toe pampering, consider a three-night spa package. Prices start at $945; the tab includes three spa treatments, a manicure or pedicure, a customized fitness or nutrition session, and three meals per day.

River Country Tips

■ Don't arrive expecting to find a water park of Typhoon Lagoon or Blizzard Beach sophistication or proportions. River Country (just one-seventh the size of Typhoon Lagoon) is much more quaint and contained.

■ Know that the park may close because of inclement weather or capacity constraints.

three nights, $750 for four nights, $1,281 for seven nights. Base prices for fully equipped two-bedroom Town Houses are $678 for three nights, $890 for four nights, $1,526 for seven nights. Cost per additional person sharing the same accommodation is $275 for three nights, $353 for four nights, $587 for seven nights. Rates are higher during peak seasons. All prices are subject to change.

Reservations: Stays at the Disney Institute must be booked in advance. Call 800-496-6337 for information; 800-282-9282 for reservations.

Water Parks

River Country

Disney's original watery playground holds its own with the sort of old-fashioned swimming hole Tom Sawyer would have tried to keep a lid on: a walled-off cove of Bay Lake furnished with rope swings and a ship's boom that swimmers may also enter via two fast-moving water flumes. A white-water raft ride deposits passengers into this freshwater hole a bit more gently. River Country's other swimming area has charms of its own. A 330,000-gallon pool ensconced in man-made boulders, it is fitted out with two steep chutes that stop seven feet above the water's surface; unlike the swimming hole, it's heated during cooler months. River Country honors its rustic Fort Wilderness surroundings with a short-but-sweet nature trail along the lake's edge that offers a peaceful retreat among egrets and a telescopic perspective of Bay Lake.

KNOW BEFORE YOU GO: River Country is located in the northwestern corner of Fort Wilderness on a shore of Bay Lake roughly opposite the Contemporary. The park is usually closed for refurbishment for at least one month each year (typically around September and October; call 824-4321 for exact dates). During the summer, crowds may push capacity as early as 11 A.M.; when the magic number comes up, only guests arriving via WDW transportation or with tickets in hand will be admitted, until crowds subside later in the day, generally around 3 P.M. When peak capacity is reached, no one is admitted until throngs ease up. The park may also close due to inclement weather.

How to get there: Buses from the TTC and the Wilderness Lodge, and boat launches from the Magic Kingdom and the Contemporary, deliver passengers within walking distance. Buses transport all other guests from the Fort Wilderness parking lot to the park entrance.

Where to eat: Guests may bring their own food and beverages (no alcohol or glass containers). Pop's Place, offering barbecue and baked beans, is the main snack stand. Shaded picnic areas are available.

Vital statistics: Hours vary, but are generally 10 A.M. to 7 P.M., with extended hours in effect during the summer (call 824-4321 for current times). Adult admission is $16.91, including tax. River Country admission is also included with a Length of Stay Pass and a Five-Day World Hopper Pass. Dressing rooms are available, and lockers and towels may be rented.

Typhoon Lagoon

The centerpiece of this 56-acre state-of-the-art water park—ostensibly a small resort town transformed by nature's wrath—is a surf lagoon larger than two football fields that incites happy pandemonium with every 4½-foot wave it unleashes. But there are also two speed slides (which drop 51 feet at 30 miles per hour), three quick and curvy body slides, and a trio of white-water raft rides (one of which accommodates foursomes) that send tubers rollicking through caverns and waterfalls. It's all encircled by a lazy floatable river in which swimmers—or more accurately, inner-tube innards—leisurely beat the heat.

KNOW BEFORE YOU GO: Typhoon Lagoon is located near Downtown Disney off Buena Vista Drive. Pools are heated during the winter, and the park is typically closed for refurbishment for at least one month each year (usually around November and December; call 824-4321 for exact dates). During warmer months, the throngs arrive early, often filling the parking lot before noon; when this happens only those arriving via WDW transportation will be admitted, until crowds subside around 3 P.M. When peak capacity is reached, no one is admitted until throngs thin out. The park may also close due to inclement weather.

How to get there: Direct buses from the TTC, and all WDW resorts except the Grand Floridian, Contemporary, Polynesian, Wilderness Lodge, and Fort Wilderness (which require transfers at the TTC).

Where to eat: Guests may bring food and drinks into the park (no alcohol or glass containers permitted). Of the two main snack stands, Leaning Palms offers a larger selection than Typhoon Tilly's. Shady picnic areas are close at hand.

Typhoon Lagoon Tips

■ Tidal conditions in the lagoon change every hour, alternating (with warning) between gentle waves and surf city. Since the pool surface is concrete, water-going shoes are a plus for body surfing.

■ For time checks, look to the shrimp boat marooned atop Typhoon Lagoon's makeshift mountain; it sounds its horn and shoots a 50-foot flume of water into the air every 30 minutes.

■ Bad weather or capacity crowds can prompt the park to close.

■ Women will find that one-piece suits fare better on the speed slides here.

Blizzard Beach Tips

■ The chairlift that transports guests to the summit of Mount Gushmore affords a wonderful view, as does an observatory located at the summit itself.

■ Women will find that one-piece suits fare better on the speed slides here.

■ Inclement weather or maxed-out crowds can cause the park to close.

■ The concrete pathways can get hot, making cool, watergoing shoes a coveted commodity.

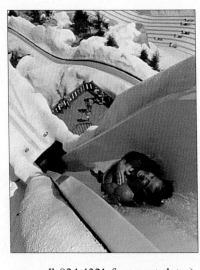

Vital statistics: Hours vary, but are generally 10 A.M. to 5 P.M., with extended hours in effect during summer months (call 824-4321 for current times). Adult admission is $26.45, including tax. Entry to Typhoon Lagoon is included with a Length of Stay Pass or a Five-Day World Hopper Pass. Dressing rooms are available, and lockers, towels, and inner tubes may be rented. Singapore Sal's stocks beach basics.

Blizzard Beach

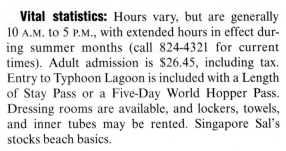

Disney legend has it that this 60-acre water park—Walt Disney World's newest and largest—is the melted remains of a failed Disney ski resort. Call it a not-so-little white lie. The bottom line on this place built around a "snow-covered" man-made peak called Mount Gushmore: It has some amazing runs. Chief among them is a ski jump–turned–speed slide that sends riders feet-first down the watery equivalent of a double-black-diamond run (a 120-foot drop at a 66-degree angle, in which speeds reach 60 miles per hour). A second speed slide plunges from 90 feet. Less intimidating highlights include an extra-long white-water raft ride accommodating five people per raft, an eight-lane "racing" water slide, and flumes that slalom. For cool yet calm, there's a lazy floatable creek that encircles the park (though it does at one point run through a cave dripping with ice-cold water) and a free-form pool with gently bobbing waves.

KNOW BEFORE YOU GO: Blizzard Beach is located near the Disney-MGM Studios. All pools are heated during the winter; the park is typically closed for refurbishment for at least one month each year (usually January and February; call 824-4321 for exact dates). During the warmer months, the throngs descend upon Blizzard Beach early in the day, and the parking lot frequently closes before noon; when this happens, only guests arriving via WDW transportation will be admitted, until crowds ease up around 3 P.M. When peak capacity is reached, no one is admitted until the throngs subside. The park may also close due to inclement weather.

How to get there: Buses are available from all WDW resorts and theme parks.

Where to eat: Guests may bring their own food and drinks (no alcohol or glass containers permitted). Of the four snack stands, Lottawatta Lodge is the largest and most centrally located. Picnic areas are nearby.

Vital statistics: Hours vary, but are generally 10 A.M. to 7 P.M., with extended hours in effect during the summer months (call 824-4321 for current times). Adult admission is $26.45, including tax. Entry to Blizzard Beach is included with a Length of Stay Pass or a Five-Day World Hopper Pass. Dressing rooms are available, and lockers and towels may be rented. The Beach Haus stocks fun-in-the-sun essentials.

Natural Distractions
Fort Wilderness

Simply put, no place on WDW property is better equipped to satisfy yens related to the great outdoors than this campground and recreation area, set on 700 forested, canal-crossed acres on the shore of the World's largest lake. (For information about campsites and other accommodations at Fort Wilderness, see *Checking In*.) Between its wonderfully canoe-worthy canals and its guided fishing excursions, Fort Wilderness gives anglers unparalleled access to the Bay Lake's largemouth bass. A marina invites guests to strap on waterskis and to rent all manner of boats for explorations of the lake. (See "Sports" earlier in this chapter for more details on fishing and boating). Escorted trail rides and a three-quarter-mile hiking trail deliver nature lovers into peaceful areas where it's not uncommon to see deer, armadillos, and birds. Myriad pathways provide inspiring venues for joggers and cyclists (bikes are available for rent), and tennis, volleyball, and basketball courts are scattered about the property. While the two swimming pools and the white-sand beach are open only to campground guests, the River Country water park (described on page 176) is close at hand. In the evenings, hayrides and the World's best dinner show, the Hoop-Dee-Doo Musical Revue (see *Dining & Entertainment* for details), keep things humming.

Fort Wilderness Tips

■ Experience the natural beauty of Fort Wilderness via a tandem bicycle (they can be rented from the Bike Barn for $4 per hour or $9 per day).

■ Because getting to and from this area can be a chore (inquire at a WDW resort Guest Services desk as to the most efficient route), it's worthwhile to combine a visit to Fort Wilderness with an excursion to River Country.

Discovery Island Tips

■ Although its possible to make a circuit of the island in about 45 minutes, we recommend allowing a couple of hours; pushing through the exhibits any faster inevitably undercuts the experience.

■ Bring your camera, plenty of film, and if you think you might want to sit out on the island's short beach, a towel; this is not lounge chair territory. If you decide to check out the beach, walk down toward the shipwreck at the edge (a holdover from the isle's original Treasure Island days) and see whether the shaded settee there is open for roosting.

■ Peek into the animal care facility (back by Toucan Corner), where veterinarians may sometimes be observed treating and feeding some of their charges.

KNOW BEFORE YOU GO: Fort Wilderness is east of the Contemporary resort on a wooded plot stretching south from Bay Lake to Vista Boulevard. It is open year-round.

How to get there: Preferably by car, for efficiency's sake. Guests at WDW-owned properties and those with River Country tickets may take boat launches from the Magic Kingdom, Wilderness Lodge, or the Contemporary resort. Buses from the TTC transport guests with a WDW resort ID or a multi-day admission pass.

Getting around: Only vehicles bound for campsites are permitted beyond the guest parking lot. Fort Wilderness is serviced by an internal bus system that links all recreation areas and campsites (buses circulate at 20-minute intervals from 7 A.M. to 2 A.M.). Guests who prefer greater independence can rent bikes or electric carts from the Bike Barn.

Where to eat: The Settlement Trading Post and the Meadow Trading Post stock staples; there's also Trail's End Buffet for all-day dining.

Vital statistics: Admission to Fort Wilderness is free. Reservations for waterskiing trips ($82 per hour for up to five people) must be made 48 hours ahead (call 824-2621). The Bike Barn in the Meadow Recreation Area is the place to pick up trail maps and to rent bikes ($3 per hour, $12 per day; tandems also available); canoes ($6 per hour, $10 per day); rods and reels ($4 per hour, $8 per day); fishing poles ($2 per hour, $4 per day); and electric carts (about $35 for 24 hours; reservations necessary; call 824-2742). Hayrides depart twice nightly from Pioneer Hall and last about an hour ($6; call 824-2900). Trail rides depart four times daily from the Tri-Circle-D Livery near the visitor lot; reservations suggested ($17; call 824-2621 up to two weeks ahead).

Discovery Island

This lush landfall for nature lovers—a 12-acre wildlife sanctuary smack in the middle of Bay Lake—allows guests to come face-to-face with one of Disney's most animated cast of characters. A zoological who's who, it features upwards of 100 species of birds, reptiles and mammals; some roam freely about the island, and all can be observed in the course of an exquisitely shaded (self-guided) three-quarter-mile footpath.

WORTH NOTING: The island's best entertainment—a 20-minute avian extravaganza called Feathered Friends—incorporates parrots, birds of prey, and a few of their feathered peers in a show that makes impressive use of the birds' natural behaviors. Reptile Relations is more educational, revealing how to tell alligators from crocodiles, for example (hint: look at their teeth). The two performances are generally scheduled back-to-back and occur several times daily; check a schedule on arrival.

Among the island's most intriguing sights are families of small busybody primates (young can often be observed clinging like tiny puffballs to their mothers' backs), a lagoon full of honking hot-pink flamingos, a walk-through aviary bespeckled with impossibly vibrant scarlet ibis, and prehistoric-looking Galápagos tortoises weighing up to 500 pounds (these endangered creatures move with such astonishing subtlety they could conceivably transport glass houses on their backs). Discovery Island's huge American exhibit features both primates and birds in an innovative setup that effectively blurs the lines between habitats while preserving the animals' separate domains. Elsewhere on the island, two extraordinary-looking Indian fishing cats provide informal (if inapplicable) fishing lessons from their own stocked stream. Also notable is the island's Malay argus pheasant, which greets onlookers with an unbelievably human "woo-woo" sound best described as the catcall to end all catcalls.

KNOW BEFORE YOU GO: Despite its isolated feel, the island is just minutes away from the resorts fronting Bay Lake and adjoining Seven Seas Lagoon, and from the Magic Kingdom itself.

How to get there: Boats depart from the Magic Kingdom, River Country, Fort Wilderness, and the Contemporary resort. Last boats to the island push off about an hour and 15 minutes before closing.

Where to eat: Guests may bring food or nonalcoholic beverages, or grab a bite at the Thirsty Perch (the main snack stand) or the Outback (an outpost). We suggest bypassing the picnic area near the Thirsty Perch for the quiet alcove of tables back by the Outback snack stand.

Vital statistics: Discovery Island is open 10 A.M. to 6 P.M., except during the summer months, when hours are extended to 7 P.M. Admission for adults is $11.61; Discovery Island admission is also included with a Length of Stay Pass and a Five-Day World Hopper Pass.

Did you know...

Discovery Island has two bald eagles, but it displays only one at a time because the pair simply do not get along.

From casual to posh, Disney dining offers a delicious world of possibilities.

Dining &
Entertainment

I t's late in the book and we're sure you must be dying of hunger by now, so we'll begin by quickly running through the food specials. But first, you'll be happy to hear that the outfit you are wearing at this moment, plus shoes, will be just fine for most any WDW restaurant (assuming that you didn't get all gussied up to read this chapter, and that you're not in your pajamas or reading on the job). And second, atmosphere—the sort that mere ambience wouldn't recognize—is a specialty of the house (you won't simply dine on seafood here, you'll do it cheek-to-cheek with a bustling coral reef or within the effervescent context of a New England clambake). Sampler platters include such unfamiliar cuisines as Norwegian and Moroccan. And if you're looking for some sophisticated eats, you're in luck. In response to patrons' demands for fresher, more imaginative fare, Disney recently revised its purchasing system to give its chefs greater freedom. With WDW's chefs doing their own grocery shopping (more accurately, blanketing the country to find the most flavorful ingredients) and having more fun, not to mention flexibility, in the kitchen, the World's menus have finally closed their historic gap with discriminating taste buds. As an example of the quality of dining that can now be found all over Walt Disney World, consider Artist Point restaurant, which features the likes of just-hooked king salmon, creatively prepared and served with hard-to-get pinot noirs from the Pacific Northwest. But we're getting carried away, and you're hungry and need to make a decision. Our

"Restaurant Guide" will help; it cuts to the chase and describes the best dining opportunities for adults in the World.

Of course, you also need to be thinking about what you want to do later, so let us quickly outline the basics. For your nighttime entertainment, you will not simply find a tremendous variety of clubs; you'll find them shoulder-to-shoulder in a section of Downtown Disney called Pleasure Island that takes the hassle out of club-hopping. The place gets going early and doesn't turn into a pumpkin until 2 A.M.; dress is weekend casual.

Next door to Pleasure Island, you'll find new excuses to stay out late in Downtown Disney West Side. This waterfront area's ultra-hip pair of

clubs provide opportunities to groove to live blues and dance to a Latin beat (complemented, if you wish, by Mississippi Delta or Cuban cuisine). A more sedate alternative is a first-run movie in the newly expanded 24-screen theater here or, coming late this year, an original, sure-to-be-spectacular production by none other than Cirque du Soleil under the big top.

Take a stroll along the BoardWalk and you'll stumble upon nostalgic snacks such as caramel apples and saltwater taffy, plus a brewpub, an old-fashioned dance hall that brings retro swing to the cutting edge, a sports bar with more TVs than Sony, and a casual sing-along spot with dueling ivory ticklers. Look around the other resorts and you'll discover hotel lounges that defy their ho-hum genre and make nightcaps an event—by evoking a locale such as Polynesia or the Old West, and by specializing; there's an outstanding wine bar, a beer lover's paradise, and several enterprising lounges that offer choice microbrews or beer by the yard.

Please, take your time, and when you're ready to think about after-dinner entertainment, know that this chapter's "Nightlife Guide" provides the complete scoop on Pleasure Island, Downtown Disney West Side, and BoardWalk, as well as compelling spots in the theme parks and resorts.

Bon appétit!

RESTAURANT GUIDE

The dining scene at Walt Disney World has evolved into a vast array of possibilities that span the price, cuisine, and atmosphere spectra. It stretches from the theme parks to the resorts and beyond, also encompassing the Downtown Disney Marketplace, Pleasure Island, and Downtown Disney West Side. Memorable dining experiences abound for adults who prefer meals to fast-food fixes. Peruse the World menu and you'll find such diverse combos as meat loaf with a side of "Father Knows Best," tiramisu served with an aria, and a sumptuous six-course splurge complete with harpist and Royal Doulton china.

Collectively, WDW's many eateries can satisfy most any craving. The key is to think with your stomach as you plot your days and nights at the World. Take note of the fact that the two Kingdoms—Magic Kingdom and Animal Kingdom—are the weakest culinary links among the theme parks for adults seeking more than fast food. Recognize Epcot's World Showcase as a gastronomic stronghold, and plan to arrive with appetite and priority seating time. Note that Downtown Disney has some mouthwatering distractions—including Fulton's Crab House, Planet Hollywood, and the much anticipated arrival of Wolfgang Puck Café—that you might want to figure into your meal plan. Be sure to look beyond the restaurants at  your own hotel to consider mealtime pilgrimages to others, as the resorts contain some of the World's most pleasant dining rooms and most enticing menus. And don't neglect to discover the far-reaching dining frontier at the BoardWalk.

> Unless otherwise noted, all phone numbers are in area code 407.

We're happy to report that Walt Disney World has more tempting cuisine for the sophisticated palate than ever before, as behind-the-scenes improvements—from fresher, more flavorful ingredients to stronger wine lists—have quietly pushed the epicurean envelope. Also, healthier, more interesting grazing options in the theme parks (see our snacking suggestions in the margins of the *Theme Parks* chapter) can provide inexpensive treats that help subsidize the sit-down meals.

To ease the task of deciding among the World's innumerable eateries, we've whittled the list down to a diverse selection of full-service restaurants and more casual noshing spots that we recommend as the best adult bets. The intention is not to diminish the value of establishments not included, but to underscore the greater appeal certain restaurants hold for adults.

Fare Thee Well

This restaurant guide is not a comprehensive listing of the World's eateries, but a selective roundup of the best adult dining and snacking venues. Those restaurants designated as "Standouts" are dining rooms and fast-food places whose exceptional flair, distinctive fare, and/or terrific setting have earned our highest recommendation. "Good Bets" are additional locales that offer consistently rewarding dining experiences.

Priority Seating, Explained

A system known as priority seating takes the place of reservations for all WDW restaurants, with the exception of most dinner shows. Disney established priority seating to prevent logjams created by no-shows and late-shows. You receive a seating time, but must check in at the restaurant to become eligible for the next available table. (Our advice: Arrive 15 to 20 minutes early.)

If the system works as intended: (1) those with priority seating will be seated at or near their assigned time; and (2) walk-ins will have a shot at any open tables. To make arrangements, call WDW-DINE (939-3463) up to 60 days ahead. Because procedures are subject to change, it's best to confirm policies with WDW-DINE.

Our dining recommendations, which touch down all over the World and provide options for all taste buds and budgets, are presented within four distinct contexts—in the theme parks, in the resorts, elsewhere within WDW boundaries, and off-property. Within each of these locales, we have roped off for extra consideration those restaurants that offer some of the most consistently rewarding dining experiences. Under the heading "Standouts," you'll find stellar places to grab a great bite on the quick; moderately priced restaurants with exceptional flair; and extra-special havens worth every hard-earned dollar for their distinctive food and setting. Under the designation "Good Bets," we've corralled additional locales, also highly regarded, that we've come to know as fine places to have a meal. Because Walt Disney World's theme parks are unique terrain calling for both firm arrangements and flexible eating plans, we have included recommendations for fast-food as well as full-service options.

Individual entries offer characterizations for each restaurant and provide such essential information as location, price, and the meals served there (represented by B, L, and D for breakfast, lunch, and dinner, with S symbolizing availability of snacks). As an indication of what you can expect to spend for a meal, we have classified restaurants as very expensive (dinners $30 and up); expensive (dinners $18 to $30); moderate (dinners $8 to $18); or inexpensive (dinners under $8). The prices represent a typical meal for one person at a restaurant (steak at a steak house, for example, and a burger and fries at a fast-food spot), not including drinks, tax, or tip. As a rule, tabs for breakfast and lunch are lower, but consistent with the price category we've assigned to the restaurant.

We also denote in each entry the necessity of reservations or priority seating (a system that has replaced reservations at WDW restaurants). In the adjacent margins, we explain priority seating and outline protocol for booking tables in and around the World. For the rundown on dinner shows, strategies to eating your way around the World, and the scoop on where to find an afternoon tea, dining rooms with terrific views, late-night bites, great wines by the glass, and more, check the margins. A final word of advice: You might *not* want to read this section on an empty stomach.

In the Theme Parks
Full Service

STANDOUTS

AKERSHUS (Norway, Epcot's World Showcase): In a world in which many international cuisines have gone from trendy to almost trite, this is an alluring taste of the unfamiliar. The ambience of a medieval Norwegian fortress—marked by dramatic cathedral ceilings, stone archways, iron chandeliers, leaded-glass windows, and the occasional red carpet—is not to be denied. Nor is the delicious novelty of the all-you-can-eat Norwegian smorgasbord served here. Known as *koldtbord* (or "cold table"), the buffet includes both hot and cold selections. There's plenty for the unadventurous palate, from creamy potato salad to savory Norwegian meatballs; but don't stop there. This is your chance to sample well-prepared signature dishes that don't often leave Scandinavia; there's smoked mackerel, herring prepared every which way, mashed rutabagas (don't wince; they're good), and a whole lot more. It all washes down quite nicely with a tall draft of Ringnes beer. Wine selection is limited. Priority seating suggested. Moderate to expensive. L, D.

BISTRO DE PARIS (France, Epcot's World Showcase): An intimate bistro that puts on romantic airs rather than the usual bustle. If you think the decor, with its evocative interplay of brass sconces, milk-glass chandeliers, mirrors, and leaded glass, is convincingly French, wait until you swallow your first morsel. The sophisticated menu—created by three of France's top chefs (Paul Bocuse, Roger Vergé, and Gaston Lenôtre)—is executed with a

---

How to Book a Table

■ **IN THE THEME PARKS:** Priority seating is suggested for nearly all full-service restaurants in the Magic Kingdom, Epcot, and Disney-MGM Studios (see individual entries); simply call WDW-DINE. For same-day arrangements in the Magic Kingdom, report to City Hall; in Epcot, use the WorldKey screens at Guest Relations; in the Disney-MGM Studios, go to the corner of Hollywood and Sunset boulevards. Same-day arrangements can also be made at the restaurants. Note that limited priority seating is available for Rainforest Café, Animal Kingdom's only full-service restaurant.

■ **IN WDW RESORTS:** Priority seating for restaurants at Disney hotels may be made by calling WDW-DINE (see individual entries to determine necessity). For reservations at any of the full-service eateries at the Swan, call 934-1609; for the Dolphin, call 934-4858.

■ **ELSEWHERE AT WDW:** In lieu of priority seating, any necessary reservations at Downtown Disney and the Hotel Plaza Blvd. resorts may be made using the number provided in the restaurant entry.

Smoker's Alert

rich authenticity that will astonish any unsuspecting gourmand. This is hearty dining of the sort that inspires a sudden need for a nap, so we're glad this restaurant sticks to dinner. Although you might want to take a stroll around the promenade to walk off your escargots, rack of lamb, and chocolate soufflé. The impressive wine list is *très* French. Priority seating suggested. Expensive. D.

50'S PRIME TIME CAFE (Disney-MGM Studios): In a word: cool. This good-humored retreat to the era of "I Love Lucy" is an amusing amalgam of comfort food, kitschy 1950s-style kitchen nooks, and attentive servers of the "No talking with your mouth full" ilk. Expect that Mom or her favored offspring will meddle in your affairs here ("Did you wash your hands? All right then, what color was the soap?"). And recognize that the best fun is had by doing some regressing of your own. One Prime Time regular we know—a troublemaker appropriately in his early fifties—has gotten major entertainment mileage from such lines as "Mom, she says I'm a tattletale!" and "Mom, can I sleep over at Susy's house? Her parents aren't home and she's afraid to be alone." As for the fare, it's tasty home cooking as it used to be (heavy on the meat and potatoes), served forth in generous-to-the-point-of-grandmotherly portions. Most guests find it honors their memory of pot roast, s'mores, and root beer floats. In fact, order a peanut butter sandwich and you could very well be asked if you'd like a side of Marshmallow Fluff. Beer and wine are served. Priority seating suggested. Moderate. L, D, S.

GARDEN GRILL (The Land, Epcot's Future World): When your assigned priority seating time comes due at this lazy susan–turned–dining area (it rotates slowly above the rain forest, desert, and prairie scenes visited by the Celebrate the Land boat ride below), you are politely informed by a "farmhand" that you have some chores to do. Bessie has been milked, apparently, but the table hasn't been set. And so it is that you are seated, only to have to stand and harvest your place setting from the center of the table. As the meal and the setting progress, you steal through a squawking rain forest, observe a strong wind kicking up desert sand, watch buffalo graze on a prairie, and visit a farmhouse (request a table on the lower tier for the best view). It's the evocative, ever-changing scenery and the farm-fresh fare that make the Garden Grill perhaps the best spot for adults to dine in the company of characters. Mickey and pals make rounds at each meal. The full country breakfast is served family-style, as are lunch and dinner, which feature vegetables grown in The Land's greenhouses, catfish (also cultivated here), rotisserie chicken, and hickory-smoked steaks. Save room for the cinnamon ice cream–topped warm apple crisp. When all's said and done, you're glad you did your chores. Priority seating suggested. Moderate to expensive. B, L, D.

HOLLYWOOD BROWN DERBY (Disney-MGM Studios): The Studios' most gracious dining is found at this faithful revival of the original cause célèbre, which opened on Hollywood and Vine back in 1926. Dressed to the nines in chandeliers, palm trees, and celebrity caricatures, the restaurant stokes the appetite with its signature Cobb salad, fabulous grapefruit cake, and main dishes along the lines of seared salmon, grilled steaks, and light pasta dishes. The wine list is excellent. Priority seating suggested. Expensive. L, D.

LIBERTY TREE TAVERN (Liberty Square, Magic Kingdom): This homey restaurant—the best in the Magic Kingdom—revives the spirit of Colonial America so fully in its sprawling dining rooms that you're apt to wonder how many kettles it's got going in the kitchen. The beamed ceilings are hung with candelabras, the floors are made of wide oak planks, and the paned windows were fashioned using 18th-century casting techniques. Interestingly, many of the period paintings on the walls were commissioned for use in the historical film shown at The Hall of Presidents. It all has a way of inspiring a taste for roast turkey, honey-baked ham, flank steak, and homemade mashed potatoes. Pot roast, turkey, and oversize salads and sandwiches are the call for lunch. Don't miss the apple butter and honey margarine served with the rolls. Aim for an early or late seating to

---

HOT TIP

Walt Disney World restaurants can accommodate special dietary requirements (vegetarian, low-sodium, lactose-free, and kosher meals, for example) if requests are made at least 24 hours in advance. Make your personal needs known when you make your priority seating arrangements (by calling WDW-DINE).

Secrets to Success

Hungry and in no mood to wait in line? To avoid the inevitable crunch, plan to eat an early (or late) breakfast, lunch, or dinner. Sit-down restaurants that offer table service are usually less crowded at lunch than at dinner, so you might want to make that the main meal of the day. But if it's a dinner spot you relish, choose a restaurant where priority seating is available (see page 187 for details on making these arrangements). Also, be on the watch for discounted early-bird specials, which arise on occasion from 4:30 P.M. until 6 P.M.

best experience this restaurant's charms. Also note that dinner here is a family-style character affair. Priority seating suggested. Expensive. L, D.

L'ORIGINALE ALFREDO DI ROMA RISTORANTE (Italy, Epcot's World Showcase): Adorned with massive murals that evoke the Italian countryside, this elegant restaurant inspires a "when in Rome" frame of mind from the outset. You suddenly hear an Italian grandmother's voice in your head, urging you to "eat, eat." But do you go with the specialty of the house, fettuccine Alfredo (wide, flat noodles in a rich butter and Parmesan cheese sauce)? Perhaps the chicken cacciatore? The veal sautéed with black truffles and wine, accompanied by fresh asparagus and mushrooms? It's hard to go wrong at Alfredo's, as fresh pasta is made right on the premises and fine Italian wines are in ready supply; of course, you could blow it and neglect to save room for dessert. This restaurant stands out, too, for its atmosphere, which is at once romantic and festive. Between arias, roving Italian singers have been known to choreograph a napkin-twirling tarantella. Priority seating suggested. Expensive. L, D.

TEPPANYAKI DINING ROOMS (Japan, Epcot's World Showcase): It's not exactly an authentic dose of Japanese cuisine (Tempura Kiku next door gives a closer approximation with its sushi, sashimi, and tempura), but it offers a great time and a terrific meal. Guests sit around a large, flat teppan grill and watch as a nimble, white-hatted chef deftly demonstrates just how quickly enough chicken, beef, seafood, and vegetables to feed eight people can be chopped, seasoned, and stir-fried (knives fly at speeds that could dust a food processor). Entrées are flavorful and sizzling. Because smaller parties are seated together, Teppanyaki becomes a social affair, and it's a fine place for singles. Priority seating suggested. Expensive. L, D.

TONY'S TOWN SQUARE (Main Street, Magic Kingdom): We have nothing against the main dining room (it's quite charming), but the bright and airy atrium at this Victorian-style Italian restaurant rates among the most pleasant dining environs in the Magic Kingdom. Something about the terrazzo floors, hanging plants, ceiling fans, and the view of Town Square beckons. The *Lady and the Tramp* theme is endearingly subtle, and the fare is reliably good, from the waffles to the Caesar salads, pizzas, and sautéed shrimp. For dessert, try Tony's Italian pastries and a cup of cappuccino or espresso. Priority seating suggested. Expensive. B, L, D.

GOOD BETS

AU PETIT CAFE (France, Epcot's World Showcase): Order a *niçoise* salad with a side of passersby; this Parisian sidewalk café is the best scoping spot in all of World Showcase and a great primer for the pastries of Boulangerie Pâtisserie around the corner. No priority seating translates here as "don't arrive famished." First-come seating. Moderate. L, D, S.

BIERGARTEN (Germany, Epcot's World Showcase): Prepare for the best of the wurst. A buffet of hearty traditional German cuisine (don't miss the potato salad, red cabbage, spaetzle, or sauerbraten) and rousing oompah-style performances are the main attractions in this vast yet charming makeshift courtyard. Adding to the fun are long communal tables, 33-ounce steins of Beck's beer, and a selection of German wines and liqueurs. Follow it up with apple strudel or Black Forest cake. Priority seating suggested. Moderate to expensive. L, D.

CHEFS DE FRANCE (France, Epcot's World Showcase): With three of France's best chefs—Paul Bocuse, Roger Vergé, and pastry guru Gaston Lenôtre—keeping tabs on this nouvelle French kitchen, the broth is far from spoiled. We love the thought of their Lyons-style onion soup and the luscious ways in which they fill a puff pastry. Modest wine list. Priority seating suggested. Expensive. L, D.

CINDERELLA'S ROYAL TABLE (Cinderella Castle, Magic Kingdom): Go for the grand medieval setting rather than the American fare (which, incidentally, includes Caesar salad topped with lobster, scallops, and shrimp for lunch; prime rib and grilled swordfish for dinner). Priority seating is necessary for the daily character breakfast, and for lunch and dinner. Expensive. B, L, D.

Cheap Eats

Here are our suggestions for spur-of-the-moment fast food:

■ **Cosmic Ray's Starlight Café** (Tomorrowland, Magic Kingdom)

■ **Sunshine Season Food Fair** (The Land, Epcot's Future World)

■ **Cantina de San Angel** (Mexico, Epcot's World Showcase)

■ **Kringla Bakeri og Kafé** (Norway, Epcot's World Showcase)

■ **Backlot Express** (Disney-MGM Studios)

■ **Hollywood & Vine** (Disney-MGM Studios)

■ **Tuskers** (Africa, Animal Kingdom)

Grape Expectations

Grownups who are surprised by the fine dining (and snacking) all over the World will be absolutely delighted at the selection of wines to accompany their food. From the pavilions of World Showcase to the lounges and restaurants of the WDW resorts, here are our favorite ways to sample the fruit of the vine.

■ Weinkeller (Germany, Epcot's World Showcase): Daily tastings from the shop's 250 varieties. Don't miss the rich, flowery dessert wines, gloriously sweet (and not inexpensive).

■ La Maison du Vin (France, Epcot's World Showcase): Tastings and sales from the country synonymous with wine. Another chance to sample top-quality vintages before you buy a whole bottle.

•CONTINUED ON NEXT PAGE

CORAL REEF (The Living Seas, Epcot's Future World): It's all about sneaking bites of fresh fish and shellfish under the watchful eyes of sea turtles, dolphins, and gargantuan groupers. Every table has a panoramic view of the living coral reef; some are right up against the glass. Priority seating suggested. Expensive. L, D.

CRYSTAL PALACE (Main Street, Magic Kingdom): A Magic Kingdom landmark of sorts, this restaurant could be a Victorian garden if not for the existence of walls and a ceiling. Nonetheless, it provides a pleasant escape from the crowds on Main Street and the widest variety of any meal in the park. The buffet is driven by fresh seasonal produce, including a salad bar, deli bar, and pasta for lunch, and adding spit-roasted beef, chicken, shrimp, and carved meats for dinner. Winnie the Pooh and Tigger, too, wander about during all meals. Priority seating suggested. Expensive. B, L, D.

MAMA MELROSE'S RISTORANTE ITALIANO (Disney-MGM Studios): A pleasantly removed bastion of red-checkered tablecloths and thin-crust pizzas baked in wood-burning ovens. Priority seating suggested. Moderate to expensive. L, D (during busy seasons).

MARRAKESH (Morocco, Epcot's World Showcase): It's not every day that you can slip into an exquisitely tiled Moroccan palace and expect to be entertained by belly dancers and musicians as you polish off a sampler plate of distinctive Moroccan cuisine, such as couscous or kebabs. The volume of the music here can be a drawback. Priority seating suggested. Expensive. L, D.

ROSE & CROWN PUB AND DINING ROOM (United Kingdom, Epcot's World Showcase): The menu ventures only a tad beyond fish-and-chips and meat pies, but the pleasant dining room offers a front-seat view of the lagoon, and the pub's downright neighborly. Priority seating suggested. Moderate to expensive. L, D, S.

SAN ANGEL INN (Mexico, Epcot's World Showcase): The lights are low, the mood is romantic, and there is a smoking volcano poised almost tableside. If that's not enchantment enough, there's a mystical pyramid and a moonlit river. The menu? You may need to bring the table candle closer to read it, but you'll find Mexican fare from margaritas to chicken mole. Don't miss the chips and salsa. Priority seating suggested. Expensive. L, D.

SCI-FI DINE-IN THEATER (Disney-MGM Studios): The dishes are more creative than those at your average drive-in theater (huge salads, sandwiches, and the Cheesecake That Ate New York, for instance), but it still takes a backseat to the campy moonlit setting. Tables resemble 1950s-era convertibles and are parked next to working drive-in theater speakers. Science fiction and horror trailers play on a large screen. Wine and beer are available. Priority seating suggested. Moderate to expensive. L, D.

Fast Food

STANDOUTS

BACKLOT EXPRESS (Disney-MGM Studios): Shady and inconspicuous (it's tucked away by the Indiana Jones Epic Stunt Spectacular theater), this is a sprawling spot with both indoor and outdoor seating and unusual potential for quiet. Paint-speckled floors and assorted auto debris give you an idea of the decor. Chicken Caesar salads, grilled chicken sandwiches, chili, and brownies are among the more tempting fare. Beer is available. Inexpensive. L, D, S.

•*CONTINUED FROM PREVIOUS PAGE*

■ Victoria & Albert's (Grand Floridian): The World's most upscale dining room boasts an equally grand wine list. Best bet: For $25, you can get four glasses of wine specifically chosen to complement individual courses on the prix fixe menu.

■ Artist Point (Wilderness Lodge): Want to know why pinot noir and grilled salmon are a match made in heaven? Here's where to find out.

■ Martha's Vineyard (Beach Club): Two-ounce samples from this lounge's savvy list of vintners are a delicious way to explore wine regions across the country.

■ California Grill (Contemporary): The list has great depth and breadth, including a fine selection of California wines by the glass; it changes daily to complement new dishes. Inquire about the weekly wine tastings. Real zinfandel is red, not white, and they've got the Ravenswood to prove it.

S.O.S. for the Sweet Tooth

The following theme park spots are sure to satisfy:

- ■ **Main Street Bake Shop** (Main Street, Magic Kingdom)
- ■ **Main Street Confectionery** (Main Street, Magic Kingdom)
- ■ **Fountain View Espresso and Bakery** (Epcot's Future World)
- ■ **Boulangerie Pâtisserie** (France, Epcot's World Showcase)
- ■ **Delizie Italiane** (Italy, Epcot's World Showcase)
- ■ **Süssigkeiten** (Germany, Epcot's World Showcase)
- ■ **Kringla Bakeri og Kafé** (Norway, Epcot's World Showcase)
- ■ **Starring Rolls Bakery** (Disney-MGM Studios)
- ■ **Sweet Success** (Disney-MGM Studios)

BOULANGERIE PATISSERIE (France, Epcot's World Showcase): The chocolate croissants, blueberry tarts, apple turnovers, and such here are timeless. Follow your nose, and don't neglect to notice the sweet temptation aptly known as the Marvelous. Kronenbourg beer and French wines are also offered. Inexpensive. S.

CANTINA DE SAN ANGEL (Mexico, Epcot's World Showcase): Forget for a moment the *churros*, the frozen margaritas, the chicken tostadas, and the Dos Equis drafts—this place has fresh watermelon juice. When the weather cooperates, the outdoor lagoonside seating makes it taste even better. Inexpensive. L, D, S.

COSMIC RAY'S STARLIGHT CAFE (Tomorrowland, Magic Kingdom): A one-size-fits-all establishment that's the choicest spot to get fast food in the Magic Kingdom for two reasons: variety and elbow room. Burgers, salads, and rotisserie chicken all have a place on the menu. Inexpensive. L, D, S.

FOUNTAIN VIEW ESPRESSO AND BAKERY (Innoventions Plaza, Epcot's Future World): This ode to pastries, desserts, and specialty coffees is a veritable adult oasis any time of day. Wine and beer are also available. Inexpensive. B, S.

HOLLYWOOD & VINE (Disney-MGM Studios): An Art Deco–style cafeteria with Tinseltown flourishes, this is the ticket when you want to make it quick. Expect standard cafeteria fare, and the heartiest breakfast at the Studios. Beer and wine are served. Inexpensive to moderate. B, L, D, S.

KRINGLA BAKERI OG KAFE (Norway, Epcot's World Showcase): Simply a super place for a sweet fix or a light lunch. Among the tasty morsels to be had here are potato salad, yogurt, open-face sandwiches (roast beef, turkey, salmon, and chicken salad), sweet pretzels called *kringles*, and *vaflers* (heart-shaped waffles fresh-made as you wait and topped with powdered sugar and preserves). Ringnes beer is on tap. The outdoor seating area is shaded by a grass-thatched roof. Inexpensive. L, D, S.

LE CELLIER (Canada, Epcot's World Showcase): If you've forgotten the charms of cafeteria-style dining, this peaceful wine cellar–like spot serves up lots of savory reminders (Canadian cheddar cheese soup, for one). You can eat a hearty meat-and-potatoes meal with no need for priority seating. Then there's the potential for a bowl of strawberries with whipped cream. Inexpensive to moderate. L, D, S.

MAIN STREET BAKE SHOP (Main Street, Magic Kingdom): This dainty spot is renowned for quick breakfasts (from bagels to fresh baked cinnamon rolls) and enormous fresh-from-the-oven cookies (from chocolate chip to Snicker-doodle). Inexpensive. B, S.

SOMMERFEST (Germany, Epcot's World Showcase): Here, quick sustenance takes such classic forms as bratwurst, soft pretzels, Black Forest cake, German chocolates, Beck's beer, and German wine. The nicely shaded outdoor seating area sports a festive mural. Inexpensive. L, D, S.

STARRING ROLLS BAKERY (Disney-MGM Studios): Have croissant and cap-puccino; will travel. This is the place in the Studios to get the day off to a sweet start or to take an impromptu cookie or coffee break under umbrella-shaded tables. A little-known fact: It's got some good sandwiches of the tuna salad and ham-and-cheese variety, to boot. Inexpensive. B, L, S.

SUNSHINE SEASON FOOD FAIR (The Land, Epcot's Future World): This bumper crop of food stands, located directly beneath the hot-air balloons on The Land pavilion's lower level, is the best place in Epcot to strap on the ol' feed bag and graze. It's a finicky eater indeed who can't find temptation among this court's countless soups, salads, baked goods, pasta, sandwiches, barbecue, baked potatoes, ice cream, and refreshing libations. The eating's significantly more peaceful here outside prime dining hours. Inexpensive. B, L, D, S.

GOOD BETS

AUNTIE GRAVITY'S GALACTIC GOODIES (Tomorrowland, Magic Kingdom): A good pit stop for frozen yogurt, fruit smoothies, and health-conscious snacks if you're in the neighborhood. Inexpensive. S.

No Priority Seating Needed

If you're caught without priority seating arrangements in the theme parks, you can usually snag a table at one of these recommended full-service or cafeteria spots (especially if you're willing to wait a bit):

- **Au Petit Café** (France, Epcot's World Showcase)
- **Le Cellier** (Canada, Epcot's World Showcase)
- **Hollywood & Vine** (Disney-MGM Studios)
- **Tempura Kiku** (Japan, Epcot's World Showcase)

Animal Kingdom Eats

Stomach growling? The restaurants in this park push the fast-food envelope by offering healthier choices in knockout settings. The standouts: Africa yields Tuskers, for chicken done every which way. In Safari Village, it's Flame Tree Barbecue, for dramatic views and, of course, tasty barbecue; and Pizzafari, for gourmet pizzas and wood-roasted chicken Caesar salads. In DinoLand U.S.A., try Restaurantosaurus, for its setting—a paleontologists' campsite—rather than the McDonald's-style fare. If you *must* dine in a full-service restaurant, note that Rainforest Café, at the park's entrance, is the only option.

CATWALK BAR (Disney-MGM Studios): This cool loft of a prop storage area is more than a lounge; it's a great place to prop yourself above the madding crowd for a plate of chilled shrimp. Inexpensive. S.

COLUMBIA HARBOUR HOUSE (Liberty Square, Magic Kingdom): This spot distinguishes itself from the rest of the fast-food crowd by emphasizing things from the sea—among them, clam chowder, fried fish, and harpoons (the latter are strictly for decor). Bypass the tables in the main room for one of the quiet nooks upstairs. Operates seasonally. Inexpensive. L, D, S.

LOTUS BLOSSOM CAFE (China, Epcot's World Showcase): The menu's on the short side, but what's here—basic Chinese takeout—is a good call when hunger strikes and you're in the neighborhood. Outdoor tables line the sidewalks. Inexpensive. L, D.

PLAZA ICE CREAM PARLOR (Main Street, Magic Kingdom): Simply the park's most bountiful stash of ice cream. Head here when you want a choice of flavors, not a Mouseketeer Bar. Inexpensive. S.

PURE AND SIMPLE (Wonders of Life, Epcot's Future World): The place merits attention by offering healthy pickings along the lines of fruit smoothies, multigrain waffles with fruit toppings, tuna pitas with reduced-calorie mayonnaise, and papaya juice. Another plus: It's rarely mobbed. Inexpensive. B, L, S.

YAKITORI HOUSE (Japan, Epcot's World Showcase): Perched among hillside gardens, this spot (named for the specialty of the house, savory skewered chicken) is one of the most relaxing settings in Epcot for a quick and satisfying bite. Kirin beer and sake are also available. Inexpensive. L, D, S.

In the Resorts

STANDOUTS

ARTIST POINT (Wilderness Lodge): The Pacific Northwest theme of this restaurant is beautifully announced in two-story-high landscape murals, while tall red-framed windows look out to Bay Lake. Artist Point's hallmark is its knack for translating the fresh seasonal ingredients from the Pacific Northwest into flavorful creations. An excellent example is the wild steelhead salmon marinated in whiskey, then roasted and served on a smoking cedar plank, accompanied by winter squash. The berry cobbler is heavenly, and takes so perfectly to vanilla ice cream that you make room no matter how full you think you are. It's just the fork-licking finale you'd expect from a restaurant that bucks tradition and puts desserts first on its menu. The wine list features some of the best pinot noirs coming out of Oregon right now. The cumulative effect is an artist's palette for the sophisticated palate. Priority seating suggested for breakfast (a character affair) and for dinner. Expensive. B, D.

BEACHES & CREAM SODA SHOP (Yacht Club and Beach Club): Every inch a classic soda fountain, it's the site for egg creams, malts, and milk shakes, plus burgers we happen to think are the best in the World. Continental breakfast is also offered. First-come seating. Inexpensive to moderate. B, L, D, S.

BIG RIVER GRILLE & BREWING WORKS (BoardWalk): Not only a standout for its fresh-brewed ales—this unassuming place delivers huge portions of satisfying pub grub. The straightforward please-all menu runs from burgers and steaks to lobster pot pie and yellowfin tuna. The kitchen takes full advantage of the ready availability of great beer for its sauces, and yes, that Rocket Red Ale Chicken is as good as it sounds. The small, partitioned dining area somehow gives the room a cozy air in spite of the factory motif. This restaurant tends to be more low-key than the other BoardWalk eateries, and makes for a particularly peaceful retreat during the day. Seating is available outside on the boardwalk. First-come seating. Moderate. L, D, S.

BONFAMILLE'S CAFE (Port Orleans): This restaurant offers an absolutely endearing introduction to Creole cooking in a casual courtyard setting that neatly

Best Burgers

The juiciest, tastiest burgers in the World are served up at Beaches & Cream Soda Shop, between the Yacht Club and the Beach Club.

The Inside Scoop

evokes New Orleans' French Quarter. The menu tells the tale of Memere, the fictional matriarch who inspired Bonfamille's; the story's parting words— "Loosen up your belt and enjoy what you've put past your tongue"—are all the more relevant after you've experienced the portions served here. Try the jambalaya or a roast beef po'boy with a bottle of Dixie Blackened Voodoo Lager. Or try something else, but do loosen your belt a little beforehand. Priority seating available for dinner. Moderate. B, D.

CALIFORNIA GRILL (Contemporary): The fresh seasonal ingredients credo gets an artistic interpretation at this casual feast for the eyes (and stomach) on the Contemporary's 15th floor. Chefs at this acclaimed restaurant keep no culinary secrets as they prepare dishes in the exhibition kitchen. The West Coast theme shines through in such market-fresh dishes as alderwood-smoked salmon with whole roasted onions, and oak-fired beef tenderloin with Sonoma foie gras and a zinfandel glaze. If there's a bit of a din in the dining room it's partly because of unsuppressible raves and the wait staff's collective ability to elaborate on any dish, ingredient, or wine. The star-studded wine list, ranging from traditional chardonnays to new-wave viogniers, is a striking mix of greatest hits and good finds, quite a few of which are available by the glass. Also drawing a crowd: the Grill's divine California-style pizza and fine sushi bar. Home-baked desserts along the lines of tangerine soufflé provide the finishing touches, as do sweeping views of the Magic Kingdom. Priority seating suggested. Expensive. D.

CAPE MAY CAFE (Beach Club): The all-you-can-eat New England clambake held nightly in this whimsical, beach-umbrella-decked dining area is among the best values at Walt Disney World. The groaning board includes mussels, fish, peel-and-eat shrimp, corn-on-the-cob, ribs, red-skin potatoes, chowders, and salads. Lobster is available for an extra charge. If you like, dessert can be milk and cookies (or fruit cobbler). Priority seating suggested for breakfast (served with a side of characters) and for dinner. Moderate to expensive. B, D.

FLYING FISH CAFE (BoardWalk): Expect an earful when you ask about the catch of the day at this compelling eatery bound and determined to serve seafood "so fresh it has an attitude." Fun, sophisticated decor from the designer of the Contemporary's California Grill elevates the appeal, as does the availability of wonderfully fruity champagne concoctions called "Coasters." As an example of the (exhibitionist) kitchen's knack for light, creatively prepared dishes, consider barbecue-glazed salmon with sweet-corn pudding and potato-wrapped yellowtail snapper. Menu items vary daily, but steaks and vegetarian choices are usually offered. Whatever you do, save room for the chocolate lava cake (voted "Best Dessert in Central Florida" by at least one restaurant critic). Priority seating suggested. Expensive. D.

NARCOOSSEE'S (Grand Floridian): Within the conspicuous octagonal building (with veranda) that looks out over Seven Seas Lagoon, you'll find a casual restaurant whose open kitchen presents such not-so-casual fare as filet mignon and Maine lobster with rock shrimp stuffing. You'll also discover knockout grilled swordfish marinated in garlic olive oil and basil, or roasted grouper with crabmeat crust, on the recently revised "Floribbean" menu—a combination of Floridian and Caribbean influences, if you didn't guess. Note: This is not your secluded romantic retreat; there are yards of beer being downed, and children are not scarce. But the food is excellent, and the wine selection quite good. Priority seating suggested. Expensive. L, D.

OLIVIA'S CAFE (Old Key West): We like the Key Western manner with which Olivia's approaches its theme; certainly, the enthusiastically laid-back setting and menu convey the spirit of the leisure-centric locale. Oh, there are menu selections that work the theme hard—salads with Key lime–honey Dijon dressing, conch chowder, and Key Lime Kooler, a creamy blend of rum and Key lime juice—but there are just as many offered strictly for fun. Cases in point: pork chops with plum barbecue sauce, grilled shrimp on a sugarcane skewer served with coconut rice, and frozen strawberry margarita tart. All things considered, it's worth a detour. Wine, beer, and specialty drinks are served. On Wednesday and Sunday, breakfast comes with characters. Menu changes seasonally. Priority seating suggested. Moderate. B, L, D.

VICTORIA & ALBERT'S (Grand Floridian): Indulgent without being too haute to handle, and stunningly luxurious without being pretentious, this grande dame of the Walt Disney World dining scene is in a class all its own. The six-course prix fixe menu changes daily, always offering an array of fish, poultry, beef, veal, and lamb selections as well as a choice of soups, salads, and desserts. The delectable $80-per-person adventure begins with the arrival of hors d'oeuvres. As an example of what could follow, consider Oriental shrimp dumplings, chicken consommé with pheasant breast, poached Maine lobster with passion fruit butter,

Don't Miss the Boat

Here's your chance to sail the Seven Seas (and Bay Lake) on a private 44-foot yacht, complete with cocktails and catered cuisine. Docking at the Grand Floridian, the vessel transports up to 12 passengers day or night. To make arrangements, inquire at Guest Services upon arrival.

Two for Tea

Teatime with all the trimmings—scones, dainty sandwiches, and pastries served on bone china—is 3 P.M. at the Garden View lounge at the Grand Floridian. An extensive selection of teas and tasty accompaniments are offered every day until 6 P.M. (first-come seating).

mixed greens with raspberry–pinot noir vinaigrette, Stilton cheese with pears poached in burgundy wine, and a dark chocolate and strawberry soufflé. Perfect portions keep it all surprisingly manageable. The beautifully appointed room is well designed for intimate dining. The strains of a harp or violin provide a romantic backdrop. The wine list is encyclopedic, and the wine pairings (you'll pay about $25 more for four selected glasses) provide fitting complements. At the end of the meal, you're presented with a souvenir menu and a red rose. In sum, an extremely expensive, extremely special experience. Jackets are required for men. Priority seating necessary. Very expensive. D.

YACHTSMAN STEAKHOUSE (Yacht Club): Our stomachs couldn't possibly be as big as our eyes at this carnivore's paradise, where on at least one occasion a server has kindly saved us from ourselves. The generous portions begin with truly massive rolls and continue with the imperative spicy fried onion skillet and the signature garlic-and-cheese "smashed" potatoes; of course, there's no skimping on the excellent and expertly prepared aged beef entrées (prime rib, filet mignon, and chateaubriand, to name a few), so good luck finding room for a piece of white-chocolate macadamia nut pie or chocolate mousse cake. While the menu emphasizes steak, it also includes seafood and chicken dishes. This atmospheric restaurant is possessed of country club elegance and is filled with intimate dining nooks perfectly suited for special occasions. Both the wine and beer lists are extensive. Priority seating suggested. Expensive. D.

GOOD BETS

BOATWRIGHT'S DINING HALL (Dixie Landings): Moderately priced Cajun specialties are the draw at this unique eatery, where the centerpiece is a riverboat under construction, boat-making tools are mounted on the walls, and tables are set with condiment-filled toolboxes. Try the baby-back ribs with Cajun dirty rice. Full bar. Priority seating available. Moderate. B, D.

CONCOURSE STEAKHOUSE (Contemporary): If homemade potato chips speak to you, you'd like to sample the best mashed potatoes in the World, or you just want a quick, civilized bite one step removed from the Magic Kingdom, here you have it. Individual pizzas are a good bet for lunch. Priority seating suggested. Moderate to expensive. B, L, D.

GRAND FLORIDIAN CAFE (Grand Floridian): Tall, wall-length windows incorporate the hotel's central courtyard into this inviting restaurant's potted-palm greenery. It's a pleasant spot morning, afternoon, and evening, and a reasonably priced way to check out the World's poshest resort. The café's tasty seasonal dishes have a southern flavor, and the menu includes many light selections. Try the citrus french toast with cinnamon, crab cakes with Key lime remoulade, or the braised mango chicken. Excellent wine selection. Priority seating available. Moderate. B, L, D.

JUAN & ONLY'S (Dolphin, 934-4884): It'll cost you a few pesos, but for Texas-size portions of exceptional Mexican fare, head for this colorful spot. Whether you take a white-corn tortilla chip to the Seven Sins Dip is up to you. There's *cerveza*, margaritas, and both red and blond sangria by the pitcher, and the bar stocks rare tequilas. Smoking permitted. Reservations suggested. Moderate to expensive. D.

KIMONO'S (Swan, 934-1609): This is the call for good sushi (prepared as you watch) and tempura in a peaceful lounge styled with bamboo and kimono accents. A respectable wine selection is complemented by sake, Japanese beers, and specialty cocktails. The calm is occasionally interrupted with karaoke. Smoking permitted. Reservations accepted. Moderate to expensive. D, S.

Walt Disney World Microbrews

- Lodge House Brew at Territory lounge (Wilderness Lodge)
- Monorail Ale at Outer Rim (Contemporary)
- Fulton's Honey Wheat Lager (Fulton's Crab House)
- Harry's Safari Beer at Harry's Safari Bar (Dolphin)
- Flying Fish Brewing Co.'s Extra Pale Ale and Extra Special Bitters at Flying Fish Café (BoardWalk)
- Three house ales and two ever-changing specialty brews handcrafted at Big River Grille & Brewing Works (BoardWalk)

We (Almost) Never Close

The following hotel eateries offer a limited selection 24 hours a day during busy seasons (hours are subject to change):

- **B-Line Diner**
  (Peabody Orlando)

- **Captain Cook's Snack Company**
  (Polynesian)

- **Crumpets Café**
  (Grosvenor)

- **Food and Fun Center**
  (Contemporary)

- **Gasparilla Grill & Games**
  (Grand Floridian)

- **Roaring Fork**
  (Wilderness Lodge)

- **Tubbi's** (Dolphin)

- **Watercress Pastry Shop**
  (Buena Vista Palace)

MAYA GRILL (Coronado Springs): Floor-to-ceiling windows overlooking a lake, warm hues, and soaring columns lend a certain splendor to this large dining room. The leather chairs, Mission-style furnishings, and stone carvings not unlike those made by Mayan artisans for their temples and palaces complete the decor. The Mayan hunting tradition plus their proximity to the sea is the inspiration behind no-fuss dishes that demonstrate the appeal of seafood, lamb, pork, and steaks prepared over an open wood-fired grill. If each bite resounds like a quick trip across the border, there's good reason: The restaurant is operated by one of Mexico's premier restaurateur families. Priority seating suggested. Moderate. B, D.

'OHANA (Polynesian): The beauty of this family-style dining experience—a South Pacific feast prepared in the restaurant's prominent open-fire cooking pit—is that the hickory-grilled skewers of turkey, pork, shrimp, chicken, and beef just keep coming. (Whatever you do, don't miss the turkey.) Lo mein noodles, rice, and dumplings are among the accompaniments, and the passion fruit crème brûlée is a fine dessert. To make the most of 'Ohana's romantic setting, which features exotic wood carvings under a vast thatched roof, request a table that's right up against the windows overlooking Seven Seas Lagoon. This puts you a comfortable distance from the sweltering grill and the route where the exuberant children's coconut-rolling contest is held, but still in prime position to be serenaded by traditional Polynesian songs. Priority seating suggested for breakfast (a character affair) and for dinner. Expensive. B, D.

PALIO (Swan, 934-1609): A spirited Italian trattoria worth noting as a trusty source for imaginatively prepared homemade pasta, tasty pizza baked in wood-fired ovens, and traditional veal and seafood dishes. Peroni and Moretti beers are featured in addition to Italian wines. Smoking permitted. Reservations suggested. Expensive. D.

WHISPERING CANYON CAFE (Wilderness Lodge): For savory eating that does not stop until you say "when," consider this family-style restaurant a good (if awfully rowdy) candidate. At dinner, apple-rosemary rotisserie chicken, maple-garlic pork spareribs, and smoked barbecue beef brisket are certain to satisfy. (Lunch sandwiches are served à la carte.) Priority seating suggested. Moderate. B, L, D.

Other World Options

STANDOUTS

FULTON'S CRAB HOUSE (between Pleasure Island and the Downtown Disney Marketplace): Walk the gangplank onto this would-be riverboat (formerly the *Empress Lilly*) and with one glance around you're prepared to book passage. Still, the polished woods, brass detailing, and nautical nostalgia of the restaurant are secondary to the impressively fresh seafood served therein. The extensive dinner menu changes with the day's arrivals. Suffice it to say that it's not unusual for Hawaiian albacore tuna (accompanied by, say, crab bordelaise and corn-whipped potatoes) to be spotted next to Great Lakes walleye pike (with garlic chips and herb rice). Standbys include cioppino, a San Francisco–style stew with seafood galore in a tomato broth; roasted garlic chicken; crab, lobster, and vegetable platters; and filet mignon. Try the mushroom potato haystack. For a quicker fix, or for a reasonable lunch, the ravishing raw bar at the adjoining Stone Crab lounge suits. Operated by Levy Restaurants of Chicago. Priority seating suggested for breakfast (a character event) and for dinner. Expensive. B, L, D, S.

GOURMET PANTRY (Downtown Disney Marketplace): Okay, so it's not a restaurant. But this shop is bursting with inspiration for casual meals, picnics, and even self-catered boating excursions on Buena Vista Lagoon. When we mention the terrific heros sold by the inch, specialty salads, Godiva chocolates, cookies, wine, and spirits, we're merely hinting at the soup-to-nuts inventory. Inexpensive. B, L, D, S.

PLANET HOLLYWOOD (Pleasure Island): This branch of the international chain, ensconced inside a 120-foot-diameter sphere, gave the World's dining lineup its first celestial jolt. The hordes who assemble to gain entry to this restaurant are rewarded with a mind-boggling three-dimensional collage of movie memorabilia that couldn't possibly be digested in one meal. But there's more to this fun-filled

---

Appetizing News

Among the fruits of the expansion reshaping the entertainment landscape of the Downtown Disney area are some key addenda to the World's dining lineup. In addition to Wolfgang Puck Café (we've taken the liberty of describing it as a standout), two restaurant-nightclubs recently opened on the West Side. See our "Nightlife Guide" for further details.

■ **Bongos Cuban Café:** The tastes and sounds of Cuba and Latin America dovetail at this tropical-themed hot spot created by singer Gloria Estefan and her husband.

■ **House of Blues:** An eclectic menu with New Orleans taste buds (think étouffée, jambalaya, barbecue, and a Sunday gospel brunch) distinguish the adjoining restaurant of this club part-owned by Dan Aykroyd.

Dining Rooms with Knockout Views

- ■ **California Grill** (Contemporary)
- ■ **Narcoossee's** (Grand Floridian)
- ■ **'Ohana** (Polynesian)
- ■ **Maya Grill** (Coronado Springs)
- ■ **Cap'n Jack's Oyster Bar** (Downtown Disney Marketplace)
- ■ **Fulton's Crab House** (between Pleasure Island and the Downtown Disney Marketplace)
- ■ **Planet Hollywood** (Pleasure Island)—No windows needed here!
- ■ **Rose & Crown Dining Room** (United Kingdom, Epcot's World Showcase)
- ■ **Cantina de San Angel** (Mexico, Epcot's World Showcase)
- ■ **Coral Reef** (The Living Seas, Epcot's Future World)
- ■ **Garden Grill** (The Land, Epcot's Future World)
- ■ **Arthur's 27** (Buena Vista Palace)

planet than meets the eye: The menu has creative flair and depth (consider blackened shrimp, Far East chicken salad, vegetable burgers, pasta primavera). Desserts are outstanding (try the butter pecan rum cake or Arnold Schwarzenegger's mother's apple strudel). Smoking permitted. No reservations or priority seating, alas, just extremely long lines (try between 1 P.M. and 5 P.M.). Moderate. L, D, S.

PORTOBELLO YACHT CLUB (Pleasure Island): This polished yet casual piece of nautica is simply one of our favorite places to visit on an empty stomach. Menu standouts include a variety of luscious thin-crust pizzas baked in a wood-burning oven, *farfalle primavera*, and *spaghettini alla Portobello*, a seafood medley served over pasta in a light tomato and wine sauce. As an example of the extraordinary qualities of the desserts here, we offer the testimony of a Portobello regular regarding the restaurant's rich layer cake with chocolate ganache frosting, chocolate toffee crunch filling, and warm caramel sauce: "*Cioccolato paradiso* got me through twenty hours of labor." Portobello also offers some tempting specialty coffees and an impressive wine list. It's open until 1:30 A.M. Owned and operated by Levy Restaurants of Chicago. Smoking permitted. First-come seating. Expensive. L, D, S.

WOLFGANG PUCK CAFE (Downtown Disney West Side): This casual yet groundbreaking restaurant marks the L.A. chef's Florida debut and brings creative California cuisine to the fore. The avant-garde chef's signature gourmet pizzas, pastas, rotisserie chicken, and other specialties are prepared in the two-story restaurant's display kitchen. Incidentally, his wife, noted interior designer Barbara Lazaroff, fashioned the geometric patterns, ceramic mosaics, and glass expanses that make up the convivial interior. Priority seating suggested. Moderate to expensive. L, D. The Wolfgang Puck Express counter here (there's also one at the Marketplace) offers pizzas, chicken salad, and focaccia sandwiches that defy most definitions of fast food. First-come seating. Inexpensive to moderate. L, D, S.

GOOD BETS

ARTHUR'S 27 (Buena Vista Palace, Hotel Plaza Blvd.; 827-3450): In the imposing check category, this gastronomic gem offers a lofty view of Downtown Disney from its 27th-floor perch. Large booths, each equipped with a window, make for wonderfully intimate dining. House specialties include duckling, Florida Gulf shrimp, and veal medaillons. The wine list is excellent. Jackets are required for men. Smoking permitted. Reservations necessary. Very expensive. D.

BASKERVILLES (Grosvenor, Hotel Plaza Blvd.; 828-4444): It doesn't take a detective to surmise the Sherlock Holmes theme of this memorabilia-laden restaurant, notable for its prime-rib dinner buffets. Smoking permitted except during character meals (breakfast Tuesday, Thursday, and Saturday; dinner Wednesday) and Saturday's reservations-only dinner show. First-come seating. Moderate. B, L (seasonally), D.

CAP'N JACK'S OYSTER BAR (Downtown Disney Marketplace): This attractive pier house perched over Buena Vista Lagoon is the place to socialize over mason-jar drafts and fresh seafood. The strawberry margarita's a keeper, as are the peel-and-eat shrimp, conch chowder, clams on the half shell, and crab cakes. Besides offering some of the most reasonably priced meals around, the restaurant also fetches some fine sunsets. First-come seating. Moderate. L, D, S.

OUTBACK (Buena Vista Palace, Hotel Plaza Blvd.; 827-3430): Despite its similar meat-and-potatoes inclinations, the place has no relation to the chain of the same name. While gator chowder and kangaroo-shaped butter are certainly among the restaurant's more unforgettable traits, we like it for the baby-back ribs, shrimp, and steaks. Smoking permitted. Reservations suggested. Moderate. D.

For the Love of Chocolate

When only a chocolate fix will do, the new Ghirardelli's Soda Fountain and Chocolate Shop makes a sweet retreat—and the perfect place to pause between shops at the Marketplace for a root beer float, a malt, or a peek at the antique chocolate-making equipment. On the West Side, try the southern-style confections at the Candy Cauldron or smoothies and desserts at Forty Thirst Street. On Pleasure Island D-Zertz is the sweetest solution.

A Virtual Film Festival

The exceptional AMC Theatres cinema at Downtown Disney West Side offers more than a little incentive to give aching feet a rest. First-run motion pictures are shown in a whopping 24 plush theaters, all of them equipped with an advanced sound system called THX that was developed by George Lucas. Call 827-1300 for showtimes.

NIGHTLIFE GUIDE

Those who find the energy to hit the town after a hard day's recreation are rewarded with a whole new world of amusements and entertainment. Among the myriad ways to take advantage of a second wind (and find a third) at Walt Disney World, Pleasure Island is the most obvious. This single-admission complex of clubs and restaurants trumpeted as Disney's playground for adults is just that. It has knockout improvisational comedy, smooth jazz, raging dance clubs, and much more, rolled into one neat package that creates a populace of happy nomads.

And that's just the prix fixe menu; à la carte nightlife options abound. Paramount among them is Downtown Disney West Side, a new (as of summer 1997) waterfront entertainment pocket next door to Pleasure Island. BoardWalk, the happening entertainment strip right in Epcot's backyard, has earned its place on our don't-miss list. But the theme parks also offer a few notable watering holes for early birds, and the resorts in and around the World rally to the adult cause with a tempting slate of lounges and clubs to suit every taste. Tally it all up and you have sufficient incentive to take even the faintest breeze of a second wind for all it's worth: havens for wine lovers and havens for beer drinkers; gems that enchant and gems that rock; places to shoot the breeze and places to shoot pool; desirable digs for singles and desirable digs for couples. The key is knowing where to find them.

In the pages that follow, we present the best nightlife in the World. First, you'll receive a thorough orientation to Pleasure Island, complete with a walking tour; next, an introduction to Downtown Disney West Side, the World's newest nighttime destination; then an informed briefing on the clubs found along the BoardWalk. The final section of this guide completes the nightlife picture with our report on other recommended clubs and lounges located on WDW property. This is structured as a listing. Under the heading "Standouts," we have singled out those places both quiet and jumping that are worth going out of your way for or simply a joy to have nearby. Within the designation "Good Bets," we have corralled the best of the rest—additional clubs and lounges worth checking out, particularly if you're in the area. *Cheers!*

Pleasure Island

This bustling metropolis—a six-acre island consumed entirely by clubs, restaurants, stage shows, and shops—can be counted on to fill the entertainment void when Walt Disney World's theme parks and golf courses have closed for the day. We'd liken the atmosphere of this most adult venture (guests must be 18 or joined at the hip to a parent to be admitted to clubs, and Mannequins disco is strictly 21 and up) to a four-alarm block party. Pleasure Island's vigor and longevity are bolstered by its unique interpretation of the calendar—the place celebrates more New Year's Eves in a year than Dick Clark could know in four lifetimes ("Auld Lang Syne" and confetti cannons join special effects–enhanced fireworks as nightly rituals). It tosses a nod to most every nightlife niche. And

although it's perhaps more fun once you've cased out your favorite hangouts, it is possible to experience all of Pleasure Island's clubs in one whirlwind night, and this is the course we recommend for first-time visitors.

While the main draw here is certainly the clubs, Pleasure Island's shops are open from 11 A.M. to 2 A.M. and its restaurants serve lunch as well as dinner. There is no admission fee until 7 P.M., when a single cover charge of $19.03 (including tax; good for entry to all clubs) applies to all but restaurant- and movie-goers. Length of Stay Passes and Five-Day World Hopper Passes include Pleasure Island admission. The drinking age in Florida is 21, and proof of age is required at the gate and at most club entrances. While the clubs don't close down until 2 A.M., note that last call is sounded at about 1:30 A.M.

Before we take you on a club-hopping tour of Pleasure Island, a few words about practicalities are warranted. For starters, the restaurants on and around Pleasure Island are among WDW's best. Portobello Yacht Club and Fulton's Crab House don't shut down their galleys until midnight; and Planet Hollywood takes orders right up to 1 A.M. For reviews of the key dining spots here

A Sense of Place

Pleasure Island's clubs are described here in the order they are encountered after you pass through the turnstiles.

Pleasure Island Tips

■ Only the Adventurers Club and Rock 'n' Roll Beach Club are up and running at 7 P.M. The Comedy Warehouse opens at 7:30 P.M., with the rest kicking in at 8 P.M. These times are subject to change.

■ It's fun to club-hop, but you can't do it with a glass in your hand. Plan ahead, and ask that your last drink be served in plastic. Conveniently, most places keep a stack of cups near the door.

■ Caught with your pockets empty? Have a chat with the ATM located just past the stairway at the Rock 'n' Roll Beach Club.

■ The Adventurers Club and the Comedy Warehouse are the island's only nonsmoking venues.

•CONTINUED ON NEXT PAGE

and throughout Downtown Disney, consult this chapter's "Restaurant Guide" (the immediately relevant section begins on page 203). For snacking, carts stand by with such things as crêpes. Of the several clubs that serve food, the Pleasure Island Jazz Company is the only one venturing beyond pub grub. The Missing Link Sausage Co. sates with hot dogs and sausages, and D-Zertz serves the sweet tooth. For details about transportation to and from Pleasure Island, consult the "Transportation" section of the *Planning Ahead* chapter.

To give you a sense of location, clubs are described here in the order they are encountered after you pass through the main turnstiles. But Pleasure Island is an open invitation to serendipity—truly a club-hopper's paradise—and its varied venues are ideally explored according to mood and energy level. Generally, you'll find that Mannequins, right inside the gate, is not one best encountered cold. Better warm-ups are the Comedy Warehouse, Rock 'n' Roll Beach Club, 8Trax, and BET SoundStage Club. For a relaxing interlude, we suggest the Pleasure Island Jazz Company and the Adventurers Club.

A Walking Tour

As you bear down on Pleasure Island, note that the parking lot here is a highly trafficked place requiring pedestrian vigilance. Either take advantage of valet parking or resist the urge to look up at the cluster of neon lights and skyward lasers until you've crossed over to the sidewalk where the ticket booth sits. Once here, do all the neck-craning and people-watching you please (everyone else is), and be sure to pick up an entertainment schedule.

The main entrance lies directly ahead. After presenting your ticket in exchange for a lovely plastic bracelet, you pass (limbo if you like) under the neon archway and into the pleasuredom itself. The first building on the left houses **Mannequins**, a pulsating den of incredible special effects and current techno-pop tracks that puts a unique spin on the standard club scene with a huge, rotating dance floor. It takes its name from the many mannequins, all related to the dance world, found throughout. The only venue on Pleasure Island reserved strictly for patrons 21 and older, Mannequins is a club in the urban mold, and it attracts a dressed-to-impress crowd. The music here is cranked so loud that a jet could pass through virtually unnoticed; yet somehow the place is packed all night long with revelers who actually employ verbal communication in their flirtations. If you can stand the volume, you may take pleasure in the fact that the circulating dance floor gives a little boost to your dance skills and allows for exceptionally easy scoping, whether you're dancing or on the sidelines.

Explosive modern dance shows are staged here nightly, and on Thursday night the music runs to retro-progressive. The club is entered (via an elevator) on the third floor, a level that enjoys the same volume as the rest of the club, and offers little beyond a bit of privacy and a perch from which to view the action below. Ditto the second floor. As for drinks, Mannequins offers a full bar but emphasizes the bubbly, serving champagne by the glass or by the bottle, from Piper Sonoma to Dom Perignon. This club is popular with both locals and visitors, so be prepared to encounter a line at the door, especially on weekends.

Directly across from Mannequins you will see a warehouse-like structure. This is the site of the **Pleasure Island Jazz Company**, the island's most sophisticated entity. Cool, uninhibited jazz and blues are the order at this live-music venue, which runs the gamut from 1930s to contemporary tunes and features both local and national talent. A relaxing interlude from the rowdier scenes, the place is dimly lit and dotted with small cocktail tables that encourage intimate conversation. If you're up for some quality entertainment in a romantic atmosphere; if you're too pooped for anything beyond snapping your fingers; if you're hankering for a jazzy libation, a nice bottle of wine, or a bite on the other side of the fast-food tracks, the Jazz Company will take care of you. The menu here covers all bases. For under $10 you'll find the likes of shrimp quesadillas and crème brûlée. Whether you're thirsty or not, check out the drink descriptions. From "the cookie dough of wine" to a red with "enough velour texture to do Ricardo Montalban proud," they're a hoot. Muddy Waters is paid tribute in a terrific specialty coffee with Bailey's, Frangelico, and a hazelnut finish. If it's too hot for coffee, try a Kinky Sax. To snag a good table, aim to arrive about 20 minutes before showtime.

Onward. Make a right turn out of the Jazz Company, and you're on due course for the **Rock 'n' Roll Beach Club**. As the club's surfboard stairway comes into sight, you'll notice Pleasure Island's gradually sloping main strip leading off to the left. At the top of the stairs, you enter a rollicking dance spot featuring excellent bands that is much easier on the eardrums than Mannequins, and substantially more laid-back (perhaps due to its surfer sensibility). Between

•CONTINUED FROM PREVIOUS PAGE

■ A reggae band performs along the waterfront behind 8Trax during selected summer weekends and at other times.

■ To snag a good table at Pleasure Island Jazz Company, arrive about 20 minutes before showtime.

■ At the Comedy Warehouse, aim for an earlier show for the shortest queue, and know that it's possible but not likely to get in on the fly.

Virgin Daiquiri, Anyone?

Soft drinks, fruit juices, and tasty specialty drinks sans alcohol are available at all Pleasure Island clubs. Just ask the bartender.

sets, some of the wackiest deejays you'll ever see keep the classic rock and current pop coming even as they're bouncing like oversize Super Balls off the walls of the prominent audio booth. While dancing is definitely a big deal here—the dance floor is generally packed, primarily with twentysomethings—there's more to do than twist and shout the night away, and many guests enjoy the three-story club's great music and casual atmosphere without so much as stepping

onto the lowest level. They shoot pool, play air hockey and pin-ball, and hang out at tables over-looking the dance floor to eat the house pizza, people-watch, and sip a beer. Roving souls should note that the Rock 'n' Roll Beach Club's specialty drinks are available in refillable 16-ounce squeeze bottles.

From the Rock 'n' Roll Beach Club it's a right turn, then a short walk (you'll pass several shops and then see it on your left) to our next gig, **8Trax**, a place so thoroughly seventies that "YMCA" is a scheduled event (12:30 A.M.). In this rather rocking joint you'll see a lot of people with goofy (lowercase, that is) grins on their faces and hear a continual stream of "Omigod, this is the song....We have to dance to this one....No way....I completely forgot about this song." Suffice it to say that the *Saturday Night Fever*–style dance floor is not only an extraordinarily popular destination but an infinitely fascinating eyeful. Decor tends toward the psychedelic. Specialty drinks include Brady Bunch Punch. And some off-the-beaten-vinyl-sofa nooks are given over to beanbag chairs and a built-in game of Twister. On occasion, the club rocks to the beat of a different decade: the eighties. Note: 8Trax offers burgers and chicken sandwiches on Friday and Saturday nights, and the small courtyard out back is a good place to have a smoke or sneak a kiss.

Moving along, the next club on the horizon (veer left out of 8Trax and cross the street) is Pleasure Island's biggest enigma—the **Adventurers Club**. This elegant and eccentric parlor takes after the salons of 19th-century explorers' clubs, and is decked out with photos, trinkets, and furnishings that document the awfully far-reaching (and far-fetched) travels of its card-carrying members.

On the surface, it's a quiet place, filled with comfortable chairs; the official club drink, the Kungaloosh, is a tasty frozen number with strawberry and orange juices, blackberry brandy, and rum. But penetrate the recesses of the Adventurers Club and you'll notice some pretty odd characters milling about, stumble upon some rather curious corners and goings-on, and ultimately be invited into a hideaway library (where those odd characters put on a rather curious show, complete with haunted organ). A few hints to making the most of this intriguing parlor: Grab a stool at the main bar downstairs, and ask the bartender for a raise; read the captions for the displayed photos; and don't miss the mask room. Finally, note that this is a nonsmoking venue.

Right next door to the Adventurers Club is the new **BET SoundStage Club**, opening early this year. The club, formerly the home of the Neon Armadillo Music Saloon, will be reincarnated as a den for soul, rhythm and blues, hip-hop, and jazz. It will be the kind of place you'd like to think Aretha Franklin might frequent, with all due respect (pun intended). The club's snack menu favors light munchables sure to cure even the worst case of the blues. Of course, the folks dressed in cowboy boots and Stetsons who have (clearly) come to Pleasure Island with one thing in mind need not despair. They can just sidestep a couple of doors down to the newest space for kicking up their heels, which will replace the Fireworks Factory restaurant. The line dancing is expected to commence this spring.

Next Stop, Church Street Station

If one pocket of ready-made nightlife isn't enough, Church Street Station is old Orlando's version of the block party as institution. While there's plenty of shopping and dining, the attractions are five distinctive clubs whose beautifully restored decor is so flush with antiques the Church Street folks call them showrooms. **Rosie O'Grady's Goodtime Emporium** puts the make on Bourbon Street with live Dixieland jazz and flaming hurricanes. **Apple Annie's Courtyard** could be a Victorian garden but for its hefty frozen drinks. The **Cheyenne Saloon and Opera House** boasts tasty barbecue and Grand Ole Opry–style country-and-western music in a polished-wood setting. **Phineas Phogg's Dance Club** plays Top 40 hits in a (why ask why?) ballooning museum setting; Wednesday's nickel beers are an Orlando institution. And the **Orchid Garden Ballroom** is not the waltz palace you might imagine; the bands leave their oboes at home in favor of rock 'n' roll. A single $16.95 admission charge permits entry to all clubs. Doors close: 1 A.M. weekdays; 2 A.M. weekends. Located about 20 miles from Walt Disney World; 129 W. Church St., Orlando; 422-2434.

After-Dark Dazzle

■ The Magic Kingdom's extended curfew during busy seasons (generally summers and holiday periods) means the relaxed atmosphere and, yes, romance of the park in the early-evening hours are more accessible. It also means nightly fireworks and performances of SpectroMagic.

The Fantasy in the Sky fireworks display is six minutes of pyrotechnics worthy of a Fourth of July finale. And the incredible SpectroMagic fiber-optic light parade is not to be missed; if there are two performances, aim for the later one, when the prime viewing spots (anywhere along Main Street) are easier to snare, thanks to little ones' needing to go beddie-bye.

•CONTINUED ON NEXT PAGE

Our next order of business is not a club but a forum known as the **West End Stage**, which provides much of the juice for Pleasure Island's street party. Live bands perform here nightly (thanks to recruitment efforts, there's now one big-name act a month on average). While you won't find any seating to speak of in the plaza that fronts this stage, you may very well sight full-blown adults dancing under the stars. And unless you are allergic to confetti, this is the place to be when the nightly New Year's Eve countdown reaches its pyrotechnic climax (showtime is 11:45 P.M.). Sure, the premise is a bit contrived, but it's a good way to gather some new energy, and you'd be surprised how many couples jump at the chance for an extra New Year's Eve smooch before joining the rest of the crowd in singing "Auld Lang Syne."

In any case, the most strategic spot to take it all in (since you'll be standing anyway) is the queue for the **Comedy Warehouse**, located right across the plaza from the BET SoundStage Club. Get there no later than 11:30 P.M. (the next show is at 12:20 A.M.) to get a jump on any New Year's revelers who might have the same idea. The Comedy Warehouse, a perennial favorite, is the sort of club in which you prop yourself on a stool in a tiered studio and hope you don't fall off laughing. The rule here: Drink in sips, because the troupe of five lightning-quick improvisational comedians does brilliant and absolutely hilarious things with assorted suggestions from the audience, and the zingers usually come without warning.

Every performance is different, but you can expect the audience to provide some pretty challenging raw material ("Okay, we need an occupation" nets the likes of "rutabaga farmer"), and count on the troupe to rise to the occasion with spontaneously composed and accessorized products (generally songs, stories, and skits). Suffice it to say that when these comics go head-to-head in do-it-or-die improv competitions (and they do), they do not go down quickly.

Beer, wine, and mixed drinks are served, and popcorn is the preferred snack. While the performances here are well worth waiting for, hard-core humorists will often begin lining up a good hour before curtain time for the later shows, making it an increasingly tougher seat to get. A queue attendant keeps count, so you won't wait for nothing. Some additional tips: Aim for the earlier shows, and know that it's possible but not likely to get in on the fly. Also note that this is a nonsmoking venue.

Downtown Disney West Side

The newest kid on the entertainment block, the West Side has joined the Marketplace and Pleasure Island to make a triple-header of the alluring distraction zone known as Downtown Disney. Like Pleasure Island, its neighbor to the east, Downtown Disney West Side is a colorful lakeside strip of clubs, restaurants, shops, and energy. Unlike Pleasure Island, this be-there-or-be-square area is ungated, even after dark. Here, guests pay as they play, springing for cover charges only at establishments they decide to patronize. Note that smoking is permitted in designated sections of House of Blues and Bongos Cuban Café.

The easternmost spot at Downtown Disney West Side is the **AMC Theatres** complex, a colossal celebration of the silver screen (make that *screens*—there were 24 at last count). The marquee is au courant, the seats are roomy and plush, and the sound system's first-rate (it was developed by George Lucas). Call 827-1300 for showtimes (which get started at about 1 P.M.).

If you prefer a diversion with an added dimension, start a conga line and head for **Bongos Cuban Café**, directly across the promenade. Created by singer Gloria Estefan and her husband, Emilio, the bright, boisterous club parades the flavors and rhythms of Cuba and other Latin American entertainment centers. This is a place in which mere foot tapping is uncommon (sit still and your friends are

---

•*CONTINUED FROM PREVIOUS PAGE*

■ Epcot's World Showcase, which stays open until at least 9 P.M. year-round, assumes a sparkling beauty at night. Disney takes superb advantage of this by presenting IllumiNations, a nightly symphony of fireworks, festive music, lasers, and dancing water fountains that rates among the most spectacular displays the World over. The 20-minute show, generally ignited at closing time, is visible from any point along the promenade.

■ Another of Disney's best nighttime shows is Sorcery in the Sky at the Disney-MGM Studios. Ten minutes of dazzling fireworks set to music from *Fantasia* and other classic films, it can be seen nightly anytime the park is open late. Best viewing is on Hollywood Boulevard.

Sure to top the list of favorites is the much awaited arrival of Disneyland's Fantasmic!, coming to a new amphitheater behind Tower of Terror late this year. The brilliant show takes you inside Mickey's dreams as he conducts dancing fountains, swirling stars, and a delightful musical score. Animation projected onto water screens on the lake helps tell the story, which climaxes in a visit from Disney's nightmare-inducing villains. A battle ensues, powered by flaming special effects and leading to a character-filled finale.

■ The Electrical Water Pageant, a 1,000-foot-long string of illuminated floating creatures, makes its beautiful yet boisterous way around Bay Lake each night. You can usually view the parade at 9 P.M. from the Polynesian, 9:20 P.M. from the Grand Floridian, 9:35 P.M. from the Wilderness Lodge, 9:45 P.M. from Fort Wilderness, and 10:05 P.M. from the Contemporary.

The Rest of the West

With no pesky Pacific Ocean standing in its way, Disney's westward expansion just might go on forever. One of several works in progress is the future home of Cirque du Soleil, a most extraordinary circus ensemble. Wipe out all thoughts of Bozo-style antics; this is not your typical big-top production. Scheduled to make its West Side premiere in late 1998, Cirque features a cast of 70 performing a dazzling mix of acrobatics and modern dance. Wild costumes and dramatic original music add to the fun. It may not be The Greatest Show on Earth, but it certainly promises to be one of the most captivating. Also in the works is DisneyQuest, a mammoth entertainment center featuring high-tech games with a distinctive Disney flair.

apt to begin shaking you). So count on swaying in your seat to the sizzling sounds of live salsa, and should the mood strike you later in the evening, push back the tables and dance around the three-story pineapple. Cover charge varies.

When you've had your fill of the fruit fly fandango, plot a moonlight stroll along the shore of Buena Vista Lagoon. Melt away the Miami mentality with a dose of cool: **House of Blues.** The massive music hall here is like a songbird that's constantly changing its tune—only much funkier. It has enough seating for Pat Boone and 1,999 other soul men and women. Inspired by one of America's proudest musical traditions, the club also serves up jazz and country, with an occasional R & B, gospel, or rock medley tossed into the mix. You can buy tickets (usually about $5 to $30) through Ticketmaster in advance (839-3900) or at the box office up until showtime. Can't live without a House of Blues cap or T-shirt? Take It Easy Baby—that's the name of the shop stocking all things blues-related, including CDs, books, even guitars. Incidentally, the powers behind House of Blues include actor/Blues Brother (and world-renowned Conehead) Dan Aykroyd.

BoardWalk

While merely strolling the boards of this nostalgic new entertainment district a short walk from Epcot provides a delightful escape to simpler times, the temptations en route are tough to resist. Cotton candy vendors, savory dining, and rolling chair rides aside, BoardWalk gives the World things it has long needed— a sports bar, a brewpub, an elegant dance club—and more. In addition to being an appealing resort (see *Checking In* for a complete description), BoardWalk is a great adult hangout. There's no admission charge, although Jellyrolls and Atlantic Dance charge a cover (no cover weekdays, $3 weekends, at Jellyrolls; $3 weekdays, $5 weekends, higher for big-name acts at Atlantic Dance); you must be 21 or older to enter. All of the bars and clubs, described below, stay open until 2 A.M. Smoking is permitted.

High on the hit list is **ESPN Club**, a sports bar so over the top it practically has referees. Between the sports commentator, the ballpark fare, and the more than 70 televisions (some in the restrooms) broadcasting games in progress, no unnecessary time-outs are taken. Check an entertainment schedule for news on any major-league special events that might be happening (and try those hot wings).

Several first downs away, the **Big River Grille & Brewing Works** invites you to bend the ol' elbow right under the brewmaster's nose. Five first-rate specialty ales, including two that change with the seasons, are crafted on the premises. It's a tough job, but someone's got to polish off the beer bread and raise a glass to the hard-working brew maestro. After trying the beer sampler (tastes of all five ales for $4.25), we heartily waved on the Tilt Pale Ale house brew. Hot beer pretzels and other appetizers from the restaurant menu are available at the bar until the kitchen closes around 11 P.M., providing fitting accompaniments to tastings. (Stick around and you'll see that the sleek metal stools are surprisingly comfortable.)

Walk a few short strides into the dueling-pianist realm of **Jellyrolls** and you're soon crooning and swaying along with the rest of the congregation to songs from the 1970s to the present. As an example of the musicians' versatility, consider this sampling of what was played in one set: "The Devil Went Down to Georgia," "Joy to the World," and a Kermit the Frog rendition of "Rainbow Connection." The music comes uninterrupted (except by the wisecracking pianists themselves). Soon you're wondering how you got so hoarse. So you head next door to **Atlantic Dance**. One look at this old-fashioned swing club and you want to take a twirl on the dance floor. A revolving roster of retro-swing bands (think Harry Connick Jr. and the Brian Setzer Orchestra) take full responsibility for the sound track. You're free to dance, order hors d'oeuvres or desserts, and if you like, enjoy one of 25 martinis and a premium cigar on a balcony overlooking the water. From this perspective, the game highlights on the ESPN Club's monitors seem miles away. But they're not, and so when your mood shifts, you venture back to settle the score. Such is an evening at BoardWalk.

Whatever Ales You...

In addition to BoardWalk's brewpub, the Big River Grille & Brewing Works, visiting beer lovers should remember these names: Crew's Cup (at the Yacht Club, with three beers on tap and 34 worldly brews) and The Laughing Kookaburra Good Time Bar (at the Buena Vista Palace, with 80 labels). For a roundup of WDW microbrews, see page 201.

WDW Dinner Shows

When it comes to dinner shows, Disney leads the pack. The elaborately themed productions offer set menus with generous portions, generally accompanied by unlimited alcoholic and non-alcoholic beverages, and welcome guests in casual attire.

Reservations are required and may be booked up to two years in advance by calling WDW-DINE (939-3463). Special dietary requests are honored at all the shows, with advance notice. Prices were correct at press time but are subject to change.

The best of the lot (and toughest reservation) is the Hoop-Dee-Doo Musical Revue, held in Pioneer Hall at Fort Wilderness. The show incorporates

•CONTINUED ON NEXT PAGE

Other World Options

STANDOUTS

CALIFORNIA GRILL LOUNGE (Contemporary): The companion lounge to the exceptional California Grill restaurant offers what amounts to box seats for the Magic Kingdom fireworks in a casual setting that does California wine country proud. What more could you want? How about weekly wine tastings (one ounce for $1.50) of your choice of nearly 100 wines. Doors close: 1 A.M.

CATWALK BAR (Disney-MGM Studios): It only sounds like a precarious setting to imbibe. This prop-laden lounge in the rafters of the Soundstage restaurant is dim, cool, a giant step removed from the crowds, and the prop collection features some extraordinary items: sofas and coffee tables you can put your feet up on. Don't forget to get yourself a drink (an iced tea or a screwdriver perhaps?) or something to eat while you're up. Doors close: varies with park closing.

CREW'S CUP (Yacht Club): When it comes to beer, the Crew's Cup runneth over with 34 worldly brews. Consider the warm copper-accented decor, the scintillating aromas wafting in from the neighboring Yachtsman Steakhouse, and the potential for four-cheese garlic bread and New England clam chowder, and you have an even better idea of why we are putty in this lounge's hands. Doors close: midnight.

THE LAUGHING KOOKABURRA GOOD TIME BAR (Buena Vista Palace, Hotel Plaza Blvd.): At "the Kook," a live band perched above the large bar plays Top 40 music Tuesday through Saturday for a crowd ranging in age from 25 to 40 (a deejay sits in on Sunday and Monday). If you'd rather listen than dance, snag a spot in one of four seating areas, including a small bar with a skylight on the upper level. Some 80 beers are on hand. Daily happy hour. No cover. Doors close: 2 A.M.

MARTHA'S VINEYARD (Beach Club): Flights of fancy (two-ounce sampler tours of select whites and reds) are the indulgence of choice in this wine lover's paradise. However, the wines may be ordered separately as well, in both full-glass and sample sizes. First-rate seafood appetizers and desserts are served until 10 P.M. But do you book the Opus One flight or the Ultimate Chardonnay (Gallo Estate to Far Niente, with stopovers at Grgich Hills and Cakebread)? Decisions, decisions. Doors close: 11 P.M.

MATSU NO MA (Japan, Epcot's World Showcase): A serene setting where—in addition to sake, beer, cocktails, and green tea—you can imbibe a stunning vista of Epcot. Sushi and sashimi are also served. Doors close: varies with park closing.

ONLY'S BAR & JAIL (Dolphin): While certainly a restaurant bar, this atmospheric slammer is a good place to do time, especially if you're a margarita lover. There are several different kinds, based on tequila gradations rather than fruity flavors; we steer you toward the Tijuana Cadillac. Sangria by the pitcher and hot tortilla chips with salsa complete the picture. Doors close: 11:30 P.M.

ROSE & CROWN PUB (United Kingdom, Epcot's World Showcase): We've always loved this cheeky classic—for its pretty polished-wood and brass decor, its rich Irish, Scottish, and British drafts, and its neighborly feel. So we weren't so surprised during a recent visit to overhear a gentleman asking a fellow behind the bar to please let Jerry (a bartender not present) know that he was sorry he'd missed him. "Next time," he said hopefully. You needn't be a fan of shandies or black and tans to appreciate that. There's even a pub singer. Doors close: varies with park closing.

•CONTINUED FROM PREVIOUS PAGE

whoopin', singin', dancin', and audience participation in a Frontier hoedown. Country vittles include ribs, fried chicken, salad, corn-on-the-cob, baked beans, and strawberry shortcake. There are three seatings, at 5 P.M., 7:15 P.M., and 9:30 P.M.; adults pay $37, plus tax and tip.

At the Polynesian resort, hula skirts, ukuleles, and fire dances add to the fun at the lakeside Polynesian Luau, which takes guests on a whirlwind journey from New Zealand to Samoa. The meal, served family-style, features tropical bread, roasted chicken, spareribs, rice, and tropical fruit dessert. Nightly seatings are at 6:45 P.M. and 9:30 P.M., and the outdoor shows are presented rain or shine, canceled only when temperatures drop below 50 degrees; adults pay $37, plus tax and tip.

The Biergarten restaurant in the Germany pavilion at Epcot's World Showcase hosts five nightly shows during which performers in lederhosen or dirndls create an Oktoberfest celebration, with yodeling, dancing, and musicians playing everything from accordions to cowbells. Seating here is family-style (eight to a table), and guests have full run of a buffet that includes bratwurst, sauerbraten, rotisserie chicken, homemade spaetzle, red cabbage, and German potato salad. Adults pay $14.75, plus tax and tip; desserts cost extra. A musical trio entertains during the lunch buffet ($10.95 for adults).

Scenic Cocktail Spots

- **California Grill Lounge** (Contemporary)
- **Matsu No Ma** (Epcot's World Showcase)
- **Atlantic Dance** (BoardWalk)
- **Narcoossee's** (Grand Floridian)
- **Stone Crab** (Fulton's Crab House, between Pleasure Island and the Marketplace)
- **Cap'n Jack's Oyster Bar** (Downtown Disney Marketplace)
- **Outer Rim** (Contemporary)
- **Top of the Palace** (Buena Vista Palace)
- **Toppers** (Travelodge, Hotel Plaza Blvd.)

STONE CRAB (between Pleasure Island and the Downtown Disney Marketplace): Like the local heartthrob who happens to be loaded, this gorgeous riverboat-bound bar stacks the odds even more in its favor with an excellent raw bar, prime water views, and a honey-wheat house brew. It doesn't just make Bloody Marys from scratch (as in hand-squeezed tomatoes and fresh-grated horseradish), it garnishes them with shrimp. No wonder it attracts so many sophisticated stowaways. Doors close: 2 A.M.

TERRITORY (Wilderness Lodge): This scenic spot of Wilderness is marked by wood-carved grizzlies and a muraled map of the western Frontier that "unfolds" over the ceiling. If you swear you see the image of a certain mouse branded on the backside of a pony, you're right. While this lounge can be swamped with diners-in-waiting during prime mealtimes, it more often inspires lingering. Hearty appetizers and a light lunch menu that extends through 4 P.M. add to the appeal. But the true toast of the Territory is Lodge House Brew, a microbrewed light beer with a hint of honey that's a Wilderness Lodge exclusive. Doors close: midnight.

TOP OF THE PALACE (Buena Vista Palace, Hotel Plaza Blvd.): Show up to toast the setting sun and you're provided with a complimentary glass of champagne, not to mention fine wines by the glass and delectable desserts courtesy of the adjacent Arthur's 27 restaurant. Miss the sunset and you've still got reason to propose a toast: an enviable view of Epcot's IllumiNations fireworks (nightly) and live entertainment (weekends). Doors close: 1 A.M.

GOOD BETS

CAP'N JACK'S OYSTER BAR (Downtown Disney Marketplace): This pier house jutting out over Buena Vista Lagoon scores with a convivial atmosphere, a mean strawberry margarita, and a bar conducive to people-watching. It also offers reasonably priced sunsets and beautiful seafood (or is it the reverse?). Note that if you want to sit at the bar, the line out the door doesn't apply. Doors close: 10:30 P.M.

COTTON CO-OP (Dixie Landings): This one's nothing fancy. Just your unassuming nook that happens to have a fireplace, ready access to chicken wings and spicy Cajun onion straws, and a steady gig Tuesday through Saturday with a sing-along-inspiring entertainer. Anyway, we've cottoned to the place in general and to the Mississippi Mud Slide (a frozen Chambord-Bailey's blend in a chocolate-swirled glass) in particular. Drinks and music stop at midnight, but the doors never close.

GURGLING SUITCASE (Old Key West): This travel-size bar is too small to warrant a special trip, but it has such a great name we'll take any excuse to mention it. For drinks, we like the one with Amaretto, crème de banana, pineapple and orange juices, and a dash of cherry brandy. Tell the bartender you're looking for a Sultry Seahorse. Doors close: midnight.

HARRY'S SAFARI BAR (Dolphin): Long live Harry's for its house brew, its big-deal appetizers (giant prawns, stuffed mushrooms, and escargot), and its heady Headhunter (vodka, gin, rum, tequila, and sweet tropical juices). Add draft beers by the yard and a tempting slate of nonalcoholic beverages and you've got a divine welcome to the jungle. Doors close: 11 P.M.

MIZNER'S (Grand Floridian): If you look past the house orchestra that sets up shop nightly outside this second-floor alcove, you'll find a mahogany bar with fine ports, brandies, and appetizers. Doors close: 1 A.M.

NARCOOSSEE'S (Grand Floridian): You've got to love a lounge that's thoroughly surrounded by Victoriana and nervy enough to serve yards (and half yards) of beer. Doors close: 10 P.M.

OUTER RIM (Contemporary): A sleek spot that keeps one eye on the monorail and the other on Bay Lake. When the vista fades to black, the bar's contemporary charms more than pick up the visual slack. This is the spot to sample Monorail Ale, a full-flavored microbrewed amber available only at the Contemporary. Try the ice-cold spirit-soaked fruits. Doors close: 1 A.M.

TOPPERS (Travelodge, Hotel Plaza Blvd.): The place wears several hats—dartboards and pool tables serve the sports crowd, wall-length windows offer prime views of Epcot's IllumiNations, and large-screen rock music videos inspire the movers and shakers. Daily happy hours feature half-price drafts and wines. Doors close: 2 A.M.

RAINFOREST CAFE (Downtown Disney Marketplace): When the restaurant is mobbed, we like to take in the thunderstorms and waterfalls from the central mushroom-capped bar. We simply saddle an unwitting zebra or giraffe (the animal bar stools are strictly hoofs-to-hips) and chase our tails. Try a Raspberry Rainfall or fresh-squeezed juice. Doors close: 11 P.M. weekdays; midnight weekends.

Two-step to the Table

Disney's All-American Backyard Barbeque features all your favorite Fourth-of-July fixin's fortified by a lineup of live entertainment. As an instructor gives line dance lessons, a country band whoops it up Nashville-style. Disney characters also appear at this seasonal show, presented near River Country. Cost is $35 for adults. For reservations, call WDW-DINE.

Index